This is the first comprehensive evaluation of Charles Taylor's work and a major contribution to leading questions in philosophy and the human sciences as they face an increasingly pluralistic age. Charles Taylor is one of the most influential contemporary moral and political philosophers: in an era of specialisation he is one of the few thinkers who has developed a comprehensive philosophy which speaks to the conditions of the modern world in a way that is compelling to specialists in various disciplines. This collection of specially commissioned essays brings together thirteen distinguished scholars from a variety of fields to discuss critically Taylor's work. The topics range from the history of philosophy, truth, modernity and postmodernity, theism, interpretation, the human sciences, liberalism, pluralism and difference. Taylor responds to all the contributions and re-articulates his own views.

Philosophy in an age of pluralism

Philosophy in an age of pluralism

The philosophy of Charles Taylor in question

edited by
James Tully

with the assistance of
Daniel M. Weinstock

CAMBRIDGE
UNIVERSITY PRESS

Published by the Press Syndicate of the University of Cambridge
The Pitt Building, Trumpington Street, Cambridge CB2 1RP
40 West 20th Street, New York, NY 10011–4211, USA
10 Stamford Road, Oakleigh, Melbourne 3166, Australia

© Cambridge University Press 1994

First published 1994

Printed in Great Britain at the University Press, Cambridge

A catalogue record for this book is available from the British Library

Library of Congress cataloguing in publication data

Philosophy in an age of pluralism: the philosophy of Charles Taylor
in question / edited by James Tully with the assistance of Daniel M.
Weinstock.
      p.   cm.
Festschrift for Charles Taylor.
'Bibliography of the works of Charles Taylor': p.
Includes bibliographical references and index.
ISBN 0 521 43150 6 (hc). – ISBN 0 521 43742 3 (pb)
1. Taylor, Charles, 1931– . 2. Philosophy, modern – 20th century
I. Taylor, Charles, 1931– . II. Tully, James, 1949– .
III. Weinstock, Daniel M.
B995.T3P48 1994
191–dc20   93–46337   CIP

ISBN 0 521 43150 6 hardback
ISBN 0 521 43742 3 paperback

CE

Contents

Contributors

CHARLES TAYLOR is Professor of Philosophy at McGill University. He received his BA from McGill University in 1952 and his doctorate from Oxford University, All Souls College, in 1961. He has taught at McGill University since 1961. From 1976 to 1981 he was the Chichele Professor of Social and Political Theory in the University of Oxford, and Fellow of All Souls College. He has been a guest professor at many universities in North America and Europe and received numerous distinguished awards. He is Fellow of the Royal Society of Canada and Fellow of the British Academy. The bibliography lists his many publications. Le Prix Léon Gérin, the most prestigious honour given by the government of Québec, was awarded to him in 1992 for his outstanding contribution to the intellectual and civic life of Québec.

PATRICIA BENNER is Professor of Nursing in the Department of Physiological Nursing at the University of California, San Francisco School of Nursing. Her most recent publication is *The primacy of caring: stress and coping in health and illness* (1989). She is editor of *Interpretive phenomenology for the study of experimental learning, caring, and ethics in health and illness*, and, with S. Phillips, of *The crisis in care*, both of which will be published shortly.

SIR ISAIAH BERLIN is Fellow of All Souls College, Oxford, and Fellow and Past President of the British Academy. His most recent publications are *The crooked timber of humanity* (1990), *Conversations with Isaiah Berlin*, edited by Ramin Jahanbegloo (1992), and *J. G. Hamann: the magus of the north* (1993).

VINCENT DESCOMBES is Directeur d'études at the Ecole des hautes études en sciences sociales in Paris. His most recent publications are *The Barometer of modern reason* (1993), *Proust* (1992) and *Modern French philosophy* (1988).

JEAN BETHKE ELSHTAIN is Centennial Professor of Political Science and Professor of Philosophy at Vanderbilt University. Her most recent publications are *Woman and war* (1987), *Power trips and other journeys* (1990) and, as editor, *Just war theory* (1992).

CLIFFORD GEERTZ is Harold F. Linder Professor of Social Science, Institute for Advanced Study, Princeton, New Jersey. His most recent publication is *Works and lives: the anthropologist as author*. His book *After the fact: two countries, four decades, one anthropologist* will be published shortly.

METTE HJORT is Assistant Professor of English and Director of Cultural Studies at McGill University. Her most recent publications are, as editor, *Rules and conventions: literature, philosophy, social theory* (1992), and *The strategy of letters* (1993). Her translation of Louis Marin's *The destruction of painting* will be published shortly.

SUSAN JAMES is Lecturer in the Faculty of Philosophy in the University of Cambridge and Fellow of Girton College. Her most recent publications are, as editor with Gisela Bock, *Beyond equality and difference* (1992), and 'Spinoza the stoic' in *The rise of modern philosophy*, edited by Thomas Sorell (1992).

GUY LAFOREST is Associate Professor of Political Science at the Université Laval, Sainte-Foy, Québec. He is co-editor of the *Canadian Journal of Political Science*. His most recent publications are *Trudeau et la fin d'un rêve Canadien* (1992, forthcoming in English translation), *De la prudence* (1993), and, as editor, a collection of articles by Charles Taylor on Canadian federalism, *Reconciling the solitudes* (1993).

MICHAEL L. MORGAN is Professor of Philosophy at Indiana University in Bloomington. His most recent publications are *Platonic piety: philosophy and ritual in fourth-century Athens* (1990) and *Dilemmas in modern Jewish thought: the dialectics of revelation and history* (1992). His book on post-Holocaust Jewish thought will be published shortly and he is currently working on Stoicism in sixteenth- and seventeenth-century philosophy.

RICHARD RORTY is University Professor of Humanities at the University of Virginia. His most recent publications are *Objectivity, relativism and truth* and *Essays on Heidegger and others* (1991).

QUENTIN SKINNER is Professor of Political Science in the University of Cambridge and Fellow of Christ's College. His most recent publication is, as editor with Nicholas Phillipson, *Political discourse in early modern Britain*. His book *Renaissance eloquence and the philosophy of Hobbes* will be published shortly.

RICHARD TUCK is University Lecturer in History in the University of Cambridge and Fellow of Jesus College. His most recent publications are *Philosophy and government 1572–1651* (1993) and, as editor, Hobbes' *Leviathan* (1991). His Carlyle Lectures in Oxford University for 1990–1, *Political thought and the international order from Grotius to Kant*, will be published shortly.

JAMES TULLY is Professor of Philosophy at McGill University. His most recent publications are *An approach to political philosophy: Locke in contexts* (1993) and, as editor, Pufendorf's *On the duty of man and citizen* (1991). His Seeley Lectures in the University of Cambridge for 1993–4, *Strange multiplicity: constitutionalism in an age of diversity*, will be published shortly.

DANIEL M. WEINSTOCK is an Assistant Professor in the Department of Philosophy of the Université de Montréal. He received his Doctorate in political philosophy from Oxford University in 1991. He has published articles on various topics in moral and political philosophy, and is currently completing a book on the challenge posed by pluralism to liberal political thought.

Preface

It is great honour to edit this collection of outstanding articles on the philosophy of Charles Taylor. The contributors are distinguished scholars in their fields who have shown a critical interest in Taylor's work over the years of its development. Their contributions, written specifically for this *Festschrift*, pose questions on a variety of critical issues in Taylor's philosophy that are at the leading edge of debates across the humanities and social sciences. In his wide-ranging reply Taylor responds by re-articulating the fundamental features of his philosophy in a new and thought-provoking manner, which will, no doubt, set the stage for further debate.

Charles (Chuck) Taylor is one of the best known and most widely respected philosophers of the present age. In an era of specialisation he is one of the few thinkers who has developed a comprehensive philosophy which speaks to the conditions of the contemporary age in a way that is compelling to specialists in the various disciplines and comprehensible to the general reader. Here he is in the rare company of scholars such as Sir Isaiah Berlin and Richard Rorty. Whereas his works such as *The explanation of behaviour* (1964), *Hegel* (1975), and *Philosophical papers* (1985) are addressed primarily to specialists, *Hegel and modern society* (1979), *The ethics of authenticity* (1992), *Reconciling the solitudes* (1993) and *Multiculturalism and 'the politics of recognition'* (1992) are written for a more general audience. The magisterial *Sources of the self: the making of the modern identity* (1989) seeks to address both.

The contributors address a wide range of topics in Taylor's philosophy from an equally wide range of perspectives. Indeed, the volume is a virtual compendium of the leading challenges facing philosophy and the humanities as they enter the demanding age of pluralism at the dawn of the twenty-first century. It might be helpful to the reader if I mention one thread that runs through the entire fabric, bearing in mind that it is just one thread, and perhaps not Ariadne's, through the labyrinth that Taylor and his questioners seek to explore.

Taylor's work can be seen as an attempt at a philosophical reflection on modernity which, unlike earlier comprehensive philosophies, does not lay down *the* comprehensive framework in which such reflection must take place. That is, he accepts that the present age is plural in two respects. First, as Isaiah Berlin has famously argued, there is an irreducible plurality of values, and cultures. Second, there is also a plurality of forms of reflection: any form of reflection will be partial to some extent; conditioned by the author's culture, tradition, philosophical genre, gender, ethnicity, language and other factors. In his reply, Taylor draws out the implications of this pluralism and criticises contemporary philosophers such as Jürgens Habermas and John Rawls whom he believes have failed to take it sufficiently into account.

All the contributors are in agreement on the plurality of the present age, but each responds to it in a distinctive way. For Taylor it does not follow, as it does for many postmodern writers, that any form of comprehensive reflection on modernity is rendered impossible; that one must simply *accept* the irreducible plurality of cultures, values, and disciplines. Rather, it is possible to say something more than 'this is my view' or 'the view from my culture, gender, etc.' It is possible to recast the philosophical task of a 'reflection on modernity' as an invitation to a philosophical *conversation* with the diverse voices of modernity and their respective sources and traditions. The objective of such a conversation is not to articulate the Hegelian 'objective spirit', as Taylor points out in his reply to Vincent Descombes, or to reach agreement on a fundamental set of universal principles, as he argues in his reply to Richard Tuck. The aim of the conversation is rather to see if the seemingly incommensurable values, conceptual frameworks and other characteristics of modernity can be articulated in a more comprehensive account, and (as Taylor responds to Isaiah Berlin) *reconciled*, not once and for all but in the course of the conversation, by various means (such as the better account, fusion of horizons, aberration, narrative, re-articulation, moral sources, hypergoods, and other conceptual tools he has developed).

Hence, although Taylor retains the Hegelian aims of comprehension and reconciliation, he has reformulated the nature of philosophical reflection to recognise and affirm, rather than to overcome, irreducible plurality and the conditional nature of any reconciliation. As all the contributors acknowledge, and Michael Morgan and Patricia Benner especially emphasise, his conversational form of philosophical reflection and articulation yields unparalleled insights into the complex identity of modernity. Nevertheless, this form of recognition of plurality raises a crucial question which is posed by Isaiah Berlin with his characteristic clarity in the introduction and taken up in various ways by all the contributors. The initial condition of recognising modern plurality must be that the interlocutors in a dialogue speak in their own diverse terms, traditions, aims and demands. The starting point must be, so to speak, a plurality of conversations. The question is whether the dialogue remains a negotiated plurality of criss-crossing and irreconcilable conversations, as with Mikhail Bakhtin and Wittgenstein (on one interpretation), or whether it is possible to re-articulate and transvalue the plurality of conversations into a plurality of interlocutors within one common mode of conversation in which their differences could then be reconciled. As Taylor succinctly puts his view in reply to Isaiah Berlin, 'I still believe we can and should struggle for a "transvaluation" (to borrow Nietzsche's term *Umwertung*) which could open the way to a mode of life, individual and social, in which these demands could be reconciled' (p. 214).

To pose this question in a slightly different form: in delineating the conditions of the conversation and the sources of modern pluralism, has Taylor not quietly enframed the entire plurality of conversations in the terms, sources, traditions and telos of reconciliation of his particular genre of conversation, masquerading as universal? Susan James, for example, questions whether his foundational distinctions between inner and outer and ancient and modern must be necessary features of any reflection on modernity. Could different stories about the sources of modernity not be told in which these distinctions would blur or become less foundational (as she nicely puts it)? Taylor's equally basic adherence to the scheme/content distinction in his account of truth is questioned by Richard Rorty. In a similar manner Quentin Skinner questions whether the role Taylor accords to theism and the way he embraces certain goods are as constitutive of all articulations of modernity as he presumes. Jean Elshtain wonders if he has been unduly optimistic in his affirmation of modern ordinary life. Clifford Geertz calls into question the fundamental distinction Taylor makes between the natural and social sciences. The way in which he interprets modern European literature as the source of modern expressivism is questioned by Mette Hjort. Daniel Weinstock, Richard Tuck and Guy Laforest question his construal of rights, liberalism and nationalism. In a longer (or future) volume similar sorts of questions could and should be raised by feminists, aboriginal writers, moderns who do not derive their moral sources from European traditions, or modern Europeans who draw on different European sources, and other contributors.

Although the contributors address specific aspects of Taylor's philosophy and of current debates in the humanities and social sciences, it is also important to see that they question the adequacy of the comprehensive philosophy Taylor has developed to overcome both the shortcomings of traditional philosophy and the nihilism of postmodern relativism in the face of the plurality of the contemporary age. The virtue of philosophy cast in a conversational mode is that the questions of adequacy posed to it are taken as interlocutions in the conversation itself. As every student of Taylor's philosophy knows, the initiation of a conversation always involves casting at least some of one's own conceptual net over the other conversationalists in an uncritical manner, no matter how self-critical one tries to be, and Taylor is no exception to his own hermeneutic rule. Accordingly, his reply to questions is neither the traditional defence of a water-tight theory against all objections nor the postmodern acceptance of the relativity of one's own formulation. Rather, his response consists in trying to do justice to the contributors' questions by re-articulating them in a way that reduces the exposed bias and partiality in his initial formulation and points towards the reconciliation of outstanding differences by means of further discussion, *within* the comprehensive conversation in which his replies seek to show his questioners to be engaged, thereby offering pragmatic proof of his philosophy.

It is up to readers to say how successful he is and, in so doing, to contribute to the conversation – or conversations – themselves.

Acknowledgements

I would first like to thank all the contributors for their original and outstanding contributions as well as for their generous cooperation. My special thanks go to Daniel Weinstock for his immensely helpful assistance and his translation of the contribution by Vincent Descombes. I am most grateful to Jeremy Mynott for initiating the project and for his continuous solidarity. Richard Fisher, as always, navigated the volume through the Press with a steady and expert hand. The volume has also benefited more than I can say from Quentin Skinner's advice and encouragement at every stage.

For their unwavering support an incalculable debt of gratitude is owed to six exceptional defenders of the kind of interdisciplinary enquiry *Philosophy in an age of pluralism* exemplifies and seeks to promote: Gretta Chambers, Chancellor of McGill University; William C. Leggett, Vice-Principal (Academic); Michael Percival Maxwell, former Dean of Arts; John McCallum, Dean of Arts; James McGilvray, Chair, Department of Philosophy; and David F. Norton, William C. MacDonald Professor of Moral Philosophy.

Iris Hardinge and Anh Do have my gratitude and admiration for processing the entire script with efficiency and patience. We are all most grateful to Natalie Oman for her meticulous and substantive proofreading, and to Lori Clifford for her assistance.

Finally, on behalf of everyone let me thank Chuck Taylor, former teacher of Mette Hjort, Guy Laforest and Daniel Weinstock, and friend and colleague of all of us, for his thought-provoking and inspiring works and deeds, and for the intellectual engagement, compassion and *générosité* of his reply.

Introduction

Sir Isaiah Berlin

The contents of this volume will without doubt be occupied with a broad examination and discussion of Charles Taylor's views and position as a thinker, and I shall therefore confine myself to a purely personal expression of my conception of his personality and outlook. Let me begin by saying that I have known him since 1956 and felt the deepest friendship and admiration for him ever since. He is a man of acute intelligence, total intellectual and moral sincerity, unswerving integrity, and a remarkable insight into a variety of philosophical traditions, their central animating ideas, uncluttered by ingenious and sometimes highly complicated means of defence against actual or possible objections. His view of social and political life, to which he has devoted his thought, is imaginative, generously receptive, deeply humane and formed by the truth as he sees it, and not as it ought to be in accordance with dogmatically held premises or overmastering ideology. This gives to his work an authenticity, a concreteness, and a sense of reality which some of his less open-minded, proselytising, not to say formula- and ideology-ridden allies and disciples do not always show. He is vastly superior to them all, and, as I can testify from my own experience, a genuine source of continuous inspiration even to those who hold views very different from his own.

The chief difference between my outlook and that of Charles Taylor is that he is basically a teleologist – both as a Christian and as a Hegelian. He truly believes, as so many in the history of thought have done and still do, that human beings, and perhaps the entire universe, have a basic purpose – whether created by God, as religious Christians and Jews believe, or by nature, as Aristotle and his followers, and perhaps Hegel (whose attitude on this point seems to me somewhat ambivalent), have taught. Consequently, everything that he has written is concerned with what people have believed, striven after, developed into, lived in the light of, and, finally, the ultimate goals towards which human beings as such are by their very natures determined to move. Hence his interest, for example, in Johann Gottfried Herder (a source of great mutual sympathy between us), who was perhaps the first thinker to emphasise that people are what they

1

are because they live in a continuous stream of cultural, moral and spiritual development; that this stream is one which does not bear individuals alone but entire societies to which they belong; and that this notion of belonging, and of movement in a direction intrinsic to cultures and societies in terms of which alone their lives, their thoughts and their feelings can be understood, is intrinsic to being a human being. Charles Taylor and I share our evaluation of Herder's central idea that to belong to society is an intrinsic human need, like the need for food or security or shelter or freedom, and indeed, that self-realisation cannot be obtained in isolation from social life, but only in the framework of, for Taylor much more than for me, the organic structure of the culture or society into which they are born and to which therefore they cannot help belonging.

At this point, we part ways, I think. I do not believe in teleology. I do not deny that society and cultures develop in a certain fashion – nobody can understand either human beings or history who does not grasp that. But like Spinoza, Hume and other thinkers less sympathetic to Taylor than they are to me, I believe that purposes are imposed by human beings upon nature and the world, rather than pursued by them as part of their own central natures or essences. I think that Taylor believes in essences, whereas I do not. I believe that it is human beings, their imagination, intellect and character that form the world in which they live, not, of course, in isolation but in communities – that I would not deny; but that this is in a sense a free, unorganised development – which cannot be causally predicted. It is not part of a determinist structure, it does not march inexorably towards some single predestined goal, as Christians, Hegelians, Marxists and other determinists and teleologists have, in varied and often conflicting ways, believed and still believe to the present day.

What, for example, attracts Taylor in Marxist ideas, I believe – and he seems to me to have been influenced by these in a fascinating fashion in both his metaphysical and social views – is the notion that human beings can only rise to their full stature and develop all the potentialities which belong to them as human beings, if human society is liberated from oppression, exploitation, domination, which are inevitable consequences of, indeed, embodied in, modern capitalism, but with their roots in various formations in the past. He believes, unless I am much mistaken, that such liberation can be obtained only by the creation of a rational society in which human beings understand the world, both animate and inanimate, themselves, and the causal factors of the material world with which natural scientists deal. In this enlightened state, and in it alone, they will be free to pursue the ends for which they are created, both individually and, above all, socially. The vision is of a human society acting in a harmonious and interactive collective fashion, in which citizens bound together by the common use of untrammelled reason, free communication and mutual understanding, can alone live freely and progress.

I wish I could believe this, but I do not. I will not take this occasion for expounding my own views, only to say that I believe in a multiplicity of values, some of which conflict, or are incompatible with each other, pursued by different societies, different individuals, and different cultures; so that the notion of one world, one humanity moving in one single march of the faithful, *laeti triumphantes*, is unreal. The incompatibility of equally valid ideals in different societies at different periods, and of the various values and ends of individual human beings of whom these societies are composed – these and these alone, not a cosmic plan, determine what the total outcome of human behaviour must be, even if the individuals cannot themselves tell what the result of these interacting activities will turn out to be. These consequences, which only privileged observers can analyse, do not emanate from concrete universals or super-individual entities, but consist of what, in Aristotle's phrase, men do and suffer, their acts and purposes, the entire web of individual and social experience.

But I must not go on about our differences. Let me repeat that Charles Taylor is a noble, gifted and deeply interesting thinker, every one of whose works has stimulated and excited me, as it has many other readers. His unique position among social and political philosophers is due as much to his humanity and his empathy with differences of groups, individuals, societies and nations, which prevent him displaying any degree of dogmatism or narrow insistence on some cut and dried schema in which alone salvation is believed to lie, which, whatever one may think of his central beliefs, cannot fail to broaden the outlook of anyone who reads his works or listens to his lectures or, indeed, talks to him. He is, in short, a great fertilising force, a creative and original thinker than which there cannot be anything more wonderful to be. I salute him after many years of our friendship from all my heart, and hope that he will continue his very fruitful activity for many years to come. Even those who disagree with him as profoundly as, in some respects, I do, have gained, and are bound to gain, very greatly by it.

Part I

Foundations

1 Internal and external in the work of Descartes

Susan James

Sources of the self tells a story of unfulfilled promises and temporary resolutions and ends with an unsatisfied yearning for moral authority which is sometimes nostalgic, sometimes utopian. The sense of loss which permeates Charles Taylor's book is itself interwoven with one of its central organising themes, the movement he identifies within the Western philosophical tradition from a belief in an external guarantor of moral values to a confident reliance on the internal guarantee of reason – to what? Our inability to complete this dialectic, to avoid either simply reiterating its earlier moments or subsiding into a helpless relativism, is a failure which consigns us, in Taylor's view, to the angst and bewilderment of modernity. We cannot draw comfort from the idea of an external source of value, independent of us and yet binding; nor can we look inwards to our rationality as the source of incontrovertible moral truths. Unanchored, our moral values and commitments are merely ours, the ones we happen to cleave to, and the absence of a deeper justification for them breeds an apt and profound disquiet.

The stages of this unfinished story are represented in *Sources of the self* by three key figures: Plato, Descartes and 'us'. To focus on them alone is to simplify Taylor's historical argument, which reveals in its detail both the complexity and the chronological unsteadiness of the process he aims to trace. None the less, Plato and Descartes are for him the purest exemplars of positions which shape the rest of the philosophical tradition and continue to trouble us. Platonic virtue, according to Taylor, consisted in the contemplation of an external cosmic order to which we belong and which is intrinsically good. Descartes marked the beginning of a transition to the view that the route to virtue lies within, in the correct use of our internal capacity to reason. Nowadays, however, philosophical argument has rendered both these views untenable, so that 'we' find ourselves at a loss.

The latter half of this story is in many ways a familiar one. Throughout the twentieth century, philosophers have grappled with the limitations of a Cartesian ego divorced from the physical world yet armed with a capacity to assess the rationality of its own judgements. This disengaged self, as Taylor designates it, has been both a scourge and an inspiration, and *Sources of the self* suggests that it remains so. A scourge, because it gives rise to a sceptical problem which philosophers seem unable either to solve or abandon. An inspiration, because the Cartesian ego represents the conceptual apotheosis of an Enlightenment rationalism which, as Taylor rightly insists, continues to play an important part in our self-understanding.

How, then, can we escape from this impasse? At the end of his book, Taylor holds out the possibility that we can turn our backs on part of the story he has told and return to a God who is the external arbiter of right and wrong. In this essay, however, I should like to consider another route which, while it may not lead to a completely safe haven, may at least rescue us from despair. Suppose we adopt two of Taylor's guiding principles: that our modern conception of the self is historically constituted, and that the way to trace its development is to focus on a sequence of philosophical texts (rather than, say, literary or historical ones). Just as Taylor's account of a self divided by the split between inner and outer emerges from a study of the philosophical tradition, so presumably will any alternative account. Why, then, should we not look again at this tradition, not for confirmation of the shifts that Taylor so sensitively identifies, but for places where his ruling categories of inner and outer carry less conviction? Rather than searching for exemplifications of this divide and dubbing them precursors of modernity, we could look instead for points where the inner tacitly depends on the outer or outer on inner, for contexts where these categories are inapposite, or for places where the line between them blurs.

This sort of investigation might awaken us to neglected features of our philosophical tradition which echo in our own self-understanding. It might extend or alter our own conception of the self in ways that would enable us to transcend the troubling dichotomy between the internal and external. Less ambitiously, it might show that we are not simply saddled with Taylor's account of an historical process that gave rise to us, and its attendant difficulties, because there are other stories we can tell. Such other stories as we can come up with may fail to dissolve the distinction between inner and outer sources of morality; but they may nevertheless provide variations and additions which place the distinction in a different light.

Perhaps Taylor will reply that his is the only story which does justice to the moral anguish that is such a pervasive and defining characteristic of modernity. However, to write the end before the beginning is surely to get matters back to front. If we insist on such a teleological stance, we deny ourselves at the outset the philosophical resources for recasting our understanding of the guarantors of morality that Taylor presents as so intractably internal or external.

In this essay I shall sketch a part of an alternative story. Taking the case of Descartes, I shall argue that his handling of the distinction between our internal capacity to reason and an external world that is itself rational is less secure and univocal than Taylor's interpretation allows, and gives rise to a substantive notion of virtue that is missing from Taylor's chapter on disengaged reason. In itself, this discussion may amount to little more than a series of footnotes to the magisterial epic of *Sources of the self*; but I hope that they may be suggestive footnotes none the less. For if, as I shall argue, the internal/external distinction is marked by ambiguities and qualifications even in the work of a philosopher who is taken to represent one of the poles of its development, it seems reasonable to suspect that a more wide-ranging exploration of the history of philosophy will serve to diffuse it still further. Such an investigation may lead us to a vantage point from which the distinction between inner and outer moral sources is less compelling, and the problems that accompany it less intractable. At the same time, it may lead us to some further questions. For example, why does the opposition between inner and outer play such a prominent part in contemporary philosophy's telling of its own history? Why does it continue to exercise such a strong hold over our imaginations?

I

Taylor's discussion of Descartes begins with an interpretation of his epistemology and then pursues its ethical implications. At each stage, the Cartesian view is characterised by contrast with a position that Taylor identifies as Platonic, or sometimes more generally as ancient. To begin with the epistemological version of this opposition, Plato held that we gain correct knowledge by opening ourselves out to the order of ontic Ideas, an order which is intrinsically good,[1] while Descartes believed that we can only start to know things when we learn to disengage ourselves from sensory experience. We must turn inward and formulate rules of reasoning which enable us to grasp the distinction between extended substance and the immaterial mind.[2] Once we come to see that the external world is a world of extended substance, we are able to understand that it is a mechanical system of bodies governed by laws of motion and drained of any moral significance. It has no meaning and sets us no ends. Instead, it is a cosmic machine that we can use to the best of our

---

[1] Taylor, *Sources of the self*, pp. 146, 155.   [2] Ibid., p. 145.

ability to realise whatever ends reason dictates to us.³ Moreover, since our bodies form part of the material universe, the bodily motions we experience as passions (a term encompassing perceptions, sensations and emotions) are equally lacking in moral value.

Since, according to this view, nothing in the external, natural world has any moral meaning, such moral sources as there are must lie within the soul. Taylor here interprets Descartes as holding that moral value resides specifically in our capacity to subject our passions to the dictates of reason by the use of the will. Only this exercise of self-control is worthy of esteem or praise, and to be virtuous is simply to be rational – to have formulated a set of sound rules and be able to stick to them in all circumstances. It is important to Taylor's argument that, in contrast to the Platonic conception, this notion of virtue does not require us to understand the true order of things; the fact that we sometimes reason our way to false judgements does not undercut our virtue, provided that we apply the rules conscientiously.⁴

Taylor grounds this account of an internal conception of reason on two epistemological contrasts, one between the substantive and the procedural, the other between the found and the built. It is in his treatment of these dichotomies, I shall suggest, that the incompleteness of his interpretation comes to light. Using the key opposition between the Platonist and the Cartesian, Taylor first argues that, while rationality is for the Platonist a substantive matter, a matter of understanding particular truths, for the Cartesian it is simply a question of grasping rules or procedures which we arrive at by investigating our own ideas.⁵

Descartes devotes a great deal of attention to devising foolproof methods of enquiry. We must break down our complex ideas into components that are intuitively clear and distinct, then carefully build them up again. So far so procedural. As he continually emphasises, however, what makes these procedures rational is the fact that they enable us to identify and hang on to clear and distinct ideas, which are guaranteed to be true. '[O]ur ideas or notions, being real things and coming from God, cannot be anything but true, in every respect in which they are clear and distinct.'⁶ This certainty in turn rests 'on a metaphysical foundation, namely that God is supremely good and in no way a deceiver, and hence that the faculty which he gave us for distinguishing truth from falsehood cannot lead us into error, so long as we are using it properly and thereby

---

³ Ibid., pp. 148–9.   ⁴ Ibid., p. 149, pp. 151f.   ⁵ Ibid., p. 145.
⁶ René Descartes, *Discourse on the method*, part IV, *The philosophical writings of Descartes*, I, trans. J. Cottingham, R. Stoothoff and D. Murdoch (Cambridge: Cambridge University Press, 1985), p. 130.

perceiving something distinctly'.[7] The rationality of the process of reasoning from one clear and distinct idea to the next surely depends on a commitment to this metaphysical foundation which ensures that it gives us a correct understanding of the world. Were this not the case, it is doubtful whether the procedure alone would count as rational.

Here, then, the procedural and substantive aspects of reason are more closely intertwined than Taylor allows, as are the categories of internal and external. A satisfactory procedural account of reasoning must deliver truths; but in order to be sure that he has satisfied this condition, Descartes has to hold the substantive view that there exists a perfect and hence non-deceiving God. 'If we did not know that everything real and true within us comes from a perfect and infinite being then, however clear and distinct our ideas were, we would have no reason to be sure that they had the perfection of being true.'[8] The validity of the internal rules thus depends on an external Deity who is the source of that supreme epistemological value, certainty.

A similar difficulty attaches to the second contrast to which Taylor appeals to elucidate the difference between internal and external standards of reason, namely that, while the Platonist finds or discovers standards of reasoning by contemplating the world, the Cartesian builds or constructs them.[9] As we have seen, the Cartesian enquirer arrives at canons of reasoning by sifting out her clear and distinct ideas and examining the relations between them. This process is an inward one in the sense that it involves considering ideas or thoughts. Is it not, however, as much a process of discovery as of construction? When we look inwards we find that some of our ideas present themselves in a singular way which allows us to identify them as clear and distinct, and marks them out as the material from which we can deduce further truths.

We have already seen that this capacity is given to us by God and depends on him. 'Every clear and distinct perception is undoubtedly something, and hence cannot come from nothing, but must necessarily have God for its author. Its author, I say, is God, who is supremely perfect, and who cannot be a deceiver on pain of contradiction; hence, the perception is undoubtedly true.'[10] In addition, however, Descartes tells us that some of our clear and distinct ideas are innate. The 'first and most important' of these is the idea of God,[11] but our knowledge of 'the

---

[7] Descartes, *Principles of philosophy*, part IV, article 206, *The philosophical writings of Descartes*, I, p. 290.

[8] Descartes, *Discourse on the method*, p. 130.   [9] Taylor, *Sources of the self*, p. 147.

[10] Descartes, *Meditations on first philosophy*, Fourth meditation, *The philosophical writings of Descartes*, II, trans. J. Cottingham, R. Stoothoff and D. Murdoch (Cambridge: Cambridge University Press, 1985), p. 43.

[11] Descartes, *Meditations on first philosophy*, Fifth meditation, p. 47.

simplest and best known principles', of such common notions as 'Nothing comes from nothing' and 'It is impossible for the same thing to be and not be at the same time', is also 'naturally implanted in our minds.'[12] These ideas are not constructed. They are there waiting for us. And if we did not have within our minds a stock of clear and distinct ideas, Cartesian reasoning would never be able to begin.

Here, then, the metaphors of finding and making do not seem to lie neatly on either side of the external/internal divide but across it. The Cartesian enquirer looks inward but this does not mean that she constructs the standards of reasoning she arrives at. At least part of her task is to discover her own innate ideas, and employ them in the task of investigating the immaterial soul and the material world.

One final aspect of Taylor's distinction between internal and external conceptions of reason which remains troubling concerns the dependence of human enquirers on God. Employing another point of comparison, Taylor emphasises that, while Augustine had achieved certainty by coming 'to see more and more that God acts within him',[13] Descartes portrays a self-sufficient thinker for whom 'the certainty of clear and distinct ideas is unconditional and self-generated'. For this enquirer, God's existence has become 'a theorem in *my* system of perfect science'.[14]

Once again, however, this characterisation seems strained. Descartes does of course offer an argument for God's existence and arrives at its conclusion by the usual steps which take him from one clear and distinct idea to another. In this sense, God's existence is a theorem, reached by internal reasoning rather than, say, by contemplating nature. But this does not imply that the clear and distinct ideas that go into the proof of God's existence are 'unconditional and self-generated'.[15] By the end of the *Meditations* we are meant to understand that, unless a veracious, independently existing God had been there all along, the argument would never have got started. In the first place, if God had not endowed us with some clear and distinct ideas we would never have been able to form a conception of valid argument. Clear and distinct ideas are therefore not entirely self-generated. In addition, our understanding of both material and immaterial substances, and of the means to find out about them, is shown to be not unconditional, but conditional on the existence of a God who does not, and will not, deceive us.

So far I have argued that Descartes' clear and distinct ideas, which are essential to our capacity to reason, do not fit easily into the dichotomies that Taylor employs to elucidate his overarching contrast between inter-

---

[12] Descartes, *Principles of philosophy*, part I, article 49; part IV, article 203.
[13] Taylor, *Sources of the self*, p. 156.
[14] Ibid., p. 157.   [15] Ibid., p. 157.

nal and external modes of reasoning. Insofar as clear and distinct ideas are true, they play a more than procedural part in reasoning and straddle the line between procedure and substance. Insofar as we are able to discover the clarity and distinctness of ideas that are innate in us, it is an oversimplification to describe them as built and constructed. There remains an overwhelming sense in which the clear and distinct ideas with and about which we reason are internal: they are quite simply *in* the mind. They are the correct representations which mirror the material world for us, and also give us access to such abstract realms as mathematics. However, we can only appreciate that this is what clear and distinct ideas are if we understand ourselves as part of an ordered universe created by a veracious God. An appreciation of our internal power to reason thus depends on an appreciation of our part in a universe which extends outside us. Once again, internal and external intertwine.

II

In the second part of his chapter Taylor goes on to argue that 'Descartes' ethic, just as much as his epistemology, calls for disengagement from world and body and the assumption of an instrumental stance towards them'.[16] In particular, it rests on a novel understanding of what the passions are, and gives rise to a revolutionary account of the point of controlling them. The first purported novelty here is that Descartes regards the passions as functional; they 'dispose our soul to want the things which nature deems useful for us, and to persist in this volition: and the same agitation of the spirits which normally causes the passion also disposes the body to make movements which help us to attain these things'.[17] As functional mechanisms they are, however, not entirely reliable: 'the utility of the passions consists simply in the fact that they strengthen and prolong thoughts in the soul which it is good for the soul to preserve and which otherwise might be erased from it. Likewise the harm they may cause consists entirely in their strengthening and preserving these thoughts beyond what is required, or in their strengthening and preserving others on which it is not good to dwell.'[18] To function optimally, the passions must be kept under the control of reason. But the point of subjecting them to reason is not simply to ensure that the soul thinks beneficial thoughts and that appropriate actions follow. Rather, Taylor argues, the ability to control the passions by reason is itself morally valuable, a mark of dignity and a cause for self-esteem. To be

[16] Ibid., p. 155.
[17] Descartes, *The passions of the soul*, article 52, *The philosophical writings of Descartes*, I.
[18] Descartes, *The passions of the soul*, article 74.

virtuous is just to possess the ability to control the passions by the use of the will.[19]

How, though, does this emphasis on the moral force of self-control connect with the internalisation of reason? Once again, Taylor's answer rests on a contrast between the Cartesian view and what he at one point calls 'the Platonic–Stoic tradition of ethics'.[20] Within this latter tradition, the reason for subduing the passions is that they will otherwise prevent us from appreciating that external source of moral value, the natural order of the cosmos. The passions get in the way of moral understanding. For Descartes, the problem is said to be different. First, our ability to regulate our passions enables us to make them serve whatever ends reason recommends us to pursue. Here, Taylor implies, our rational ends are internal in that they are the result of a process of inference which is 'unconditional and self-generated'. Second, self-control is what qualifies us as virtuous. To possess virtue is not to understand something about the world, but to understand something about one's own mind, namely how to use the will to regulate passion.

In this interpretation we see again the shifts from ends to means and from substance to procedure that are so central to Taylor's argument. But has he captured the whole Cartesian story? Does Descartes back off from a conception of substantive moral ends in favour of a purely procedural notion of virtue? And does he hold that, because our passions are simply the effects of bodily motions, they have no more moral significance than the movements of billiard balls? I shall next consider these claims in a little more detail.

First, then, does Cartesian virtue consist simply in self-control, in the exercise of volition which, Descartes tells us, is 'the only, or at least the principal activity of the soul'?[21] In articles 152 and 153 of *The passions of the soul*, Descartes argues that the only thing which gives us reason to esteem ourselves, and for which we can justly be praised, is the exercise of our free will and the control we have over our volitions. To pursue virtue in a perfect manner is to use one's freedom well, that is, never to lack the will to undertake and carry out what one judges to be best.

These passages provide striking evidence for Taylor's reading. However, in assessing them it is important to remember what else Descartes has to say about the relation between the will and reason. In the first place, the will does not work alone. The art of self-control is a matter not just of willing, but of willing what one judges to be best, or what reason dictates. Moreover, Descartes holds that the will is inclined to

---

[19] Taylor, *Sources of the self*, pp. 150–2.   [20] Ibid., p. 156.
[21] Descartes, *Principles of philosophy*, part I, article 43.

follow reason and indeed cannot resist assenting to clear and distinct ideas.[22] So a reliable way (though not the only way) to ensure that one's will conforms to rationally grounded judgements is precisely to reason as clearly and distinctly as possible. Self-control therefore depends to a great extent on reason.

There are, moreover, some clear and distinct ideas which play a particularly important role in enabling the will to follow reason. In order to control our desires, Descartes argues, we need to understand the difference between things that depend on us and things that do not. 'We must recognize that everything is guided by divine Providence, whose external decree is infallible and immutable to such an extent that, except for matters it has determined to be dependent on our free will, we must consider everything that affects us to occur of necessity and as it were by fate, so that it would be wrong for us to desire things to happen in any other way.'[23] Those who clearly understand that this is what the world is like will not desire things that are beyond their control; their volitions will conform to their reason and their passions will come to nothing.

We have here an instance of the way that self-control depends upon understanding certain things about the world; the internal knack of control can only be gained by people who look outward at the world and grasp the fact that it is governed by immutable laws. Internal self-control and substantive understanding of the external world are thus closely connected. Perhaps, however, they are not equally valuable. Perhaps outward-looking understanding is only of value as a means to self-control, which is valuable in itself. This conclusion would fit Taylor's thesis; but in fact Descartes holds that the knowledge which promotes self-control is knowledge of a world that he describes, not instrumentally, in mechanical terms, but unequivocally as the work of divine Providence. To understand it is therefore to understand a God-given order and to wish it otherwise would, Descartes says, be wrong. This world looks more like an external source of moral value than a manipulable realm of functional mechanisms.

Because self-control depends on understanding in this way, people who have control are guaranteed to have other qualities which are part of an established conception of value. *Générosité*, which consists both in a person's 'knowing that nothing truly belongs to him but [the] freedom to dispose his volitions' and in 'a firm and constant resolution to carry out whatever he judges to be best'[24] is, Descartes tells us, 'as it were, the key to all the other virtues'.[25] When we understand the law-governed structure

[22] Descartes, *Principles of philosophy*, part I, article 43.
[23] Descartes, *The passions of the soul*, article 146.
[24] Ibid., article 153.   [25] Ibid., article 161.

of the world we realise that only our volitions are completely within our control; and this resolution in turn contributes to our abilities to judge correctly (we won't frustrate ourselves by desiring ends we can't achieve) and to exercise self-control (we have a clear sense of what we should be controlling). However, a virtuous person must, in Descartes' view, possess more than *générosité*; for this blend of understanding and control needs to be accompanied by several other traits which are equally essential to a virtuous life.

In some cases, these qualities depend quite explicitly on an understanding of things outside ourselves, including other people. For instance, the knowledge that people have the capacity to control their volitions makes us, so Descartes argues, more inclined to attribute their weaknesses to ignorance than to the lack of a good will. It consequently prevents us from feeling contempt for them.[26] Or, to take another case, we become humble once we see that people are all the same both in their capacity to control their volitions and in their tendency to make mistakes.[27] We are then more inclined to render each person his or her due 'and have a very deep humility before God'.[28]

In Descartes' account of some of the other qualities connected with *générosité*, strength of will is more prominent. Thus, people who possess *générosité* 'have complete command over their passions. In particular, they have mastery over their desires, and over jealousy and envy, because everything they think sufficiently valuable to be worth pursuing is such that its acquisition depends solely on themselves ... finally, [they have mastery] over anger, because they have very little esteem for everything that depends on others, and so they never give their enemies any advantage by acknowledging that they are injured by them.'[29]

Descartes also claims, however, that people of *générosité* display all sorts of other conventionally admirable traits which are less obviously connected either to having a strong will or to understanding the universe. Thus, 'because they esteem nothing more highly than doing good to others and disregarding their own self-interest, they are always perfectly courteous, gracious and obliging to everyone'.[30]

Virtue, it emerges, is a complex notion which extends beyond *générosité* as Descartes defines it. When he says that what we commonly call virtues 'are habits of the soul which dispose it to have certain thoughts'[31] we can see that strength of will is what enables us to form habits and sustain them. But only some habits are virtuous. To be virtuous, the soul must

---

[26] Ibid., article 154.   [27] Ibid., article 155.   [28] Ibid., article 164.
[29] Ibid., article 156.
[30] Ibid., article 156.   [31] Ibid., article 161.

also be disposed to have 'certain thoughts', namely those associated with courtesy, humility, courage and so on.

These points suggest that Descartes' notion of virtue is less purely procedural than Taylor's interpretation allows. To be virtuous is to possess a range of specific qualities, of which self-control is only one; and if self-control were not allied to these other qualities (humility, pity, benevolence, etc.) it would not in itself be virtuous. Furthermore, virtue is not acquired solely through the internal resource of reasoning. To become virtuous one must have a particular, substantive understanding of the laws governing the external world and of their moral significance.

What now of the passions? Taylor argues that Descartes' interpretation of the passions as the effects of bodily motions serves to drain them of moral significance. Since the mere movements of our animal spirits cannot tell us anything about the ends we ought to pursue, we are thrown back on our own rationality, on firm and determinate judgements concerning knowledge of good and evil. Taylor allows that, in order to arrive at these judgements, we have to 'take account of and conform to the dispositions of things which we find in the world, or in our own natures', including our passions. But this is not because 'this disposition essentially and of itself commands the love of all rational knowers'. Rather, to take account of it is 'the rational thing to do, where this term is now defined by the standards imposed on the orders we construct in order to live by them'.[32]

I have already tried to explicate an important sense in which the canons of Cartesian rationality are not constructed. Nevertheless, Taylor is surely right that Descartes conceives of the passions as disenchanted – or at least very nearly disenchanted. A qualifying note sounds when we recall that, although our bodies are machines, they are nevertheless machines created by God to function in particular ways. Through reason and experience, we can come to appreciate what it is for them to function well.[33] And part of this appreciation consists in knowing what our various passions are for, and what it is for them to fulfil their natural function in relation to the body, which is 'to move the soul to consent and contribute to actions which may serve to preserve the body or render it more perfect'.[34] This description suggests that we are not to view the passions entirely as the means to moral ends given by reason rather than nature. For the proper working or perfection of the body is part of divine Providence, part of the good that we have to discover in the world and to which our passions are a key.

[32] Taylor, *Sources of the self*, p. 155.
[33] Descartes, *The passions of the soul*, article 138.
[34] Ibid., article 137.

For the most part, however, Descartes does insist that our passions are functional mechanisms that are sometimes beneficial, sometimes harmful, and that they are consequently neither good nor bad in themselves. This interpretation is available to him, Taylor suggests, precisely because he sees the passions as belonging to a disenchanted world of extended substance. Since the passions are part of this world they must lack value; and since they lack value they can be viewed in instrumental terms. If, however, as I have argued, the world beyond the human soul has more moral significance for Descartes than Taylor allows, this connection will be weakened. The moral neutrality and the functional character of the passions will not follow unequivocally from their identity as bodily processes, though they may be regarded as morally neutral and functional for other reasons.

What might these other reasons be? The various ancient philosophies that Taylor discusses have in common a conception of the passions as inherently ambivalent. While they sometimes work to our advantage, they are intrinsically unreliable and often destructive. Moreover, the Stoic tradition (to which, as Taylor points out, Descartes is particularly indebted) upholds the view that only those things which are always 'in agreement with nature' or conducive to our preservation are good in themselves. The passions are consequently not good in themselves; in Taylor's terms, they are not a source of moral value. But at the same time they are understood to contribute to our natural disposition to preserve ourselves and thus serve certain non-moral functions.

This tradition offers a conception of the passions which contains the ingredients that Taylor regards as central to the Cartesian interpretation, while integrating them into a completely different account of what the passions are. For the Stoics, the passions are misjudgements rather than effects of bodily processes. Much of the innovativeness of Descartes' treatment consists, of course, in his relocation of the passions in the body; but the many Stoic strands of his argument suggest that he had precedents for viewing them as functional and as morally neutral which were separate both from his dualism and his mechanical understanding of the physical world.

To speak, as I have done, about the complexities surrounding Descartes' conception of moral value and their implications for a distinction between external and internal sources of moral value may seem to miss Taylor's point. It may be felt that I have simply drawn attention to features of Descartes' work which are left over from the Classical tradition out of which his philosophy emerged. True, Descartes retains a notion of clear and distinct ideas which mirror the world, but this is a residual Platonism. True, he keeps the Stoic idea of a world governed by

Providence, but this is at odds with his more important, revolutionary conception of a mechanical universe. Since Taylor so sensitively identifies what is historically dynamic in his *oeuvre*, it is not helpful to quibble.

Up to a point, I agree. I have indeed concentrated on some of the continuities between ancient and early modern philosophy and have tried to show that the break between Descartes' work and that of his predecessors is less wholehearted and dramatic than Taylor believes. There is no clear transition from an external to an internal notion of reason or from an external to an internal source of moral value. Perhaps, however, Descartes' reliance on the external version of these doctrines is just left over and on its way out. Perhaps the kind of ambiguities I have traced really will have vanished by the time we get, say, to what Taylor describes as Locke's punctual self.

If this were so it would vindicate Taylor's case. However, although I have only been able to discuss the single example of Descartes, it seems to me that both sides of the various distinctions which contribute to Taylor's understanding of the divide between inner and outer continue to play important roles throughout early modern philosophy. Their presence encourages me to think, as I suggested at the beginning, that Taylor's pessimistic story is not the only one we can tell. Indeed, the disengaged self may be a creation, not of Descartes nor of Locke, but of a subsequent historiography.

2 Taylor on truth

Richard Rorty

My deepest, most heartfelt, disagreements with Charles Taylor are too complicated to discuss within the word limit to which the editors have, sensibly, restricted contributors to this volume. Perhaps our most basic disagreement is whether poetry should be seen as 'a means of arranging the order of our internal lives by making an harmonious pattern of extremely complex attitudes, once thought to refer to an external order of metaphysics but now seen to be a symbolic ordering of our inner selves'.[1] Taylor says that 'such a self-enclosed reading manifestly will not do' for such writers as 'Eliot, Pound, Mann, Lawrence, Joyce, Proust or Rilke'. I think that it will do admirably. Indeed, I think that one of the most important changes for the better in recent centuries is our increasing willingness to see our poets as edifying examples of how to be mere human self-fashioners, rather than as people who open us up to something other than themselves, and perhaps other than human.

If Taylor and I tried to argue about whether one should encourage a tendency to envisage hypergoods, rather than simply arranging and balancing ordinary goods, we should probably end up talking about the details of our favourite poems and novels. For I suspect that different literary canons, and disagreement about how to read the works which appear in both our canons, lie at the bottom of our disagreement about the nature of moral experience. My reading of my canon makes me doubt Taylor's claim that we can make sense of our moral life only with 'something like a hypergood perspective'.[2] Taylor reads his favourite authors in the light of his conviction that 'the poet, if he is serious, is pointing to something – God, the tradition – which he believes to be there for all of us'. I read some of these same writers in the light of my conviction that seriousness can, and should, swing free of any such universalistic belief.

Instead of attempting to discuss these deeper differences, however, I am

---

[1] This is I. A. Richard's view of the matter, as formulated by Stephen Spender. Taylor quotes Spender at *Sources of the self*, pp. 490–1.

[2] Ibid., p. 71.

going to stick to a narrow, specifically philosophical, disagreement. I shall confine myself to a parochial topic, one about which only philosophy professors find it profitable to reflect: truth. Taylor thinks of his own attachment to hypergoods as entailing a need to defend some form of the correspondence theory of truth. I reject all forms of that theory except those which are so shallow and trivial as to be non-controversial. I think that Taylor would do better to split off universalism – the belief in hypergoods which are there for all of us – from this theory. He and I would doubtless continue to disagree about moral experience even if we came to agreement on what to say about truth, and about such related issues as the relation of language and thought to the rest of the universe. In the hope of facilitating such limited agreement, I shall bracket, in what follows, everything in Taylor's work except his rejection of what he calls 'Rorty's non-realism'.[3] I hope that my replies to some of his arguments for this rejection will help keep the exchanges between us going. These exchanges started almost twenty years ago, and I have found them invaluable. Taylor is one of the philosophers from whom I have learned most. By now he and I agree on a great deal. Whenever I find myself disagreeing with him, I reflect that I am disagreeing with a philosopher who has thought very hard and long about the topic about which we differ, and whose objections I can deal with only by getting back down to bedrock.

I

I have frequently urged, in the course of polemics against attempts to resuscitate the correspondence theory of truth, that any such theory requires the idea that the world is divided into facts, and that facts are what Strawson calls 'sentence-shaped items', items having the shape of sentences in 'nature's own language'. Taylor deplores my use of 'rhetorical flourishes' such as 'nature's own language' to describe the view of my realist (or, as I should prefer to say, representationalist) opponents. He thinks that I should not pretend, as he puts it, that 'believers in the correspondence theory are "Raving Platonists"' – people who believe that 'a vocabulary is somehow already out there in the world'.[4]

To avoid starting unnecessary hares, I am prepared henceforth to abjure all references to 'nature's own language'. I should insist, however, that this was no more far fetched a rhetorical flourish than Putnam's 'God's-eye point of view'; both flourishes are just ways of saying that

---

[3] This phrase occurs at p. 258 of Taylor's 'Rorty in the epistemological tradition', in *Reading Rorty*, ed. Alan Malachowski (Oxford: Basil Blackwell, 1990).

[4] Ibid., pp. 268–9, and also p. 262.

correspondence theorists need to have criteria for the adequacy of vocabularies as well as of statements, need the notion of one vocabulary somehow 'fitting' the world better than another. So perhaps the chastest, least rhetorical, way of making my point is to restate it as: believers in the correspondence theory have to claim that some vocabularies (e.g. Newton's) do not just work better than others (e.g. Aristotle's) but do so because they represent reality more adequately. Taylor thinks that good sense can be made of this claim, and I do not.

Taylor says that there will be 'no further problem with the proposition that the reality independent of my representations makes them true or false' once one drops the absurd notion of 'the thing-in-itself' and, with Heidegger and Wittgenstein, refuses to let an '*ex ante* theory of know-ledge' dictate to ontology. For once one has done so, once one recognises the primacy of the *Zuhanden* to the *Vorhanden*, and realises that to agree on a language is to agree on a form of life, one will find oneself 'at grips with a world of independent things'.[5]

But none of us anti-representationalists has ever doubted that most things in the universe are causally independent of us. What we question is whether they are representationally independent of us. For X to be representationally independent of us is for X to have an intrinsic feature (a feature which it has under any and every description) such that it is better described by some of our terms rather than others. Because we can see no way to decide which descriptions of an object get at what is 'intrinsic' to it, as opposed to its merely 'relational', extrinsic features (e.g. its description-relative features), we are prepared to discard the intrinsic–extrinsic distinction, the claim that beliefs represent, and the whole question of representational independence or dependence. This means discarding the idea of (as Bernard Williams has put it) 'How things are *anyway*', apart from whether or how they are described.

Taylor seems to think that neither I nor any one else would feel any 'serious temptation to deny that the no chairs claim [viz. 'there are no chairs in this room'] will be true or false in virtue of the way things are, or the nature of reality'. But I do, in fact, feel tempted to deny this. I do so because I see two ways of interpreting 'in virtue of the way things are'. One is short for 'in virtue of the way our current descriptions of things are used and the causal interactions we have with those things'.[6] The

---

[5] Ibid., p. 270, p. 264, p. 270.
[6] This is a paraphrase of Davidson's 'the truth of an utterance depends on just two things, what the words mean and how the world is arranged'. I expatiate on the point of this claim in my 'Pragmatism, Davidson and truth', in Ernest LePore, ed., *Truth and interpretation: perspectives on the philosophy of Donald Davidson* (Oxford: Basil Blackwell, 1986), pp. 344ff.

other is short for '*simply* in virtue of the way things are, quite apart from how we describe them'. On the first interpretation, I think that true propositions about the presence of chairs, the existence of neutrinos, the desirability of respect for the dignity of our fellow human beings, *and about everything else* are true 'in virtue of the way things are'. On the second interpretation, I think that *no* proposition is true 'in virtue of the way things are'.

Taylor cannot really believe that the ways we describe things, the words which make up our truth-value candidates, are simply irrelevant to the truth of our sentences and beliefs. So he might accept the first interpretation. But if he does, he opens himself to the question: can we distinguish the role of our describing activity, our use of words, and the role of the rest of the universe, in accounting for the truth of our true beliefs? I do not see how we can. To say that we cannot is to say, with Davidson, that we need to drop 'the third dogma of empiricism', the distinction between scheme and content. This means dropping the attempt to sort our propositions by whether they are 'made' true by 'the world' or by 'us' – dropping the problematic of realism and anti-realism by dropping the representationalist presuppositions of that problematic.

On my view, if we drop that distinction and that problematic, we cannot explain what we mean by 'correspondence' unless we posit something like 'the world as it is in itself', or 'the features which a thing has intrinsically, independent of how we describe it'. That is why I think that when the thing-in-itself goes, correspondence goes too, and why I think Taylor's attempt to keep the latter without the former is doomed to fail. Although the idea of the 'thing-in-itself' is in dispute, it seems to me to survive, in disguise, in the purportedly non-controversial idea that things have intrinsic, non-description-relative, features. That idea is quite distinct from the claim that most things, under most descriptions, have the features they do in entire causal independence from the way they are described.

Take dinosaurs. Once you describe something as a dinosaur, its skin colour and sex life are causally independent of your having so described it. But before you describe it as a dinosaur, or as anything else, there is no sense to the claim that it is 'out there' having properties. *What* is out there? The thing-in-itself? The world? Tell us more. Describe it in more detail. Once you have done so, but only then, are we in a position to tell you which of its features are causally independent of having been described and which are not. If you describe it as a dinosaur, then we can tell you that the feature of being oviparous is causally independent of our description of it as oviparous, but the feature of being an animal whose existence has only been suspected in recent centuries is not. That is not a distinction between 'intrinsic' and 'merely relational' features of dino-saurs. It is just a distinction between their causal-relations-under-a-description to some things (eggs) and their causal-relations-under-a-description to other things (us).

It was thought (e.g. by Kripke) that causal relations are not under a description, whereas intentional relations are. The popularity of this belief was enhanced by the Davidsonian slogan that causation, unlike explanation, is not under a description. But I think that this slogan, so phrased, is a bit misleading. What we Davidsonians should say is that the same causal relationship could be explained in many different ways, as many as there are ways of describing the things related. This amounts to saying: no matter which way you describe the things between which you are trying to find causal relations, you should be able to see (find, envisage, posit) the very same such relations between them under every description of them. (That is, if you describe them as dinosaurs and eggs, you should be able to spot the same causal relations as when you describe them as batches of molecules, or as space–time bumps). In other words, Davidson's point is (or should be) not that causal relations are more 'intrinsic' to things than their descriptions, nor that describing things as causally related to one another gets closer to the way they are 'anyway' than describing them in other ways. His point is (or should be) just that causal relations need to be kept constant under the kind of redescription in which both of the causally related things are redescribed in the same terms.

People who pride themselves on being realists may ask: *why* do they need to be kept constant? Because they *really and truly are* invariant, or merely because unity is a desirable feature of science, a useful regulative idea which would be endangered if we let causal relations vary with descriptions? I see this as a bad question, because it presupposes one more version of the scheme/content distinction. It is one more example of the fatal temptation to hold on to the distinction between 'in-itself' and 'for-us'. This latter distinction (which is *not* the same as the harmless and necessary distinction between 'is' and 'seems')[7] is the root of most of the pseudo-problems in this area of philosophy.

Putnam's well-known criticisms of Kripke's (and his own) efforts to develop a causal theory of reference make clear why describing some-thing's causal relations to other things is describing features which are no more and no less 'intrinsic' or 'extrinsic' to the thing than any other features of it, including its having been described by human beings. Once

---

[7] The difference is that is–seems is a distinction which applies to objects under a description, whereas in-itself–for-us is an attempt to distinguish between an object under no descrip-tion and a described object.

we drop the scheme/content distinction, we have no use for the distinction between the 'intrinsic' and the 'relational' features of things.

I can dramatise my basic disagreement with Taylor by taking up his contrast between our *self-* understanding and our understanding of 'independent objects'. Taylor brings up this contrast after suggesting that I might wish to say that I 'agree perfectly well with [Taylor's] post-epistemological, intra-framework notion of truth as correspondence' but think that such an intra-framework notion of correspondence is 'trivial' and 'empty'.[8] So I do, and I also resist Taylor's claim that 'this kind of truth (the post-epistemological kind) contrasts with something. It's not all the truth there is.'

'What it contrasts with,' Taylor says, 'is the truth of self-understanding. Just because we are partly constituted by our self-understandings, we can't construe them as of an independent object, in the way our descriptions of things are ... There isn't a single independent reality, staying put through all the changes in description, like the solar system stayed there, waiting for Kepler.'[9] I claim that we cannot make sense of the claim that 'the solar system stayed there, waiting for Kepler', or at least not the sense that Taylor needs to make of it. As I see it, the only difference between redescribing the solar system and redescribing myself is that I use the redescription to make true statements about the state of the solar system antecedent to my redescription whereas, in some cases, I don't use my present redescriptions to make true statements about my earlier self. In the case of a 'Sartrean' redescription which changes the redescriber (e.g. when I redescribe myself as a coward or a homosexual, thus becoming something different) I make a predicate (e.g. 'self-confessed coward', 'self-aware homosexual') true of my present self which was not true of my old self. But there are no scientifically interesting 'Sartrean' redescriptions of the solar system; large-scale astrophysical descriptions of it were, if true

---

[8] By 'intra-framework' Taylor here means a notion of truth provided by our non-representational dealings with the *Zuhanden*. He thinks these dealings not only 'show us as being at grips with a world of independent things' but provide us with the insight that 'our representations of [the world], are true or false by correspondence' ('Rorty', p. 270). As a Sellarsian psychological nominalist, who believes that all awareness is a linguistic affair, I of course am suspicious of the notion of 'non-representational dealings with the world'. But the matter is complicated by the fact that, unlike Sellars, I do not see language as *representing* anything. As I say in more detail when I return to the *Zuhanden* versus *Vorhanden* distinction below, I think that our dealings with things give us, at most, a sense of the causal independence of objects, but do *not* give us any notion of truth as correspondence. Taylor thinks (ibid., p. 271) that 'ordinary people' are believers in the correspondence theory of truth, and that my views 'might surprise and scandalize them'. I do not think that non-philosophers have any theory of truth, or any familiarity with (or use for) the distinction between 'in-itself' and 'for-us'; but I happily grant that they believe in a world of causally independent things.

[9] Taylor, 'Rorty', p. 270.

at all, always true. So if Kepler's description is right now, it was right before Kepler thought it up.

Is this difference helpfully explicated by Taylor's phrase 'staying put through all changes in description'? If this just means 'the solar system behaved the same way before and after Kepler' it is merely a remark about the causal relations between Kepler and the solar system – just as 'Pierre became a new man after he admitted his cowardice to himself' is simply a remark about the causal relations between the young Pierre's beliefs and behaviour and those of the slightly older Pierre. We do not need the idea of two kinds of truth, nor that of two kinds of reality (e.g. *Vorhandensein* and *Dasein*) to explicate the difference between these two sets of causal relationships. But if 'staying put' means 'there was a world, consisting of a multiplicity of objects differentiated by intrinsic, non-description-relative, features, waiting for somebody to come along and develop a language which cuts it at the joints by assigning a word to each object', or if it presupposes or entails that claim, things get controversial.

The strength of Taylor's position is that people like Goodman, Putnam and I – people who think that there is no description-independent way the world is, no way it is under no description – keep being tempted to use Kantian form–matter metaphors. We are tempted to say that there were no objects before language shaped the raw material (a lot of *ding-ansich*y, all-content-no-scheme, stuff). But as soon as we say anything like this we find ourselves accused (plausibly) of making the false causal claim that the invention of the term 'dinosaur' caused dinosaurs to come into existence – of being what our opponents sneeringly call 'linguistic idealists'. Davidson, however, has shown us how to make our point without saying anything susceptible to that misinterpretation. He suggests that we stop trying to say *anything* general about the relation between language and reality, that we stop falling into our opponents' trap by taking seriously problems which owe their existence to the scheme/content distinction. We should just refuse to discuss such topics as 'the nature of reference'.

This suggestion amounts to saying: answer questions about word–world relations for particular words used in a particular way by particular people, but don't answer any more general questions about such relations.[10] Treat, as Davidson advises, 'words, meanings of words, reference

---

[10] See Davidson's 'Reality without reference' on this point, especially the following passage: 'If the name "Kilimanjaro" refers to Kilimanjaro, then no doubt there is *some* relation between English (or Swahili) speakers, the word, and the mountain. But it is inconceivable that one should be able to explain this relation without first explaining the role of the word in sentences; and if this is so, there is no chance of explaining reference directly in non-linguistic terms.' (*Inquiries into truth and interpretation* (Oxford: Oxford University Press, 1984, p. 220).

and satisfaction' as 'posits we need to implement a theory of truth'[11] – a Tarski-style theory of truth for a particular, used, language.[12] Such a theory is a theory which enables us to predict the behaviour of people who make roughly the same noises in roughly the same situations. It is constructed by inspecting the apparent causal relations between speakers and their environment with the hope of eventually mapping their behaviour on to ours. Such an empirical theory is entirely irrelevant to questions about 'realism' or 'the nature of reference'.

This strategy dictates that whenever a question like '*was* the solar system waiting around for Kepler?' comes up we decline to answer. We insist that, in return for our abandoning our Kantian form–matter metaphors, our opponents abandon their anthropomorphic, pathetic-fallacy, metaphors: no more inorganic objects hoping desperately that somebody will finally find language in which to pick them out, wistfully waiting for somebody to locate the joints which divide them from their neighbours. We think that the only way to get beyond this sterile clash of uncashable metaphors is to put the burden of argument on our opponents by asking them to answer two questions: can you find some way of getting between language and its object (as Wittgenstein sardonically put it) in order to suggest some way of telling which joints are nature's (part of the content) and which merely 'ours' (just part of the scheme)? And if not, can you see any point in the claim that some descriptions correspond to reality better than others?[13]

This brings me to Taylor's distinction between matters 'arbitrable by reason' and other matters. If there were a distinction between a sentence being just plain true and a sentence being true because it corresponded to reality, then there might be some point to a distinction between 'believed because it suits our purposes better than any available alternative' and 'believed because it has survived the arbitration of reason'. For we could say that sentences believed true but not believed to correspond to reality are not arbitrable by reason, whereas those whose truth involves such correspondence are appropriate candidates for rational arbitration. If I

[11] Ibid., p. 222.
[12] I take Davidson's claim (in 'A nice derangement of epitaphs') that 'there is no such thing as a language' to mean simply that there are no sets of conventions to be learned when one learns how to talk, and no abstract structure to be internalised. In the above context, 'truth-theory for a language' just means 'theory which enables you to predict, fairly successfully, what noises or marks a speaker or group of speakers will produce in what situations'.
[13] Readers familiar with Davidson will recognise this second question as a reformulation of his point that 'the notion of fitting the totality of experience, like the notion of fitting the facts, or of being true to the facts, adds nothing intelligible to the simple concept of being true' ('On the very idea of a conceptual scheme', *Inquiries*, p. 195).

understand him correctly, this is in fact Taylor's way of aligning these two distinctions.

Taylor pictures me as saying, by contrast, 'either true by correspondence to reality or not true at all, so moral judgements (and other *Dasein*ish beliefs) can't be true'.[14] This picks me up by the wrong handle. Taylor sees me as interpreting 'all differences between "alternative language-games" non-realistically',[15] whereas I want to discard the whole project of distinguishing between what is to be treated 'realistically' and 'non-realistically'. This is why I cannot see that notions like 'corresponding' and 'representing' have anything to do with the distinction between rational arbitrament and alternative ways of settling disputes. I see that distinction as needing no fancier philosophical explication than is offered by the distinction between persuasion and force (suitably fleshed out with

[14] See 'Rorty', p. 272: 'He [Rorty] seems to be as always drawing his inference that a representation which is not made true by some independent reality might just as well not be considered a candidate for truth at all.' My inference is rather: 'since no proposition is "made" true by anything, and since no sentence is a representation of anything, all candidates for truth are on a par in respect of relation to an independent reality.' Taylor takes me to have something like a correspondence view when it comes to normal, routine, physical science, but unwilling to grant that moral reflection, or revolutionary, paradigm-changing, physical science arrives at truth in the way normal physics does. My point is rather that the difference between doing physics (either normal or revolutionary) and reflecting on one's moral character is not a matter of truth verses no truth, or of different kinds of truth, but *just* the difference between finding sentences which, if true, are (usually) always true, and finding sentences which either have to include dates or else have to be seen as changing their truth-value. The only other difference is degree of controversiality – a sociological matter without philosophical significance.

I have to admit, however, that something like the view which Taylor attributes to me, and which I am here repudiating, can be found in certain passages of *Philosophy and the mirror of nature*. There was an only half-erased decisionism in that book – an unhappy tendency to make existentialist noises, noises which presuppose a usable distinction between *Wille* and *Vorstellung*. By slowly coming to understand the thorough-going anti-representationalism of Davidson's approach to language, I have been helped to reach what I hope is a more consistent view. I should think that decisionism was hard to find in most of the texts which Taylor cites in 'Rorty in the epistemological tradition'. But I confess that as late as 1986 it still rears its ugly head. For I was still making the unhappy distinction between 'demonstrating that previous philosophers were mistaken' and 'offering redescriptions in an alternative language', instead of briskly urging that to say that one's predecessors used a bad language *is* to say that they made a certain kind of mistake. (This lapse is cited by Taylor in 'Rorty', p. 259.) Whatever dumb things I may have said in the past, I am now heartily in accord with Taylor that 'there is no automatic inference from lack of consensus to unarbitrability' ('Rorty', p. 263) and that there is no plausibility to the 'scenario of closed pictures' (ibid., p. 260). I also am happy to say that when I put forward large philosophical views I am making 'claims to truth' (see ibid., pp. 266–7) rather than simply a recommendation to speak differently. After what I admit was a good deal of wobbling and weaseling on the point, I am now prepared to go all the way with Quine in saying that there is no epistemic, methodological, or 'status' line between science and philosophy (though, of course, I am still not willing to privilege the vocabulary of physics in the way in which Quine does).

[15] Taylor, 'Rorty', p. 273.

Foucaldian warnings about insidious 'capillary' uses of power).[16] I think of all instances of persuasion, of oneself or of others, as equally cases of 'the arbitration of reason'.[17] Debates about astrophysics, how to read Rilke, the desirability of hypergoods, which movie to go to, and what kind of ice cream tastes best, are, in this respect, on a par. There is no point to asking in which of these cases there is 'a fact of the matter' or 'a truth of the matter', though there may be a point in asking whether any useful purpose is served by spending much time debating the matter.

II

So far I have been talking about passages in which Taylor employs notions which I refuse to use, and so asks questions which I refuse to answer. I turn now to the differing stories we tell about what has happened in twentieth-century philosophy, the differing narratives we construct within which to place ourselves. Taylor and I both pride ourselves on having escaped from the collapsed circus tent of epistemology – those acres of canvas under which many of our colleagues are still thrashing aimlessly about. But each of us thinks that the other is still, so to speak, stumbling about among the tangled guy-ropes, rather than having escaped altogether.

Taylor thinks that once one gets out from under epistemology one comes to an 'uncompromising realism'.[18] I think one comes to a position in which the only version of 'realism' one has left is the trivial, uninteresting and common-sensical one which says that all true beliefs are true

---

[16] But not so padded as to eclipse the distinction altogether. Some overenthusiastic Foucaldians, alas, have tried to make the term 'rational persuasion' inapplicable to *anything*; they have done so by treating even the most judicious, courteous and apparently unfettered parliamentary or academic debate as an instance of 'violence', because certain alternatives which the participants never thought of, or considered unworthy of serious consideration, are 'marginalized'. This is as pointless as saying that the debates between Democriteans and Aristotelians did violence to the alternatives which Einstein would eventually propose.

[17] Taylor (at 'Rorty', p. 262) criticises me for saying that the world doesn't 'decide between' language-games, and for reinterpreting issues (e.g. between Aristotle and Newton) which 'have been quite conclusively decided rationally' as having been 'settled on pragmatic grounds'. What I meant by saying that the world doesn't decide is that we didn't have a criterion for choosing between Aristotle and Newton in the sense in which poker players have one for deciding who takes the pot. The former decision was taken in the same way all large, complex, non-criterion-governed, rational decisions are taken – on pragmatic grounds. What could be more rational than to say that it's no longer worth the trouble adding new epicycles, re-interpreting gravitational attraction as natural motion and otherwise shoring up Aristotle's cosmology? Why bother to make a big *Vorhandensein-*versus-*Dasein* distinction to distinguish that sort of decision from the decision that it is no longer worth the trouble shoring up the distinction between my own behaviour and that of a coward by making a lot of fine supplementary distinctions, throwing in a lot of *ad hoc* excuses, etc?

[18] Ibid., p. 258.

because things are as they are. This is uninteresting because it says only that the production of true beliefs is a matter of causal relations between language-users and the rest of the universe, and that if either were different, their relations would be different. Realism becomes interesting only when we supplement plain speech and common-sense considerably by invoking what I regard as the specifically philosophical distinction between the in-itself and the for-us. Taylor sees me as bearing the burden of argument because he thinks that this latter distinction cannot simply be walked away from but must be dealt with.[19] I think that neither he nor anyone else has explained why we cannot just walk away from it, that nobody has explained what good this distinction is supposed to do us. I keep hoping that Taylor, as fervent an anti-Cartesian as I am, will join me in abandoning it. Alas, he persists in agreeing with Bernard Williams, Barry Stroud and other admirers of Descartes, that it is indispensable.

Taylor thinks that the early Heidegger helps us to avoid both a reductionistic naturalism and the boring epistemological problematic of Cartesian scepticism. He sees me (particularly because of my sympathies with Daniel Dennett and my reluctance to admit that 'there really is something it is like to be a human or a bat, but not to be a fifth-generation computer')[20] as inclined to reductionism. I see myself as a wholehearted naturalist, but one who is as anti-reductionist as Taylor himself. I should define 'naturalism' as the claim that there is no occupant of space–time that is not linked in a single web of causal relations to all other occupants; and that any explanation of the behaviour of any such spatio-temporal object must consist in placing that object within that single web. I should define reductionism as the insistence that there is not only a single web but a single privileged description of all entities caught in that web. The reductionist thinks that we need explanatory unity as well as causal unity – a way of commensurating all explanatory vocabularies, one which will give us true nomologicals connecting all these entities (thoughts and neurons, vices and hormones, actions and motions, persons and organisms). Having learned from Davidson to be satisfied with token–token identities between entities differently described, I regard myself as cleansed of reductionist sin.[21] But this redemption makes me all the more eager to insist, against Taylor, that Heidegger and Merleau-Ponty do not show us how to avoid naturalism, but merely caution us against letting naturalism slide over into reductionism.

---

[19] See ibid., p. 273.   [20] Ibid., p. 265.

[21] One of the things for which I am grateful to Davidson is his having shown us how to distinguish what is alive in naturalism from what is dead in reductionism. For more on this point, see 'Non-reductive physicalism' in my *Objectivity, relativism and truth* (Cambridge: Cambridge University Press, 1991), pp. 113–25.

Taylor and I agree that epistemology is something to get beyond, but he thinks me still 'a prisoner of the epistemological world-view'.[22] He thinks this because, as he put in an earlier essay, 'Overcoming epistemology':[23]

the whole epistemological construal of knowledge is mistaken. It doesn't just consist of inner pictures of outer reality, but grounds in something quite other ... We can draw a neat line between my picture of the object and that object, but not between my dealing with the object and that object ... The notion that our understanding of the world is grounded in our dealings with it is equivalent to the thesis that this understanding is not ultimately based on representations at all, in the sense of depictions which are separately identifiable from what they are of.

Whereas Taylor thinks Heidegger on *Zuhandensein*, and Merleau-Ponty on action and the body, help us out of epistemology, I think they keep us within it just insofar as they allow a place, however derivative, for pictures (and thus for the notions of 'representation' and 'correspondence').[24] They also help keep us within it by treating our non-linguistic causal interaction with the rest of the universe as 'grounding' knowledge rather than just plain helping to cause it. Following Robert Brandom and Mark Okrent, I want to see the *Vorhanden* as merely a special case of the *Zuhanden* by seeing words as merely a special case of tools.[25] So I do not see our dealings with the world as the framework (what Searle calls 'the Background') which makes picturing possible; I do not think that either language or knowledge has anything to do with picturing, representing or corresponding, and so I see formulating and verifying propositions as just a special case of what Taylor calls 'dealing' and I call 'coping'.

Where Taylor sees a more primordial relation with the world than representation, I see no break between non-linguistic and linguistic interactions of organisms (or machines) with the world. The only difference between such interactions is that we call interactions 'linguistic' when we find it helpful to correlate the marks and noises being produced by

---

22 Taylor, 'Rorty', p. 258.
23 'Overcoming epistemology' in *After philosophy*, ed. Kenneth Baynes, James Bohman and Thomas McCarthy (Cambridge, Mass.: MIT Press, 1987), p. 477.
24 At *Sources of the self*, p. 176, Taylor says that Heidegger and Merleau-Ponty help us see that 'radical objectivity is only intelligible and accessible through radical subjectivity'. I do not believe there is such a thing as radical objectivity; that is, I reject Bernard Williams' idea that physics can assume a point of view which ignores human needs and interests – an idea which Taylor accepts. I think that the subjective–objective distinction can be as safely and profitably neglected as the distinction between for-us and in-itself.
25 Note that this is quite compatible with saying that 'language speaks us', as Heidegger does at the outset of 'Letter on humanism'. We self-creating tool-users cause new predicates to be true of ourselves whenever we create new tools with which to create ourselves. Language can speak us even though a language is just a bunch of marks and noises thrown about in more or less predictable ways by human beings. Poets can be the unacknowledged legislators of world-historical epochs even though they are merely human beings who use marks and noises in unpredictable ways.

other entities with the ones we ourselves make – to engage in translation, as well as in other ways of explaining the behaviour of the beings we are observing.[26] So, *pace* Taylor, we cannot draw a line between the object and our picture of the object, for what Taylor calls 'picturing' the object is just more dealing with it. It is just interacting with it in a more complex way than we did before we thought up a linguistic description of it. All that we can draw a line between is the object and some other objects (the marks, noises, brain-states, or whatever, which are helping us cope with the initial object). The latter are, usually, neither pictures nor representations.[27]

III

I hope that what I have been saying shows that I am not a 'non-realist' in the sense in which Taylor takes me to be one, and that my pragmatism (or, at least, my updated,[28] more thoroughly and explicitly Davidsonised and anti-representationalist, version of it) is not subject to some of the charges Taylor makes in 'Rorty in the epistemological tradition'. But I realise that even if we put all questions about truth, realism and correspondence to one side, Taylor would still find my pragmatism too entrenched in the Enlightenment tradition, too unaware of the need for hypergoods.

I am one of those who lack a sense of (in Taylor's words) 'how deep the roots are of our fragile consciousness, and how mysterious and strange its emergence is'.[29] I am also one of those who, like Aristotle and Dewey, think that the moral life is a series of compromises.[30] But at least I can try

---

[26] For what it is worth, I agree with Dreyfus, Taylor and Searle that mark and noise-making robots which, in Dreyfus' phrase, 'lack the flexibility of a six-month old child' cannot be viewed as using a language. In particular, they cannot be viewed as having 'internalised' the language used by their programmer in her flow charts. To use a language requires interacting with the rest of the world in such a way that a radical interpreter could figure out how to translate the marks and noises one makes into sentences of the interpreter's language. It is one thing to say, with Dennett, that we can hardly avoid taking the intentional stance when trying to predict the behaviour of robots and another thing to say that they are thinking or have 'inner representations' (except in the trivial sense in which the retina bears an inner representation of what is before the eye, or that inside the thermostat there is a representation of the temperature of the room). The basic anti-MIT thrust of the arguments about intentionality which Dreyfus, Taylor and Searle have been offering all these years now seems to me right, even though I do not see the use of Searle's notion of 'intrinsic intentionality' or of Nagel's notion that robots lack a vital ingredient called 'something it is like to be . . .'.

[27] Sometimes, of course, they *are* pictures or representations, as when we use an illustrated dictionary, or a map, or a field guide to identify birds, or wanted posters to identify criminals. Then we have representations in the proper sense – items some of whose parts can be correlated one to one with parts of the thing being represented (a condition which obviously does not hold for most sentences or beliefs).

[28] See note 14 above.   [29] Taylor, *Sources of the self*, p. 347.   [30] Ibid., p. 66–7.

to clear myself of the charge which Taylor levels at 'theories of Enlightenment materialist utilitarianism '. Such theories, Taylor says, 'have two
sides – a reductive ontology and a moral impetus'.[31] Like Dewey (and
Taylor himself) I am trying to hang on to the moral impetus. Unlike both
Dewey and Taylor I am trying to do so while dropping the very idea of
ontology (*any* ontology, reductive or otherwise – even the neutral monist
ontology of 'experience' which Dewey developed in *Experience and
nature*). I hope that this paper has shown that, whatever the other defects
of my philosophical position, I am not one of those who, as Taylor puts it,
'allows epistemology to command ontology'.[32]

[31] Ibid., p. 337.   [32] Taylor, 'Rorty', p. 264.

Part II

Interpreting modernity

3   Modernity and disenchantment: some
historical reflections

Quentin Skinner

The historian Alexander Kinglake wanted the following inscription to be placed on all churches: *Important if true.*[1] The same motto could equally well be inscribed on Charles Taylor's masterly new survey, *Sources of the self*.[2] In some measure the appropriateness of the motto is simply a tribute to the intellectual weight of Taylor's achievement, an achievement which it is a pleasure as well as an honour to be helping to celebrate in this book. But in part its appropriateness stems from the fact that Taylor's most recent message, like that of the churches, is that our present secularised outlook may be inadequate to meet the moral challenges posed by modernity.[3] It is this aspect of Taylor's philosophical position on which I should chiefly like to comment.

Taylor's wish to question and transcend our 'stripped-down secular outlook' appears in *Sources of the self* in connection with his analysis of what he takes to be 'moral imperatives which are felt with particular force in modern culture'.[4] Although Taylor states and restates his list of these imperatives at a number of different points, he cannot, I think, be said to do so at any stage with complete consistency. Without being overschematic, however, I think one can say that he distinguishes four main elements in our modern vision of 'strongly valued' goods.[5]

One characteristic component of modern moral consciousness is said to derive from the emphasis we place on the need to avoid suffering. Put positively, the value we are held to cherish is that of considering the welfare of others.[6] But Taylor is even more concerned with a second

---

[1] The proposal is recorded in Geoffrey Madan, *Notebooks*, ed. J. A. Gere and John Sparrow (Oxford: Oxford University Press, 1981), p. 11.

[2] In this chapter I draw heavily on an article I have already published about *Sources of the self*. See Quentin Skinner, 'Who are "we"? Ambiguities of the modern self', *Inquiry*, 34 (1991), pp. 133–53. For permission to cite from that earlier discussion I am grateful to the editor of *Inquiry*. For helping me to recast and strengthen my original argument I am much indebted to Raymond Geuss and Jonathan Lear.

[3] This is the formula Taylor employs in his own contribution to the symposium on *Sources of the self*, published in *Inquiry* in June 1991. See Taylor, 'Comments and replies', p. 240.

[4] Taylor, *Sources of the self*, pp. 495, 520.   [5] Ibid., p. 4, 14, 20, 42.

[6] Ibid., pp. 12–14; cf. p. 394.

aspect of our contemporary sensibility, our disposition to attach the highest moral importance to respecting other people's rights. We have come to think of everyone as possessing such rights, in consequence of which we have come to think of rights themselves as having a universal character. This prompts us to espouse a global ideal of justice, a value we define mainly in terms of the need to ensure that human rights are recognised.[7] At the same time, we attach a no less exalted importance to our own rights to follow whatever lines of individual self-development we may choose for ourselves, which in turn means that we place a correspondingly strong emphasis on the values of autonomy and integrity.[8]

Taylor goes on to claim that our anxiety to acknowledge the rights and equal moral worth of every individual expresses itself in our culture in a distinctive style. We have come to believe, in a manner Taylor regards as unique among the higher civilisations, that the obligations and commitments of 'ordinary life' embody moral and spiritual values worthy of our deepest respect.[9] Taylor has in mind the obligations of production ('the making of things needed for life') and of reproduction (the life of 'marriage and the family').[10] For Taylor, as for Max Weber, this 'affirmation of everyday life' represents the distinctive as well as the most far-reaching legacy of Protestant spirituality. It was Puritanism that gave rise to an ethic of work and a 'companionate' view of marriage, thereby acting as the main progenitor of a bourgeois scale of values in which ordinary callings came to be seen as sanctified.[11]

Taylor's fourth and fundamental claim is that all these commitments are underpinned by a general moral outlook definitive of modernity. We have come to believe that we ourselves are the sources and creators of the values by which we live. This vision of the modern world as disenchanted, lacking any sense of God as an immanent force or morality as objectively grounded, again appears to owe a considerable debt to Max Weber. Nevertheless, Taylor develops the argument very much in his own style, retracing the steps by which we have arrived at our present position in an ambitious historical survey extending from ancient Greece to the philosophy of the Enlightenment.[12]

Taylor begins with Plato, for whom there was a 'tight connection' between 'awareness of right order in our lives and of the order of the cosmos'.[13] Taylor's main concern is to contrast this position with that of

---

[7] Ibid., pp. 10–12; cf. p. 395.   [8] Ibid., p. 12; cf. p. 314.
[9] Ibid., pp. 11–13; cf. pp. 211–12.
[10] Ibid., p. 211.   [11] Ibid., pp. 224–5.
[12] This survey occupies most of part II of Taylor's book. See *Sources of the self*, pp. 109–207.
[13] Ibid., p. 125.

Descartes, but he first notices that 'on the way from Plato to Descartes stands Augustine'.[14] Augustine still believed that our values must be founded on common standards lying outside ourselves, but also began to emphasise the more subjective notion of an inner guiding light.[15] Descartes took a second giant step towards modern subjectivity when he insisted that the sources of knowledge as well as morality must be sought entirely within us.[16] Locke went on to argue that we have no access to any innate ideas about morality or truth, inferring that all our beliefs, as well as our very personalities, must therefore be constantly re-created by our mental activity.[17] By the time we come to Rousseau, the process by which our moral values became disengaged from external standards is more or less complete. Although Rousseau may not have taken the final step, he made it easy to arrive at the conclusion that, as Taylor put it, 'the inner voice of my true sentiments *defines* what is the good'.[18]

It is crucial to Taylor's argument that these are the beliefs 'we' affirm. Sometimes, it is true, he recognises that they can hardly be treated as the values of every denizen of planet Earth. They are merely the conceptions of the self and the good 'which are at home in the modern West'.[19] But he nevertheless thinks that this 'new moral culture', which first arose in 'England, America and (for some facets) France' at the beginning of the nineteenth century, has been radiating 'outward and downward' to the rest of the world ever since.[20] Taylor is, in short, offering us a portrait of ourselves. So the first question to ask is whether the likeness is satisfactory.

It seems to me that Taylor offers a number of genuinely illuminating insights into the distinctiveness of our modern condition. He is surely right in the first place to stress the peculiarity as well as the centrality of the modern belief that individuals should be seen as bearers of rights which can in some sense be viewed as personal properties. Moral philosophers in ancient and medieval Europe were greatly concerned with the question of distributive justice, and thus with the question of what is due to us as a matter of right. But they lacked a vocabulary to articulate the suggestion that what is due to us as a matter of right is something which can in turn be called our rights. It was only during the later Middle Ages that this conception of 'subjective' right began to enter European political discourse.[21] And it was only in the course of the seventeenth century that

---

[14] Ibid., p. 127.   [15] Ibid., pp. 132–3.   [16] Ibid., p. 143.
[17] Ibid., pp. 164, 171.
[18] Ibid., p. 362.   [19] Ibid., p. ix.   [20] Ibid., p. 305.
[21] For contrasting suggestions about when exactly this came about, see Michel Villey, 'Le genèse du droit subjectif chez Guillaume d'Occam', *Archives de philosophie du droit*, 9 (1964), pp. 97–127; A. S. McGrade, 'Ockham and the birth of individual rights', in *Authority and power*, ed. Brian Tierney and Peter Linehan (Cambridge: Cambridge

the concept began to acquire that moral hegemony which it has never subsequently lost.[22]

Taylor also seems to me deeply perceptive in his comments on the modern preoccupation with everyday life and work. The Graeco-Roman vision of the good life certainly allowed no space for the development of anything resembling an ethic of work. It was a vision too firmly wedded to the presumed connection between the progress of civilisation and the enjoyment of leisure. Nor is it easy to find in premodern Europe any strong precedents for our modern belief that the lives of ordinary folk may be deserving of just as much respect as those of great heroes. The moralists of antiquity and the Renaissance were too much concerned with ideals of honour and glory for such a perspective to be admissible. Nor was their outlook fundamentally altered when these values were transmuted under Christianity into an admiration for those individuals whose way of life appeared to promise them heavenly as opposed to worldly glory. The main effect of this change was simply to replace the worship of heroes with the worship of saints. As Taylor indicates, it was only after the Reformation that the duties of everyday life came to seem a major site of moral value and commitment.

It is difficult, however, to feel altogether satisfied with Taylor's sketch of 'our' predicament. Consider first his discussion of the value of autonomy, summarised in his declaration that 'everyone in our civilisation feels the force' of John Stuart Mill's demand that we should 'accord people the freedom to develop in their own way'.[23] I am far from confident that everyone in our civilisation has heard of John Stuart Mill. But even among those who broadly concur with such views, is it really true that there is general agreement about the relationship between the idea of 'legitimate development' and 'such things as pornography'? According to Taylor, 'no one doubts' in the case of pornography that, if its prohibition endangers such development, we have a reason for relaxing social con-

---

University Press, 1980) pp. 149–65; Brian Tierney, 'Villey, Ockham and the origin of individual rights', in *The weightier matters of the law*, ed. T. Witte and F. S. Alexander (Atlanta: Scholars Press, 1988), pp. 1–31; and Brian Tierney, 'Origins of natural rights language: texts and contexts, 1150–1250', *History of Political Thought*, 10 (1989), pp. 615–46.

[22] I have in mind here especially the centrality of the concept of natural rights, and the idea of liberty as a right, to be found in seventeenth-century contractarian thought. On these themes see John Dunn, *The political thought of John Locke* (Cambridge: Cambridge University Press, 1969); Richard Tuck, *Natural rights theories: their origin and development* (Cambridge: Cambridge University Press, 1979); James Tully, *A discourse on property: John Locke and his adversaries* (Cambridge: Cambridge University Press, 1980); and Quentin Skinner, 'Thomas Hobbes on the proper signification of liberty', *Transactions of the Royal Historical Society*, 40 (1990), pp. 121–51.

[23] Taylor, *Sources of the self*, p. 12.

trols.[24] But this is exactly what a number of recent writers *do* doubt.[25] Instead of concentrating on traditional questions about the possible effects of pornography, these theorists have raised an interpretative question about its meaning or character. Rather than asking what it does, they have asked what it is. They have answered that one way to characterise pornography is to see in it an expression of violence and hatred towards women. It follows that those who claim a right to distribute such materials are claiming a right to propagate violence and hatred. But 'we' already regard such behaviour not as a right but a criminal offence, at least where racial hatred is involved. Why not in the case of women as well?

Taylor unrepentantly responds that 'we generally consider it a reason for some measure that it facilitates people developing in their own way'.[26] But this fails to come to grips with the ferocity of recent attacks on what are perceived as liberal complacencies. What is being suggested is that, even if pornography could be shown to be absolutely vital to the self-development of those who propagate and consume it, we should still have no good reason for relaxing social controls. This is one of several points at which Taylor's account of what 'we' believe appears to underestimate the extent to which a liberal consensus has been vigorously challenged by the continuing march of modernity.[27]

Consider similarly Taylor's emphasis on 'our' conviction that 'the full human life' must in part be 'defined in terms of labour and production, on one hand, and marriage and family life, on the other'.[28] Taylor's view of labour occasionally seems rather sentimental or at least unduly optimistic in tone. When he celebrates the value of work, he lays all his emphasis on the claim that, through acting as 'producers', we are able to gain the satisfaction of creating 'the things needed for life'.[29] But as recent exponents of Green politics have above all emphasised, the sad truth is that much of the labour undertaken in modern capitalist economies is not in this sense productive, while much of what is produced is not in the least needed for life. Again, Taylor appears to underestimate the extent to which 'we' have begun to reject traditional assumptions about production, and to complain at the same time that the worlds of daily labour and self-realisation scarcely intersect.

---

[24] Ibid., p. 12.

[25] The claim has been advanced with the greatest vehemence by Andrea Dworkin. For a discussion see Susan Mendus, 'Harm, offence and censorship', in *Aspects of toleration*, ed. John Horton and Susan Mendus (London: Methuen, 1985), pp. 99–112. See also S. Kappeler, *The pornography of representation* (Cambridge: Polity Press, 1986).

[26] Taylor, 'Comments and replies', p. 253.

[27] For a fuller discussion of this point see Stephen R. L. Clark, 'Taylor's waking dream: no one's reply', *Inquiry*, 34 (1991), pp. 195–215, especially at pp. 198–200 and 202.

[28] Taylor, *Sources of the self*, p. 213.   [29] Ibid., p. 211.

A further question raised by this aspect of Taylor's argument is how far it is really true that 'we' still think of marriage and family life as constitutive of our identities. Taylor's response has been to insist that it 'rather severely misidentifies' his position to suppose that this is what he believes.[30] But his disavowal seems hard to reconcile with the end of *Sources of the self*, and especially with the powerful passage in the concluding chapter where he examines the narcissism of American 'self-help' manuals. He convincingly criticises the 'thinness of ties and shallowness' which this literature implicitly recommends us to cultivate.[31] But it is striking that he makes his point by arguing that, if we insist on 'the primacy of self-fulfillment', the 'solidarities' that will be forced into second place will include those 'of birth, of marriage, of the family'.[32]

I still find troubling the way in which this contrast is drawn. One reason why the issue seems worth pressing is that historians have recently done so much to uncover the paradoxical role played by the institutions of marriage and the family in the development of modern liberal societies. Although the ideology of liberalism has always proclaimed the values of freedom and equality, liberal societies have always been underpinned by a sexual contract in which these ideals have been systematically violated. As a number of feminist historians have recently argued, the result has been to inhibit women from attaining the liberal goals of self-realisation and moral self-development.[33] Again, Taylor appears to me to underestimate the extent to which 'we' have come to accept this indictment. The institutions he invokes to save us from meaninglessness are just those which, according to many of 'us', are most likely to betray our interests and threaten our liberties.

It is not my aim, however, to criticise further Taylor's portrait of 'our' modern predicament, especially as I not only admire but feel influenced by many features of it. I now wish to take up the argument he goes on to develop about the right attitude to adopt towards the values he singles out.

Taylor makes two contrasting points, the first of which is that we cannot fail to see the story he recounts as one of 'epistemic gain'.[34] A declared foe of relativism, he goes so far as to insist that the proper view to take of our own moral evolution must be strongly affirmative. Despite the barbarism of the present century, we should recognise that we have built 'higher standards' into 'the moral culture of our civilisation' than

---

[30] Taylor, 'Comments and replies', p. 239.   [31] Taylor, *Sources of the self*, p. 508.
[32] Ibid., p. 507.
[33] For the best recent statement of the theoretical and historical case, see Carole Pateman, *The sexual contract* (Cambridge: Polity Press, 1988).
[34] Taylor, *Sources of the self*, p. 313.

ever before.[35] More than this, Taylor thinks that (to adopt the current jargon) we cannot but be 'moral realists' about our culture itself.[36] Even though we can see that our picture of the good has been historically formed, we are bound to accept that our inherited values and way of life *are* good, and constitute 'something that we have to embrace'.[37]

But does a knowledge of history really have the effect of tying us to the present in this way? My own view is that exactly the opposite tends to happen. To see why this might be so, consider again Taylor's account of our modern disposition to attach a high degree of moral and even spiritual significance to the values of everyday life and work. Before these commitments could come to figure in our contemporary sense of self-hood, a strongly contrasting picture of spirituality had to be widely challenged, a picture according to which the life of full moral commitment involved the abandonment of precisely these everyday ties. A number of rival images of political life also had to be obliterated, particularly the Renaissance ideal of the citizen not as a bearer of rights but rather as someone engaged in government who acknowledges an overarching duty to contribute to the common good. We need to recognise, in short, that the march of modernity left a number of casualties lying on the roadside of history, including such previously prominent and respected figures as the Citizen and the Monk.

Let us now suppose that, in learning this much history, we also come to understand something of the causal processes by which our modern 'everyday' values triumphed over these earlier and incommensurable images of spiritual and political life. No historian denies that the ethic of family life and work must have answered to some authentic and important aspirations among the peoples of western Europe in the sixteenth century. Had this not been so, it is hard to see how anything could ever have been achieved or legitimised in its name. At the same time, however, historians have been impressed by the number of powerful groups that had an interest in patronising and encouraging the growth of these values at the expense of older and more familiar conceptions of the moral life. It was obviously in the interests of aspiring absolutist rulers to insist that, as Hobbes puts it in *De cive*, a citizen's primary duties lie not in the public but entirely in the private and familial spheres.[38] The prize for winning this argument was to permit the concentration of more and more political power in fewer and fewer hands. It was even more obviously in the

[35] Ibid., p. 397.   [36] Ibid., pp. 6–8.   [37] Ibid., p. 347.
[38] Thomas Hobbes, *De cive*, ed. Howard Warrender (Oxford: Clarendon Press, 1983), esp. pp. 176–7. Hobbes' *De cive* constitutes a crucial document in the legitimisation of the change with which I am here concerned. Although his book is entitled *The citizen*, part of his aim is to show citizens that they ought to think of themselves as subjects.

interests of the same ruling groups to promote the view that monastic spirituality embodied a misuse of human labour and wealth. The prize in this case was to make it seem godly and progressive (rather than impious and avaricious) to confiscate the vast estates the monasteries had acquired.

What are the implications of coming to understand that these were among the causal processes that enabled the figure of the dutiful subject to replace the Citizen and the Monk? One implication, it seems to me, is that we become disturbingly aware of the sheer contingency of the process by which our values were formed. To this Taylor responds that he is 'not sure what is being claimed here'.[39] But the claim is not complicated: only three simple components are involved. The first is that a Classical and Renaissance conception of active citizenship was largely elbowed aside at a particular historical period by our modern view that citizens should be treated essentially as consumers of government. The second is that this change largely took place because a number of early-modern European states happened to evolve in the direction I have been indicating. The third is that this evolution was partly engineered by powerful ruling groups, and thus that things could conceivably have been otherwise. Taylor's response to this, if I understand him, is that my emphasis on causal factors overlooks the fact that certain ideas have an inherent force which helps explain why they supersede others.[40] To this I can only reply that the modern concept of the Subject does not appear to me to embody any greater moral force than the Renaissance concept of the Citizen. But even if it does, I doubt if this forms any part of the causal explanation of why the Renaissance ideal was successfully elbowed aside.

I have also tried to gesture at a closely connected implication which follows from accepting the kind of historical explanation I have sketched. We are left confronting the possibility that our forebears may to some degree have been coerced or even hoodwinked into exchanging their traditional pictures of spirituality and citizenship for the very different ones they subsequently bequeathed to us. This is not of course to deny that the new values unrelentingly drilled into them by Protestant pastors and humanist pedagogues were indeed valuable. But so were the old values they were at the same time urged to forget. The point is rather that the world we have lost was one that our ancestors, left to themselves, might never have wished to forsake.

What hangs on my claim that these are among the implications to be drawn from the story of the Subject, the Citizen and the Monk? My suggestion is that, once we see this much, we can see that the victory of

---

[39] Taylor, 'Comments and replies', p. 240.   [40] Ibid., pp. 239–40.

our inherited values brought losses and even deprivations in addition to the obvious gains. Taylor retorts that he has already taken sufficient account of this balance-sheet.[41] But it seems to me that what it *means* to take sufficient account of it is to recognise that we cannot hope to affirm our view of the good – the one that happened to emerge victorious – in anything like the unambiguous style that Taylor asks of us. One effect of learning more about the causal story is to loosen the hold of our inherited values upon our emotional allegiances. Haunted by a sense of lost possibilities, historians are almost inevitably Laodicean in their attachment to the values of the present time.

I turn to the other claim Taylor makes about our modern predicament. While we must embrace our present values, we must also recognise that they are in crucial ways inadequate. Taylor's sense of their inadequacy stems from his vision of modernity as the offspring at once of the Enlightenment and the Romantic movement. From the Enlightenment we have inherited an atomised conception of the individual self; from Romanticism we have derived a sense of the need to concentrate on our inner natures and explore their potentialities. The effect has been to bring to final fruition our deeply rooted tendency to look for our values entirely within ourselves. But this is not only selfish and self-absorbed, a cause of the erosion of traditional communal ties; it also has the consequence of cutting us off from wider sources of meaning and moral significance.[42]

According to Taylor, this outcome is untrue to some of the finest elements in our natures. We have a 'craving for being in contact with or being rightly placed in relation to the good'.[43] But as we 'struggle to hold on to a vision of the incomparably higher', we cannot hope to derive much comfort or inspiration from prevailing images of the self and the good.[44] The way we live now 'involves stifling the response in us to some of the deepest and most powerful spiritual aspirations that humans have conceived'.[45]

It is striking that, by contrast with so many sages who have recently bewailed our loss of spirituality, Taylor never suggests that the solution to our dilemma may lie in putting ourselves in contact with other cultures less contaminated by Western individualism and science. He looks for his solutions entirely within the resources of our own civilisation, describing his work as an attempt to 'retrieve' a number of neglected values and thereby 'bring the air back again into the half-collapsed lungs of the spirit'.[46]

---

[41] Ibid., p. 240.
[42] For the development of these claims see Taylor, *Sources of the self*, pp. 37–40 and 495–521.
[43] Ibid., p. 45.   [44] Ibid., p. 24.   [45] Ibid., p. 520.   [46] Ibid., p. 520.

I find many of Taylor's proposed remedies very congenial, although they strike me at the same time as a bit optimistic and perhaps unavoidably vague. One of his suggestions is that we may still be able to discover in the values of everyday life a haven in a heartless world.[47] A second is that we may be able to 'get outside' ourselves by enjoying the 'epiphanic' powers of art and literature. We can take advantage, that is, of the Romantic and modernist insight that great works of art bring us 'into the presence of something which is otherwise inaccessible, and which is of the highest moral or spiritual significance'.[48] Finally, Taylor suggests that we may be able to satisfy our craving to make ourselves part of some larger design by devoting ourselves to a life of public and political activity.[49]

Even if all these hopes were to be realised, however, it remains Taylor's 'hunch' that none of this would be adequate to meet the full force of 'the modern moral challenge'.[50] We need to recognise that life is a quest, and that what we are in quest of, as part of 'our telos as human beings', is a scale of values that will 'command our awe', not merely our admiration or respect.[51] Put positively, Taylor's hunch is that 'the significance of human life' needs to be explained and vindicated in theistic terms, not in our present 'non-theistic, non-cosmic, purely immanent-human fashion'.[52] If we remain 'closed to any theistic perspective' we shall condemn ourselves to our present narrow subjectivism.[53] This is why 'the potential of a certain theistic perspective is incomparably greater' than any purely secularised vision of the moral life.[54] The fullest 'affirmation of humans' requires a belief in God.[55]

I confess to being disappointed by this *dénouement*, especially as Taylor presents it with so much rhetorical skill that he makes it appear as the climax and not just the conclusion of his book. My disappointment stems from the fact that, speaking once more as an historian, Taylor's argument strikes me as incomplete in two important respects. First of all, he makes it clear that the 'theistic perspective' he has in mind is specifically the Judaeo-Christian one, with 'its central promise of a divine affirmation of the human, more total than humans can ever attain unaided'.[56] As any historian can relate, however, the outcome of imposing this perspective

---

[47] For the exploration of this theme see Taylor, *Sources of the self*, pp. 47–50, 292, 458.
[48] Ibid., p. 419.   [49] See for example (ibid.), pp. 27–30.
[50] Taylor, 'Comments and replies', p. 240.
[51] For this theme see especially Taylor, *Sources of the self*, pp. 17–20.   [52] Ibid., p. 342.
[53] Ibid., p. 506.   [54] Ibid., p. 518.
[55] This is Taylor's own summary of the point he wishes to make about theism. See his 'Comments and replies', pp. 240–1. As Taylor also notes in that passage, I placed an exaggerated emphasis on his claim in my original critique (cited in note 2 above). I am glad of the chance to correct this misunderstanding and restate my own point.
[56] Taylor, *Sources of the self*, p. 521.

on western Europe over more than a millennium was at many stages
catastrophic in human terms. The medieval centuries were marked by
frequent persecutions, while the attempt to challenge the powers of the
Catholic Church in the sixteenth century gave rise to several generations
of religious war. Given this background, the idea of recommending the
re-adoption of the same theistic perspective is, I think, likely to strike
anyone familiar with the historical record as a case of offering a cure for
our ills potentially worse than the disease.

Taylor has of course thought of this objection, and freely recognises
'the appalling destruction wrought in history in the name of the faith'.[57]
But he insists that it must be a cardinal mistake to believe 'that a good
must be *invalid* if it leads to suffering or destruction'.[58] The historical
record of Christianity gives us no reason to doubt its value or applicabi-
lity. But the fallacy in this line of reasoning is surely obvious. It is only
true that we have no reason to fear the Christian faith if we can be
confident that the horrors perpetrated in its name were unconnected with
its character or aspirations as a creed. Once again, however, it is hard for
an historian to offer such reassurances. The historical record makes it all
too evident that Christianity has often proved an intolerant religion, and
that some at least of the wars and persecutions with which it has been
associated have partly followed from its character as a creed.

I turn finally to the other way in which Taylor's argument strikes me as
incomplete. His intuition is that we need to believe in God if we are to
appreciate the full significance of human life. But it is hard for an
historian to avoid reflecting that one of the most important elements in
the so-called Enlightenment project was to disabuse us of precisely that
intuition. For Hume and his modern descendants there is no reason
whatever to suppose that human life in its full significance cannot be
appreciated in the absence of God. Not only have they argued that theism
is a dangerously irrational creed; they have added that the death of God
leaves us with an opportunity, perhaps even a duty, to affirm the value of
our humanity more fully than ever before. Their arguments strike me as
decisive, but that is not the point. The point is rather that, given the force
of their claims, the task for contemporary theism must surely be to answer
them. Theists need to convince us that, in spite of everything urged to the
contrary for the past two centuries, the case for theism can still be
rationally re-affirmed.

What, then, does Taylor take to be mistaken about the arguments
underpinning modern unbelief? What reasons can he give us for sharing
his doubts? Taylor has taken me to task, and quite rightly, for having

[57] Ibid., p. 520.   [58] Ibid., p. 519.

merely asserted my own faith in the atheistic values bequeathed by the Enlightenment. But I remain disappointed that he for his part evidently feels it sufficient to present us with his alternative hunch, without making any attempt to show us that it amounts to more than whistling in the dark.

4   Religion, history and moral discourse

Michael L. Morgan

It is a commonplace that in Western society and culture, during the past three centuries, the grip of religious traditions and beliefs has weakened. Ritual life has changed in content and scope, and its hold on people's lives has become more restricted and less vigorous. Belief in God, in divine Providence, and such matters is no longer taken for granted by the majority; religious commitment is more selective, vaguer, and without the old robustness.[1] Religious behaviour and beliefs affect people less than they once did. At least they matter differently, in more qualified ways, and without the old sense of depth and stability. The roles of religion and its primacy in everyday life and in our intellectual world are not what they once were.[2]

The precise and detailed story of the erosion of the religious dimension of Western culture, however, is not a simple one. It is not an uncomplicated and linear story of unmitigated decline without any evidence of permanence or recovery. Nor is it a single story. Religious life and belief changed in France earlier than in Germany and in different ways. And they changed later still in England and America, and there, too, differently. But, if Charles Taylor is right, the complexity of these narratives converges on a common conclusion, that the modern identity, our self-understanding as moral agents, cannot be properly comprehended without reference to its religious history. To understand who we are and what matters most to us necessarily involves retrieving the religious elements of our identity.

Some commentators on Taylor's *Sources of the self*, however, have taken him to be saying more than this about religion. Moral and political

---

[1] See, for example, Peter Berger, *The heretical imperative* (Englewood Cliffs, N.J.: Doubleday Anchor, 1979); Robert Bellah, *Habits of the heart: individualism and commitments in American life* (Berkeley: University of California Press, 1985); Michael J. Buckley, *At the origins of modern atheism* (New Haven, Conn.: Yale University Press, 1987); Peter Gay, *The Enlightenment* (New York: W. W. Norton, 1966); Owen Chadwick, *The secularization of the European mind in the nineteenth century* (Cambridge: Cambridge University Press, 1975).

[2] See Taylor, *Sources of the self*, chapter 18.

recovery require that we get clear on what our identity contains. This Taylor calls articulation, and it involves an historical interpretive analysis of the main tendencies and features that arise in and are conveyed through the history of western European culture. The result is a picture of the multiple aspects of who we are and in particular of the many goods that we value and what grounds these values. But, these readers claim, Taylor wants more than the articulation of this plurality of goods as constituents of the modern identity; he also wants us to acknowledge the theistic moral source and to accept its presence. That is, some readers have taken Taylor to be an advocate of Augustinianism, an apologist for Catholicism, a defender of theism. This they find unattractive or even in some cases repulsive. Taylor, they say, is dogmatic, naive and overconfident about religion, about the appeal and the very possibility of belief in the divine as a moral source.[3]

Taylor's enterprise encourages tolerance, receptivity and pluralism, and hence, in one sense, the dismissive and even angry criticism of his sceptical readers ought to surprise him, for one of his goals is to discredit such one-sidedness.[4] In another sense, however, Taylor's detractors may be partially right. Taylor is not only receptive to religion and its various contributions to the articulation of our modern identity; he also provides resources for advancing the religious case, for defending the plausibility of the divine–human relationship as a desirable and promising feature of our moral identity. His understanding of our moral life, its development and its structure provides religion with a kind of legitimacy that opens up once again an old avenue, the moral avenue, to the authenticity of the

[3] *Sources of the self* has been widely reviewed. Among those reviewers who are severely critical of Taylor's stance toward religion are Quentin Skinner, Bernard Williams, Jonathan Glover, Charles Larmore, George Scialabba, Jeremy Waldron and Judith Shklar. See Jonathan Glover, 'God loveth adverbs', *London Review of Books*, 12 (22 November, 1990), pp. 12–13; Judith N. Shklar, 'Review of *Sources of the self*', *Political Theory*, 19,1 (February 1991), pp. 105–9; Charles Larmore, 'Review of *Sources of the self*', *Ethics*, 102, 1 (October 1991), pp. 158–62; J. B. Schneewind, 'Review of *Sources of the self*', *The Journal of Philosophy*, 88 (August 1991), pp. 422–6; Bernard Williams, 'Republican and Galilean', *The New York Review of Books*, 37 (8 November, 1990), pp. 45–7; Quentin Skinner, 'Who are "we"?: ambiguities of the modern self', *Inquiry*, 34 (June 1991), pp. 133–53; Martha Nussbaum, 'Our pasts, ourselves', *The New Republic* (9 April, 1990), pp. 27–34; Jeremy Waldron, 'How we learn to be good', *Times Literary Supplement*, (23–29 March, 1990), pp. 325–6. See also Robin W. Lovin, 'Inescapable frameworks of meaning', *The Christian Century*, 108 (6 March, 1991), pp. 263–5; Russell Hittinger, 'Charles Taylor, *Sources of the self*', *Review and Metaphysics*, 44 (1990), pp. 111–30; George Scialabba, 'The modern man', *Dissent*, 37 (autumn, 1990), pp. 534–7; *Theology Today*, 48 (July 1991), p. 204; Alan Wolfe, *Contemporary Sociology*, 19,4 (July 1990), pp. 627–8.

[4] For Taylor's expression of just such surprise and even unhappiness, see his response to Skinner's criticisms in Taylor, 'Comments and replies', pp. 240–2: 'The paradox is that the last members of the educated community in the West who have to learn some lesson of ecumenical humility are (some) unbelievers.'

religious life and to religious belief. A generous and positive reading of Taylor's book may reveal more advocacy of religion than he might initially want to acknowledge.

What makes Taylor's work so unusual is that he raises the religious question in a way that is indirect and yet suggestive; opponents of religion have to distort and exaggerate what he says in order to mount an attack on him. He does not argue directly that God and religion *should* play a central role in our moral lives; he does show how, subject to detailed clarification, they *could* do so. If Taylor is right, then one can, after Kant but in a wholly different way, take morality with utter seriousness and conduct our moral lives within a religiously oriented world. Unlike Leo Strauss, Alan Bloom and others who might cultivate a return to other, older forms of theism, liberalism and realism in response to the threats of relativism and fascism, Taylor accepts the pluralism of both the past and the present and yet argues for independent sources that make demands on us and give our lives significance and direction. Perhaps Taylor is too insensitive to evil and too sanguine about the horrific realities with which we are confronted.[5] Still, he is clear about his differences with relativism, constructivism and naturalism. Hence, his argument can be treated as a religious response to Feuerbach, Marx and Freud as much as a refutation of Mackie, Wilson and other moral relativists.

I want to show how this is so by doing three things. First, I shall examine Taylor's account of the self and the good more carefully, to expose its religious import. Then, I shall consider how Taylor's treatment of the epiphanic art of post-Romanticism and modernism can be understood as an interpretation of the divine–human relationship as it was conceived by the religious existentialists of this century. Finally, I shall look at Taylor's account of the role of history and articulation for modern moral self-understanding and how practical reasoning about moral sources might engage the question of the advocacy of the religious life.

I

Moral argument, judgements and conduct are based on our moral instincts and intuitions as agents. Taylor proposes that we begin with these intuitions, consider them from the agent's perspective, and try to identify the background picture, the moral ontology, in terms of which they exist, function and make sense.[6] People tend to be unaware of this

---

[5] Several reviewers chastise Taylor for failing to appreciate the destructiveness of Western religion in general and Christianity in particular. See especially Judith Shklar's comments in her review in *Political Theory*.

[6] Taylor, *Sources of the self*, pp. 3–4, 8, 41.

ontology and its elements; some even are inclined to suppress it. But if Taylor is correct about the pervasiveness of what he calls strong evaluation in our moral lives and about the experience of a standard external to ourselves that such evaluation involves, then such a moral ontology is always available.[7] Moreover, genuine self-understanding, clarification, moral discipline and education require that it be identified and articulated – Taylor's term of art for the process whereby the aspects of our moral world are identified, clarified and made accessible and potent for us.[8] A phenomenological grasp of our moral conduct, then, exposes the structure of strong evaluations whereby we make 'qualitative distinctions' and orient ourselves to a good or goods.[9] To articulate a framework is to identify the moral goods that make sense of such conduct. One tries, that is, to paint the background picture that makes the most sense of our moral intuitions and conduct; the goods and moral sources specified in this picture are the ones we take to exist and to empower us as moral agents.[10]

In the case of our moral identity, the modern identity, this picture is a complex collage, a pastiche of many goods and many sources.[11] They include equal respect, disengaged reason, justice, self-fulfilment and divine will. Goods like these are preeminent, goods 'of overriding importance' that function as standards of judgement and criticism, and even though, at any time there may be a single, dominant good in one's moral ontology, the latter will contain many goods.[12] One of the goals of articulating the modern identity is to identify and clarify this plurality, both the highest, most important goods and the lesser, more immediate ones.[13] Only then can we grasp their conflicts and tensions and evaluate them.[14]

Taylor's historical articulation of the modern identity specifies the conditions necessary to give the best account of our moral life. It calls for the moral ontology that *in principle* incorporates diverse constitutive and life goods which make sense of our moral selfhood, and it describes the moral ontology that *in fact* includes God, reason, nature and much else.[15] This account shows that agency demands objectivity of the good, and it narrates historically how different features of the self developed in Western society and culture, together with different goods and a variety of modes of connectedness between the two.

The constitutive goods that ground and direct our moral beliefs and

---

[7] Ibid., pp. 19–20, 26–32, 68.   [8] Ibid., pp. 10, 18.   [9] Ibid., pp. 33, 43–4, 53.
[10] Ibid., pp. 58–9, 68–9, 72.   [11] Ibid., p. 89.   [12] Ibid., p. 62.
[13] Ibid., p. 307. Articulation, then, is one of the tools of Taylor's pluralism, his tolerance and his openness to the significance of goods that originate from a variety of sources.
[14] Ibid., pp. 72–3.   [15] Ibid., pp. 53, 62–5.

that empower our moral judgements and choices are real.[16] They are objective components of our moral universe. Why is this so? For Taylor, reality or objectivity is a function of two things: first the moral ontology or background picture that corresponds to the best account of our moral intuitions and moral experience, and second, the character of those intuitions and that experience.[17] Whatever the best account of our moral experience invokes is real, and since that account calls for self-independent goods or moral sources – nature, reason, God – then these are objectively real. There is no absolute, completely general account of these moral experiences or any other. Nor is there such an account of objectivity. But for us moral agency involves judgements and beliefs that acknowledge as standards of value things that are outside of our desires and interests. What these standards are requires articulation, identification and characterisation. And this process involves an historical enquiry into how the featured goods of our modern identity arose and underwent change. The constitutive goods and moral sources that are recognised and understood, then, are those that function for moral agents of a particular culture and historical moment, and they are the goods that such moral agents would recognise as sources for themselves if they engaged in such a process of articulation.[18]

What is the self's relation to its moral sources? How does the good resonate for the moral agent? Taylor claims that the language of moral sources, constitutive goods and life goods applies generally.[19] But the relationship between the agent and the good differs historically and culturally. At one time, the good is wholly external to the self, and the relation – of awe, love, respect, bindedness – is also external. At another time, the good is internal to the self, and the relation is one of expressiveness. And at another time still, the good is in a sense both external and internal, and the relation is one of empowerment or envitalising the self or one of reaching out, from within, to gain access to what lies beyond. Part of the process of articulation, moreover, is to clarify this complexity, to locate the good *vis-à-vis* the self and to specify how the self is related or relates itself to its moral sources.

Taylor is explicit that God has historically in Western culture been a preeminent one of these goods or sources. God is one of those realities the love of which has empowered people to do and to be good.[20] God is one of those entities that has figured in our moral ontology, has provided a standard or ground of value, and has given our beliefs and actions meaning and significance. Indeed, God and the believer's relation to God

[16] Ibid., pp. 53, 62.   [17] Ibid., pp. 68–76.   [18] Ibid., pp. 77, 80.
[19] Ibid., pp. 93–6.
[20] Ibid., pp. 92–3, 533 n. 66.

are conceived in ways that facilitate this configuration of moral selfhood and its moral sources – in terms of commandment, holiness, covenant, love, grace, and more. In a way, then, Taylor's account of articulacy, historical examination and practical reasoning serves as a vehicle of retrieval for religious discourse and religious commitment. For articulation makes an issue of human-centredness, of any suppression of objective sources of value, and of any form of reductionism to human capacities, beliefs and so on. It retrieves a receptivity to non-human goods and moral sources. Insofar as God is one such good, indeed the supreme one among those of Western culture, Taylor's account re-establishes the plausibility of the divine–human relationship as primary for our moral experience.

One might object that Taylor's account of the moral ontology that forms the background of our modern moral intuitions is tailored to incorporate the religious model. The polarity of the moral self and the good, especially that self's relation to an independent moral source, seems framed to include the divine–human relation as a paradigm case of how the self and the ultimate good are connected. There is a circularity in this situation, but it is not vicious. The moral ontology that corresponds to the best account of our modern moral intuitions will be broad enough to include all those elements that historically have contributed to those intuitions. It is hardly surprising that the religious conception of God and the goods associated with the relation to God fit this framework, since they clearly have contributed to the modern identity and its moral intuitions.

But for two reasons this circularity is not a disreputable one. One is that Taylor is not begging the question. Among other things, he is trying to articulate and thereby expose to view how the divine–human relationship figures into our moral self-understanding. This task should yield a clarification of the way that religion can be legitimately and plausibly discussed within our world. It is not a proof of God's existence, a justification of faith, or a defence of religious belief; it is an illumination of religion's place in our moral lives. Hence, the circularity in question is not vicious; it is natural and expected. For the very same thing, God and the divine–human relationship, is both initially occluded from our moral vision and subsequently clarified by Taylor's account.

Second, the poles of the circularity are separated by a portrayal of our moral agency and an account of the conditions that make it possible. This mediation does not interrupt the circularity, but it surely gives the result a credibility that it might otherwise lack. That is, it is Taylor's view that for us moral agency involves strong evaluation, as he calls it, the recognition that some things matter to us for reasons independent of our own desires and interests. As moral agents, we are in touch with moral sources that empower us and provide us with standards of value; these sources and standards constitute the goods that matter most to us. To understand ourselves fully and properly, we need to uncover what these sources are for us, how they arose, and how they function.[21] In the modern world, after the eighteenth century, they are three: nature, reason and God, and the three occur in various modes and shapes and in various interrelationships. God, conceived in different ways and in a variety of relationships with the self, has been and continues to be an influential moral source for modern agents.[22] That God has historically played such a role is an accident, but it is none the less an undeniable fact. That something – nature or disengaged reason or a drive for expression and creativity or divine will – has played this role, according to Taylor, is not an accident, at least not in the same way. As he sees it, the existence of such a locus of objective value is necessary for us – for the historical tradition of which we are a part and for us, as moral agents, today. If Taylor is right, our moral lives – judgements, intuitions and decisions – only make sense if such grounds or sources exist. Objectivity, realism and anti-subjectivism are necessary features of the modern identity.[23] They are the necessary conditions that underlie historical contingencies. Hence, they are necessary and accidental at once. These attributes do not amount to an advocacy of theism or religion, as I have indicated. But they vitiate any sense that the role for belief in God, the moral role, has been bought with tainted coin.

The language of divine command has had a prominent currency in Western religious and moral culture. But to many, Kant and Hegel among them, the divine–human relationship is not best conceived as one of master or ruler and subject; covenant should not be understood politically, at least not so as to compromise individual autonomy and dignity.[24] Indirectly and without full development, Taylor's account of agency, the strong evaluation historically situated and perspectival character of

---

[21] See ibid., pp. 4, 19–20, 26–37; also 'What is human agency?', pp. 15–44.

[22] Ibid., p. 17: forms of revealed religion continue alive but contested.

[23] Hence Taylor's doubts about naturalism, subjectivism and relativism in their various forms.

[24] Kant criticises the master–subject understanding of the divine–human covenant as exemplified, he believes, in ancient Judaism, in *Reason within the limits of reason alone* (pp. 116–18, 142). There and in the *Critique of practical reason* he defines religion as the recognition of our duties as divine commands, only to qualify this phrase: not as sanctions of a foreign will but rather as the essential content of any free will as such. Hegel appropriates and deepens the criticism in his early theological essays (*Early theological writings*, pp. 68–9, 182–205) and later in his *Lectures on the philosophy of religion*. This criticism is an implicit feature of the revised conception of divine–human encounter in Kierkegaard, Buber and others.

selfhood, moral sources, life goods and constitutive goods points in the direction of a solution to this problem: how to set aside the vocabulary of command and the relationship of compulsion and subordination while retaining the moral contribution of the belief in God and the religious life. The problem is not a new one: ever since Kant at least, it has been a prominent feature of the landscape of liberal religion in the West.

II

Taylor's theory takes us this far. His historical examination of post-Romantic art, modernism, and postmodernism takes us further, by showing how, in the modern world, God as a moral source, but not as an absolute commander, and moral agents, but not as unconditional subordinates, can be related to each other.

Taylor focuses on art and literature of the nineteenth and twentieth centuries, on poets, painters and novelists, but his analysis applies as well to religious transcendence and to the attempt by religious thinkers and theologians, to articulate a conception of faith that can meet the challenges of philosophy, biology, psychology and modern secularism. He sees post-Romantic and modernist art as oriented to epiphanies, episodes of realisation, revelation or disclosure. The work of art is 'the locus of a manifestation which brings us into the presence of something which is otherwise inaccessible, and which is of the highest moral or spiritual significance; a manifestation, moreover, which also defines or completes something even as it reveals'.[25] Such art, that is, shapes a receptivity to grace, an openness to the influence of an other that brings meaning and purpose. Dostoyevsky, Taylor argues, ponders how and when we in our lives open and block such opportunities for grace.[26] Art and poetry in the nineteenth and twentieth centuries *aim* at such moments; it is a central feature of artistic self-consciousness and the *role* of art. Moreover, realising such epiphanies or revelations is a paradigm case of what Taylor calls recovering contact with a moral source, and a special case of this renewal of a relationship between

[25] Taylor, *Sources of the self*, pp. 419, 479 ('reveals something otherwise inaccessible'). See also George Steiner, *Real presences* (Chicago: University of Chicago Press, 1989); Michael H. Levenson, *A genealogy of modernism* (Cambridge: Cambridge University Press, 1984); Sanford Schwartz, *The matrix of modernism* (Princeton: Princeton University Press, 1985). Steiner proposes a radical thesis, that 'any coherent understanding of what language is and how language performs, that any coherent account of the capacity of human speech to communicate meaning and feeling is, in the final analysis, underwritten by the assumption of God's presence ... the experience of aesthetic meaning in particular, that of literature, of the arts, of musical form, infers the necessary possibility of this "real presence"' (p. 3). As Steiner puts it, 'the wager on the meaning of meaning ... is a wager on transcendence' (p. 4).

[26] Ibid., pp. 451–2; see also 430–4.

the self and the moral source is religion and the relation to God.[27] Not only did some consider art a surrogate for religion; the relationship established by art is *like* that established by religion, when the self is located in the presence of an ultimate reality that is otherwise not accessible.[28]

In this view of things, religion transcends morality at the same time that it grounds it. Something other than, higher than, the moral law within demands awe and registers in amazement.[29] The self and God are related directly and not mediately, through the moral law. And yet, at the same time, the self is not overwhelmed and belittled. Somehow, in both epiphanic art and in modern religious thought, the self remains autonomous and becomes fulfilled even as it opens itself to the impact of the other. Taylor is emphatic about this feature of Romantic and modernist art; it is equally true for existential religious thought from Kierkegaard to Barth, Buber and Tillich.

On the one hand, the epiphanic character of modern art is akin to the orientation of modern religious thought towards faith and the event of revelation. And what is central in both is not the transparent, external presence of an independent order but rather the self's access to the source of order. Significance is grounded in the other, in a standard or presence beyond ourselves. But the significance is only accessible through the self and its capacities, its imagination, concepts, will and more. On the other hand, the self is not itself the ground of order, even if it is the vestibule to it. As Taylor puts it, 'the moral or spiritual order of things must come to us indexed to a personal vision'; in art, this is 'mediation through the imagination' or 'articulation through a personal vision'.[30] What this means is that 'modern epiphanies' – religious, artistic or moral – are all, to some degree, subjective, but at the same time they are objective. To explore how this is so is crucial to understanding them.[31]

Epiphanies and epiphanic art are about transcendence, about the self's coming into touch with what lies beyond it, a ground or source of qualitative preeminence. In Plato, such an epiphany was a receptivity to the Forms and the goal of a philosophical education that began with mathematical studies and progressed through dialectical investigation, culminating a process that involved an erotic as well as cognitive re-orientation of the soul. In Augustine and later in Luther, it was the content of the believer's recognition of his or her salvation and of the

27 Ibid., pp. 425, 454–5.
28 Ibid., pp. 439–40. In the case of religion, of course, the issue is not, however, whether the act, event, or experience is representational or non-representational; see also pp. 419, 469, 479.
29 I am alluding to Kant's account of the sublime and the moral law as its primary object. See Paul Crowther, *The Kantian sublime* (Oxford: Clarendon Press, 1989).
30 Taylor, *Sources of the self*, p. 428.   31 Ibid., pp. 428–9; see also p. 481.

receptivity known as faith. In Kant, epiphanies involved an appreciation of the primacy of the moral law within and an amazed respect in response to a confrontation with that sublime and any lesser sublime immensity.[32] In the Romantic poets, like Wordsworth, it occurred in the encounter with the simplicity and the awesome beauty of nature and with what was revealed through them, 'something . . . deeply interfused . . . a motion and a spirit, that impels/All thinking things, all objects of thought,/and rolls through all things'.[33]

Transcendence often has meant a turning to an other, to a detached, separated perspective, and a giving over of oneself to it. But, as Taylor notes, after Kant and the Romantics, it has meant more, not a selfless exposure or re-orientation alone but also a receiving that deeply involves the self, its imagination, its inner resources, its visions and its revisions. Hence, transcendence in this period always begins within and even, as in the case of the Kantian will, remains within, in a sense, finding its otherness there, in what the self shares with all rational selves, a light, if not a god, within the self. But where that divine source resists in its separateness, the relationship between the self and the divine becomes problematic and challenging. The God of Idealism, of Hegel, becomes remote, but not remote as a dominant, oppressive master;[34] however that epiphany is to be understood and the relationship with God conceived, it must express or at least meet the needs of human freedom. It must transcend, too, the limitations of moral, aesthetic and political mediations. Kierkegaard is here the crucial transition figure, as is Nietzsche to a degree; the religious analogues of Taylor's epiphanic, modernist poets are the existentialist descendants of this tradition, thinkers who are challenged by modernity to reconfigure faith as an 'epiphanic field' in which God reveals Himself to those who are open to Him.

On the Christian side, the key figures after Kierkegaard are Barth, Bultmann, Tillich, and all those who have wrestled with the relationships between revelation and history, faith and culture.[35] On the Jewish side, in Germany before the Second World War and the Nazi Holocaust, there were Franz Rosenzweig and Martin Buber; in North America, in more recent decades, there has been Emil Fackenheim. What these thinkers

---

[32] See Crowther, *The Kantian sublime*.   [33] William Wordsworth, 'Tintern Abbey'.

[34] For Hegel, the divine becomes remote, then immanent, leaving behind the oppressive detachment of the Jewish God.

[35] See Peter C. Hodgson and Robert H. King, ed., *Christian theology* (Philadelphia: Fortress Press, 1982) Gordon E. Michalson, *Lessing's 'ugly ditch': a study in theology and history* (University Park, Penn.: Pennsylvania State University Press, 1985); Schubert M. Ogden, *Christ without myth* (New York: Harper and Row, 1961; reprinted SMU Press, 1991); Hans W. Frei, 'Niebuhr's theological background', in *Faith and ethics*, ed. Paul Ramsey (New York: Harper, 1957), pp. 9–64.

share is a critical attitude towards modern culture, with its mechanism and materialism, a commitment to the primacy of the religious relationship and the revelation of God to the self, and an appreciation of the significance of human freedom and appropriation within that event of presence and disclosure.[36] Some of these thinkers saw faith and history as continuous; others saw them as discontinuous, eternity as 'metaphysically' distinct from time, history, culture and rationality. But largely they agreed that the route to the divine lay within the self, indexed to a personal – though non-subjective, communal, often traditional – vision. In the person of faith, that is, there is a receptivity shaped by the past and grounded in the freedom, the expressiveness and spontaneity, of the individual.

Martin Buber's *I and thou*, which was originally published in 1923, the revised text of a set of lectures initially presented at the Frankfurt Lehrhaus in 1922, is an excellent example of what we, after Taylor, might call an epiphanic religious text. Buber portrays human experience as historically situated and capable of two modes of relation – with the world and its contents, the I–thou encounter between two mutually engaged selves and the I–it relation between an impersonal, detached subject and its object. Within one of these modes of relation – which Buber calls dialogue, meeting, relation, concreteness or reality – God as a Thou, as the Other as mutual subject, is received and encountered. 'The extended lines of relations meet', Buber says, 'in the eternal Thou. Every particular Thou is a glimpse through to the eternal Thou.'[37] Revelation is a momentary event that depends upon both God and the agent: 'The Thou confronts me. But I step into direct relation with it. Hence the relation means being chosen and choosing, suffering and action in one.'[38] Here is Taylor's access to a moral source, the resonating in the self of a ground of significance, conceived as the dialogical encounter between a finite and an infinite self.

The human 'religious situation, his *being there* in the Presence', Buber characterises as an antinomy. In modernism, as Taylor understands it, the objective source of meaning and direction is received through the self, its creativity, its imagination. For Buber, God is encountered by a self and through a self, and the encounter somehow, paradoxically, depends both upon divine grace and power, on the one hand, and upon human freedom and receptivity, on the other. In a revealing passage, Buber compares this antinomy to Kant's third antinomy, between causality and human freedom, in the *Critique of pure reason*:

---

[36] See Taylor, *Sources of the self*, pp. 460–1.
[37] Martin Buber, *I and thou*, p. 75; see also p. 100.
[38] Ibid., p. 76.

Kant may make the philosophical conflict between necessity and freedom into a relative matter by assigning the former to the world of appearances and the latter to the world of being, so that in their two settings they are no longer really opposed, but rather reconciled ... But if I consider necessity and freedom not in worlds of thought but in the reality of my standing before God, if I know that 'I am given over for disposal' and know at the same time that 'It depends on myself', then I cannot try to escape the paradox that has to be lived by assigning the irreconcilable propositions to two separate realms of validity ... but I am compelled to take both to myself, to be lived together, and in being lived they are one.[39]

For Buber, then, the religious event, revelation, involves a meeting between the self and the divine other, an encounter that depends upon both. In the modern, post-Kantian world – after Locke, Rousseau, Hegel, and Nietzsche – no access to a constitutive good can efface human freedom. Buber's conception of revelation fits this pattern; it is an act of self-affirmation, even as it is a giving over of the self to the other.[40]

Moreover, Buber's description of revelation and its content for the self could have served as a model for Taylor. The eternal moment, revelation, is characterised as

the phenomenon that a man does not pass, from the moment of supreme meeting, the same being as he entered into it ... in that moment, something happens to the man ... we receive what we did not hitherto have ... In the language of the Bible, 'Those who wait upon the Lord shall renew their strength'. In the language of Nietzsche, who in his account remains loyal to reality, 'We take and do not ask who it is there that gives'.[41]

Buber here portrays the self as a receiver, but it is a receiver not of a content, a proposition, a truth, but rather of a 'Presence, a Presence as Power'. Furthermore, that Presence provides 'the inexpressible confirmation of meaning', a meaning that calls out to be done, to be confirmed by the self in this life and in this world. For Buber, that is, the content of revelation is not itself a set of truths or rules; it is the self's being oriented and empowered to do and to confirm the revelation as the self, from its perspective and within its historical context, understands it. There is presence, impact, influence, and then, in response, human interpretation and action.[42] 'Meeting with God does not come to man in order that he may concern himself with God, but in order that he may confirm that

---

[39] Ibid., p. 96.
[40] Compare Kierkegaard on self-choosing; Taylor, pp. 449–51. Kierkegaard, prior to Buber, acknowledges the primacy of the religious and the believer's dependence upon an unmediated relation to God.
[41] Buber, *I and thou*, pp. 109–10. The passage from Nietzsche is from *Ecce homo*.
[42] Ibid., pp. 109–12.

there is meaning in the world.'[43] This confirmation and this affirmation of God and self in the world are what Taylor calls a 'changed stance towards self and world, which doesn't simply recognise a hitherto occluded good, but rather helps to bring this about'.[44]

In discussing the modernist poetics of Pound, Eliot and others, Taylor not only applauds their goals, to invite epiphanic encounters and thereby to recover access to 'hitherto occluded good[s]'; he also appreciates their method. Their poetry, by 'juxtaposing thought, fragments, images', seeks to 'reach somehow between them and thus beyond them'.[45] As in Pound's famous Metro poem, the images and the metaphor do not represent; instead they form a space between them, and it is within this space or frame that an epiphany is invited to occur.[46]

Taylor does not call upon religious examples of epiphanic retrieval, but I believe he could have. His endorsement of Romanticism and especially of modernist poetics, together with his critical attitude towards post-modernism and recent developments – Derrida, Lyotard and even Foucault – suggest that Taylor's articulation, his historical account of our moral ontology, incorporates an advocacy of religion. At least it provides a contemporary moral and cultural discourse for the retrieval of religion and religious belief. In a sense, Taylor shows us that the world in which we live is not as bereft of the divine, of religious potentiality, as some have thought.

III

But it might be that Taylor has made room for too little. Certainly he has been cautious; his hints and admissions are few, and they play no major role in his account. He carries on his project of recovery and articulation with a commitment to openness. But if I am right, the pluralism he recommends and the type of divine–human relation he hints at are a far cry from Catholicism or indeed from any traditional, robust, substantive, authoritative religious view. Taylor is too historical, too hermeneutical and too liberal for conventional orthodoxies. And when we appreciate these commitments of his, old worries resurface, worries about revelation and tradition, about how much is sacrificed when the primacy of the religious relation to God is bought at the price of pluralism and non-exclusivity. Recall that for Buber, revelation provided a 'Presence as strength' but no propositional or imperative content. It is a challenge, then, to tie such a conception to a traditional religious heritage, and if it

---

43 Ibid., p. 115.   44 Taylor, *Sources of the self*, p. 454.   45 Ibid., p. 473.
46 Ibid., pp. 473–7.

cannot be done, then Taylor's avoidance of parochialism is not so much restraint as it is necessity.

Taylor's project is to help us understand who we are and in particular to identify and grasp the moral sources or goods that constitute our moral world. As strong evaluations, our judgements and actions require that there be such sources; Taylor's history enables us to recognise them and thereby gain a renewed access to them. It also enables us to deliberate about them, to reason about their relative influence and significance for us. There are, then, two questions about these matters that arise when we appreciate their religious character. One is whether we ought to choose to accept the divine source as valuable for ourselves. The other is how that deliberation ought to be conducted, especially if the most appropriate conception of our relation to God is like the one we saw in Buber, a kind of epiphanic receptivity where the content of the encounter is a 'Presence as strength', meaning-demanding and even meaning-confirming but not itself meaning-giving. Given such a view, one might very well wonder what, morally speaking, is to be gained or lost in the choice regarding faith. Reasoning about nature or reason, about justice or benevolence, makes a kind of sense that reasoning about such a God and such a relationship might not seem to make. Perhaps Taylor's achievement on behalf of religion and its moral role, guarded and yet provocative, succeeds at too steep a cost, for ultimately there may be too little substance in the divine–human relation to support any serious practical, moral reasoning about the religious option. Taylor may have carved out a route of access to the religious life, only to eliminate any good reasons for taking it.

Taylor would deny that the religious option has no moral content. In the modern identity, our moral imperatives arise out of the notions of freedom, benevolence and the affirmation of ordinary life; they include universal justice and beneficence, equality, freedom and self-rule, and the avoidance of death and suffering. These rules or standards, however, occur and interact differently as they are grounded in different constitutive goods or moral sources: God, disengaged reason in scientific form and the expressive self.[47] The theological source, then, is not bereft of content; it registers its own commands about justice, freedom, avoidance of death and suffering and more. But, as Taylor argues, even religiously grasped goods must come 'indexed to a personal vision'; they must resonate personally. Divine commands without personal sensibility are unacceptable.[48] In Buber, Rosenzweig, as in Kierkegaard, Barth and

[47] Taylor, *Sources of the self*, pp. 317–20, 491–2, 498–9, 511–12, 515.
[48] Ibid., pp. 511–13.

other 'modernist' theologians, this tension is expressed as the conflict
between human freedom and divine power, and it is partially accommo-
dated by making revelation prepropositional and immediate and by
relegating all interpretation and action to the level of human response.
Hence, the theistic moral source does have content – in terms of justice,
beneficence and freedom, but that content is always a human response to
a divine impact. The content is a human articulation of the meaning of the
relation to God. Meaning arises out of the human response to an encounter with God; revelation provokes meaning but does not contain it.

There is, then, a content for revelation. In Taylor's terms, practical
reasoning about goods can apply to such goods in the religious context.
Revelation – the religious epiphany – gives access to the divine; both prior
and subsequent to such events, however, the individual lives in the world;
he hopes, wants, believes, deliberates, chooses and acts, and in doing all
this, the individual recalls the past, recovers old models, patterns and
habits, and seeks to re-enact, to revise or to innovate. In short, the
moment of revelation, when an epiphanic episode takes place within a
frame or field, may be unique and even ahistorical, eternal. But what
precedes it – the framing of the field – and what follows it – the response in
the world – are both thoughts and actions complexly related to one or
more goods, life goods and constitutive goods. About these thoughts and
actions, values and principles, we can surely debate and deliberate. They
are objects of clarification and understanding, and to the degree that they
are constitutive of who we are, reflection on them is relevant to who we
may want to become, to our self and its relation to the good.[49]

As moral sources or primary goods appear on our moral horizon and as
they are articulated and defined, they become the objects of practical
reasoning, of reflection, analysis and assessment. But, how can one
engage in practical reasoning about God as a moral source? God, like any
primary good that presents itself as a constituent of our moral ontology,
threatens to 'challenge and displace other' such goods.[50] 'Our acceptance
and love of this good makes us re-evaluate the goods of the original range.
We judge them differently and perhaps experience them quite differently,
to the point of possible indifference and, in some cases, rejection.'[51] On
the one hand, then, the articulation of a moral source like God and its
placement within our moral horizon gives us access to it, empowers us
and threatens to challenge other goods already within that horizon.[52] On
the other, however, 'it is not just a matter of looking but also of arguing,
of establishing that one view is better than another. And this raises the

[49] Ibid., chapters 2 and 3.   [50] Ibid., p. 69.   [51] Ibid., pp. 69–70, especially 70.
[52] Ibid., pp. 91, 92, 93, 96.

difficult question of practical reason.'[53] How, that is, does one debate with oneself and 'rationally convince oneself' about the superiority of a particular good or source? How does a situated, meaning-laden practical reason proceed in general? And specifically, how does it proceed with regard to the assessment of the religious good?

Taylor gives the following picture of such reasoning. 'Practical reasoning ... is a reasoning in transitions ... It aims to establish ... that some position is superior to some other.'[54] Hence, such reasoning is grounded in what things mean to us, and it operates by evaluating whether a given transition will reduce confusion, avoid problems or gain in epistemic or moral content. 'The argument turns on rival interpretations of possible transitions from A to B, or B to A.'[55] But a particular moral source of good arose for us in a particular way, about which there is a narrative or story, or it was superseded, suppressed, dislocated by some other good, and about this too there is a story. Our practical reasoning, then, not only assesses possible transitions; it also retraces the paths of past transitions and registers a judgement about the desirability of a good in view of what was gained or lost in its past career for us. This is not, as Taylor warns, a matter of proving God's existence from facts about the world; rather God is 'accepted' as a constitutive good or moral source only when we see what is gained by so doing and when we are thereby 'moved' by our relation to God. When that impact is deeply felt and when that resonance is supplemented by an evaluation of the benefits gained by the acceptance of God as such a moral source, then God comes to play a central role in our moral lives. Sometimes this sense of prominence arises for us individually and directly, but more often it is mediated through our respect for powerful, moving authoritative figures, 'the founders of our traditions, those who give these goods their energy and place in our lives, [who] felt [these goods] deeply' and whom we follow in that receptivity 'even though we don't fully understand it or feel it ourselves.'[56]

For Taylor, then, the practical reasoning that endorses the superiority of a particular good for us involves narration, evaluation, recognition and a sense of being moved, of feeling deeply the good's importance for us. If the account of the divine–human relation that I sketched earlier figures as one strategy whereby the divine other is present to us within our moral horizon, it is certainly compatible with this broad, multi-faceted conception of practical reasoning. It makes available a divine presence which can move us, and it has a field or space that can be our object of interpreta-

---

53 Ibid., p. 71.
54 Ibid., pp. 72–3; and 'Explanation and practical reason', in *The quality of life*, (Oxford: Oxford University Press, 1993).
55 Ibid., pp. 72–3.   56 Ibid., p. 74.

tion, as the transitional situation in which, in life, the epiphany of the divine occurs.

Moreover, the conception of revelation does nothing to prevent an assessment of the historical transitions that have in the past relocated God and the relation to God in our moral culture. This conception of religious epiphanies, then, may leave the event of revelation without propositional or cognitive content. But it does not strip the religious domain of a content that can be considered, interpreted and evaluated. Each such episode has a substantive penumbra of receptivity or anticipation, on the one hand, and of response, on the other. In addition, the historical dominance of religious life has its own transitions, its period of genesis and of decline, when it became ascendant and when it was superseded. Both of these, and not the revelatory event itself, are the objects of practical reasoning. If Taylor is right, acceptance is as much a matter of being moved by God as believing that allegiance to Him will yield some epistemic and moral gain; this 'modernist' conception of the divine–human encounter makes both possible.

There is a tolerance, an openness, about Taylor's discussion that is appealing. His analysis of our moral lives and his history provide access for a moral discourse that facilitates defending the role of religion in modern culture and society. And even though Taylor acknowledges his own Catholicism, there seems to be a willingness on his part to learn from other religious traditions and to accept their claims on any of us. But this very openness raises an old question. Does it require that the religious traditions in question be translated into modern terms? It certainly seems so; the beneficial features of modernity, its commitments to freedom, justice, equality and benevolence, must be retained. And yet if these commitments, together with the commitment to situated selfhood and the demands of authentic existence, are non-negotiable, then how can God and religion be tied, in any significant sense, to a particular religious tradition? Do we not find in Taylor, read in a certain way, the old problem of liberal theology and neo-orthodoxy, of the tension between reason and faith, eternity and history, philosophy and theology?[57] Does Taylor really admit religious pluralism? Or has he, in the end, dissolved religious distinctiveness in a homogeneous modern identity of a very recognisable liberal cast?

I do not think that Taylor's openness to religion is discredited in this way. Given his rich sense of historical situatedness, tradition and community, it would be odd if it were. The constraints that the liberal tradition places on moral reflection and deliberation need not be incompatible with

[57] See, on this problem, Ogden, *Christ without myth*; Michalson, *Lessing's 'ugly ditch'*.

a variety of religious traditions which are distinct and yet can accommodate its principles. Taylor may not solve the religious paradox of universality and distinctiveness, of treating the central teachings of Judaism and Christianity as available and appropriate to all human existence but somehow peculiar to each community, with its texts, its formative events and its special understanding of God's acts in history. Certainly, in this book, he does not seek to do so. But this does not mean that Taylor thinks the paradox insoluble. To address this problem, however, as well as to develop his project in the direction of religious advocacy, would be beyond his goals, which, in the present circumstances, are ambitious enough.

5   The risks and responsibilities of affirming ordinary life

Jean Bethke Elshtain

'[w]e are born only once on this earth, and only one and no other historic time is given to us.'

Czeslaw Milosz

What does it mean for a political philosopher to affirm ordinary life? Indeed, what does an affirmation of this sort, urged on us by Charles Taylor, imply as to the subject matter of political philosophy and its identity in relation to the world of modern state-centred politics?[1] I have selected this theme for a closer examination in part because I have called for something similar – 'the redemption of everyday life' – and it has never been crystal clear to me what the full implications of such a summons might be were one required to work them out.[2] I agree with Taylor that 'this affirmation of ordinary life ... has become one of the most powerful ideas in modern civilization', but I also believe that this affirmation is an increasingly troubled one, harder and harder to sustain, not so much against its 'knockers' as against its ostensible supporters or 'boosters'.[3]

What are we enjoined to affirm when we locate 'ordinary life' above the heroic, history making (in the grand sense) virtues or imperatives? Taylor is surely right to suggest that the ground for controversy now is the manner of living that ordinary life which we would affirm. I suspect there are some ways to live such a life – for example, embracing a notion of untrammelled freedom and making of individual choice an absolute which brooks no constraint – that themselves signal a radical departure from the 'life of production and the family' in its redemptive and transvaluative historic meanings. In other words, I wonder if it makes the best

---

[1] Taylor is most explicit about affirming ordinary life in *Sources of the self*. Part III of this monumental work is devoted to 'the affirmation of ordinary life'. It is a theme that echoes through Taylor's *The malaise of modernity*, a decoction of the larger book. But a good number of Taylor's *Philosophical papers* also reverberate with this theme in some form.

[2] The phrase appears in Jean Bethke Elshtain, *Public man, private woman: women in social and political thought* (Princeton: Princeton University Press, 1981).

[3] Taylor, *Sources of the self*, p. 14. Taylor chastises both the adoring boosters of modernity and the grumpy knockers: both, he argues, have got it wrong, the boosters with their uncritical celebration and the knockers with their unrelenting denigration.

sense to see the controversies surrounding ordinary life, as Taylor does, as manifest conflicts within a horizon framed by its affirmation or, alternatively, whether what is at stake is not so much contestation over the individual's mode of living and affirming ordinary life as culturally sanctioned attempts to *escape* the confines of ordinary life altogether. I have in mind, for example, the attempted overcoming of embodied limits and 'natural' constraints justified by an unfettered anthropocentrism.

Perhaps we have arrived at a subjectivist impasse in a more thoroughgoing way than Taylor allows or fears. If so, the emptiness he describes as that which 'consistent subjectivism' tends towards because nothing 'would count as fulfillment in a world in which literally nothing was important but self-fulfillment', may be growing like the hole in the ozone: an obscure but real threat which no one knows how to prevent altogether and which may or may not finally destroy life as we know it.[4] I am not sure about this, but I want to put some pressure on Taylor's claim that contemporary affirmations and conceptions of freedom do not involve 'a repudiation of qualitative distinctions, [or] a rejection of constitutive goods as such', and, second, that the forces of immanentisation at work on so much of the moral horizon of late modernity yet retain, or bear within themselves, the possibility of 'the good'.[5]

Taylor claims that 'the moral conflicts of modern culture rage within each of us'.[6] My hunch, uttered more in sorrow than in a spirit of modish pessimism, is that the conflicts do not rage as they *should* within the breasts of many of our fellow citizens (my reference point here is primarily the political entity Taylor refers to as 'the great republic to the South'). My hunch is that the battle has perhaps been won for a certain sort of radical subjectivism, thoroughly immanentised, hence not terribly open to correction, reflection and reproof. In an odd way, quite different from that of the Attic warrior-citizen or the gut-wrenching proclamations of gory glory uttered by later civic humanists, this vision of self-celebrating self-expression also disdains 'mere life', the life of labour, householdery, maternity and paternity. Taylor hints at this when he notes that one version of modern subjectivism leaves no room for 'non-anthropocentric exploration' of the sources of meaning.[7]

In the following I attempt to sort through Taylor's affirmation, some might say 'exaltation', of ordinary life by means of two contrasts. The first, a historical contrast, is with the warrior's quest for civic valour and honour carried out in arenas that were defined in part against the homey and the everyday, which were thereby humbled. I draw on early Christian conceptions of ordinary life, as Taylor also does, to sharpen this contrast.

---

[4] Taylor, *Sources of the self*, p. 507.   [5] Ibid., pp. 90, 98.   [6] Ibid., p. 106.
[7] Ibid., p. 506.

In describing the historical transition from these earlier conceptions to modern views of ordinary life and the self, Taylor has not dealt with the dangerous relation between conceptions of the modern self and the modern sovereign state which has carried and transformed some of the worst features of the warrior's quest into modern political philosophy and practice. The second contrast is with the panoply of scientifically generated demands for control over human life which threaten (to the boosters the threat is a promise) to turn human procreation into a technical operation. This scientific project of self-transcendence effectively occludes a horizon of meaning and intelligibility of the sort Taylor believes we can and must retrieve.[8] Is there a specifically *political* philosophy which can attend to any of this in a compelling way? In the conclusion I suggest that Václav Havel's ethic of responsibility must be part of any satisfactory answer.

I

If one goes back to the Greeks, one discovers that war from the beginning was construed as something of a natural condition for mankind. The Greek city-state was a community of warriors whose political rights were determined in large part by the fundamental privilege of the soldier to decide his own fate. One can trace a direct line of descent from the Homeric warrior assemblies to Athenian naval democracy. Civic identity was restricted to those who bore arms. The formal definition of justice, repeated by Thrasymachus in Plato's *Republic*, was 'the interest of the stronger'. The Greek citizen army was an expression of the Greek *polis*; its creation one of the chief concerns and chief consequences of the formation of the city-state. In Sparta, the army, organised in mess groups, was substituted for the family as the basic element of the state. Another custom of the male group, homosexuality, was developed and institutionalised, most systematically at Thebes in the fourth century, to create a Sacred Band of lovers fighting side by side. Such institutions served to ensure that sense of fellowship deemed a prerequisite of disciplined courage in war, of willingness to risk death together.[9]

It need hardly be added that the civically heroic ethic enshrined in these institutions diminished the world of everyday production and reproduction – the business of metics, women and slaves. Not having the bodies of protectors, of men constituted as warrior-citizens, women were those who

[8] The example drawn from radical, technological intrusion into human reproduction is but one of many one might select, of course.
[9] For a fuller account of the tradition of armed civic virtue in the West see Jean Bethke Elshtain, *Women and war* (New York: Basic Books, 1987).

had to be defended, whose role in the household, the *oikos*, was a necessary precondition for, but not an integral part of, the structure of the dominant political warrioring world. These presumptions were geared rather rigidly towards preserving sex segregation even as they required sex collaboration to hold the overall system intact. The free space of the *polis*, though apart from necessity, existed in a necessary relation to the sphere of production and reproduction, the realms of unfreedom. This is by now a familiar tale. But perhaps it is worth one more pass. This should help us to see the many ways in which political philosophy has construed its mission in heroic or quasi-heroic terms – bringing order, curing the universe of its ills and woes – at odds with Taylor's insistent embrace of the dignity of the ordinary and everyday.

Plato places the body under suspicion – its needs and desires draw us away from virtue and true knowledge. The lower part of the soul, tied to fleshly eros, taints us, whether one is speaking of heterosexual or homo-sexual desire, although sublimated homoerotic relations between men come nearer to the Platonic ideal than any other. Those who give in to the basest form of erotic expression are tied to women and to the procreation of flesh and blood children. It does not take much stretching to assay why there is a problem for women in all this. Women are less able than men to abstract themselves from fleshliness. It is women's bodies that change form – that are procreative – reminding us all of our fleshly origins and vulnerability. It is this activity Plato downgraded to the level of what is shared with the 'beasts'; sub-rational existence in his way of thinking.

If my embodied self is not the grounding of who I am, located as it is in time and space, having particular qualities, unique characteristics, a history and so on, then the heroic abstractedness of Plato's plans for his ideal city and its sketch of the exemplary Guardians may be more likely to follow. The Guardian woman is a particularly disquieting image: that of the pacified female whose (collective) body has been disciplined in the interests of unruffled order. Plato's fears are clear: 'Have we any greater evil for a city than what splits it and makes it many instead of one? Or a greater good than what binds it together and makes it one?'[10] The monistic urge in political philosophy is here given one of its most eloquent and persuasive moments of expression. And it is an urge wholly at odds

---

[10] Plato, *The republic*, book 5, 461e-462d. I have examined, and criticised, the attraction of one strand of monistic or assimilationist feminism to Plato's erasure of bodily identity as importantly constitutive of who we are. Presumably his argument, taken seriously, appeals to all those who believe that the body is at best a nuisance and its importance is best denied or suppressed or technologically and legalistically 'corrected for'. The image of women 'in common' has also appealed to various collectivist and utopian thinkers. Some Marxists have found comfort in the prohibition or elimination of private property among the elect. We all grasp at straws from time to time.

with an affirmation of ordinary life with its messy confluence and mix of goods and purposes. But I jump ahead of my story. Let's stay with the Greeks for a moment longer.

Aristotle, by contrast, sees life in the *oikos* as the locus of those particular attachments necessary to any life in common. One cannot, as Plato does, leapfrog over particularity directly into the realm of abstract claims and ties. Plato would suffuse kinship ties throughout an entire social network. But these more general fraternal urgencies cannot emerge in those who lack, from birth, any ties to anybody in particular. Human moral development, as we know, does not work in this way. Evidence on this score is overwhelming: without concrete, special relationships, no general, broader identification follows as a matter of course. Love of what is in common must begin with particular loves. This Aristotle recognises; hence, he aims to preserve the diversity of elements, broadly construed, which comprise a precondition for the *polis* and that which is in common. The suggestion one can tease from this Aristotelian recognition is that we would be more, not less, subject to importunate demands from 'above' if we had no particular ties, links, loyalties, duties and affections 'below'.

Plato aims heroically to eliminate politics; Aristotle is a preeminent asker of political questions. Plato deeded to subsequent political philosophy an unmatched but dangerous grandeur; Aristotle an unmatched argument for the rational foundation of the polity as a necessary precondition for the realisation of human ends. Aristotle none the less articulated and justified that fateful divide between the whole (*polis*) as prior to and superior to the parts which form its necessary conditions: the parts develop to the complete but foreclosed possibilities set by their interior essences or natures.[11] Here again, I make no claims to be presenting anything other than a decoction of a long and familiar tale – at least for students of Western political thought. What Taylor offers to our rethinking of the sources of the modern self and politics is not, as some have suggested, a full embrace of the Christian moment but, rather, a canny re-interpretation of the profound challenge Christian theory and practice offers to any and all heroic construals and monistic constructions of political life and thought.

Clearly, Taylor shares the Gospel's shimmering hope that 'they might have life and might have it more abundantly'. An early Christian savant, imploring the Deity, wrote: 'We beg you, make us truly alive.'[12] The Christians construed their task as one of learning how to 'keep body and

---

[11] Aristotle, *The politics*, ed. Ernest Barker (New York: Oxford University Press, 1962), especially book I, 'The theory of the household'.
[12] The words are those of one Serapion of Thumis as quoted in Margaret Miles, *Fullness of life* (Philadelphia: The Westminster Press, 1981), p. 9.

soul together'. The body was the very condition of life itself for its creatureliness bore the mark of the Creator. The human body in Greek, then Roman, antiquity was wholly conscripted into the social order (an insight I owe to the great historian of late antiquity, Peter Brown). Brown's story goes like this: the pre-Christianised individual was not free to withhold his or her body from conscription into the extant social order. One could, with Socrates, endorse withdrawal of the soul from the body but one could not take oneself out of the group – one could not constitute one's body as a protest against its conscription as a social body in the form of the warrior, the slave or the producer of children for the city. The Classical view, then, is that the city-state or empire has complete control of human bodies for the purpose of labour, procreation and war.[13] Augustine was to argue that Rome perfected the régime of *cupiditas* run rampant, the triumph of a lust to dominate. The distinctive mark of Roman life as a *civitas terrena*, a city of man, was greed and lust for possession which presumed a right of exploitation. This became a foundation for human relationships, warping and perverting personality, marriage, family, all things.

The early Christians did endorse rendering unto Caesar that which was Caesar's, but that turned out to be minimal: obedience to laws aimed at public peace, payment of taxes, at first a refusal to serve in armies – although this is a point of controversy among scholars of early Christianity. All agree that what was not Caesar's was control of life's ultimate purpose and meaning and the human being's vocation and calling on this earth. Christian doctrine drained the empire of its claims to divinity and omnipotence. Possessing free will, the bearers of responsible moral agency, Christians could and might be called to act against the state, to resist its claims and impositions upon their bodies and minds. The notion of moral revolt against public power opened up a new range of options, duties, responsibilities, dilemmas and re-assessments. These remarkable developments did not of course usher in an era of earthly peace or an unambiguous affirmation of everyday life. For the bodies of those who continued to bear the sign of that early withdrawal from the sexual–social contract of late antiquity were lifted up and ranked as somehow 'higher' than those who tended to the tasks of procreation, who were within rather than apart from daily labour in its many senses.[14] Importantly, necessity was no longer defined *against* freedom. But this created terrific problems and temptations for political philosophy precisely because of the brake

[13] See Peter Brown, *The body and society* (New York: Columbia University Press, 1988).
[14] It is good not to make too much of this for a reciprocal relationship existed between the 'praying' and clerical classes and others in Western Christendom; but a clear overevaluation of the one to the detriment of the other is a persistent feature of the medieval West.

put on the drive to heroicise and the temptation to absolutise that order of things one has oneself defined or redefined textually.

Consider, for example, the two greatest pre-Reformation exemplars of Catholic social thought – Augustine and Aquinas. Each transforms radically the exigencies of antiquity. Taylor locates Augustine as one of the most profound articulators of our shared understanding of 'the self' as an entity having depth, a potent and reflexive inwardness. He does not spend any time on Augustine's reconfiguration of the familial in relation to the political. But this is an important part of the story, for Augustine strips the earthly city of its claims to preeminence. He locates the entire sentient human race within one category, overturning the sharp antique distinction between citizen and 'foreigner' or 'barbarian'. Most importantly, where everyday life is concerned, he finds in the household the beginning or element of the city, going on to argue that domestic peace has a relation to civic peace.

For Augustine, unlike Aristotle, the household and city, public and private, do not diverge 'in kind'; rather, aspects of the whole are borne into the parts, and the integrity and meaning of the part carries forward to become an integral part of the whole.[15] This solution, as with every powerful new entry in the world of political philosophy, trails in its wake new problems. A thorough-going isomorphism of public and private doesn't seem right either. But that isn't the issue here. The issue is that Augustine helps to lay the basis for the affirmation Taylor wants to lift up for our time. But he does something more: he defines a people as bound together by common agreement as to the objects of their love. You can, as a social thinker, assess an entire moral culture; you can ask the Taylorian questions of what sort of moral culture you inhabit. This is a point I will return to in my closing comments.

Aquinas ups the ante where *regnum* is concerned, finding more legitimacy, more of a job for earthly rule to do, more goods within its purview, than did Augustine. But the social emphasis, the refusal to effect a sharp cleavage between public and private remains. There was wisdom in this. As Isaiah Berlin observes, 'a sharp division between public and private life, or politics and morality, never works well. Too many territories have been claimed by both.'[16] For the Christian thinkers this was a rule of thumb. A resonant motif in Christian theory and practice emerged from the conviction, sanctified by the Eucharist, that the faithful could achieve a good life only in the fellowship of others. St Thomas glosses the

---

15 I tell the longer story in *Public man, private woman*, see especially pp. 64–74. In the second edition (in press) I re-affirm aspects of the 'Augustinian turn' in an epilogue. Unlike Taylor, I rely primarily on Augustine's *The city of God* rather than his *Confessions*.
16 Isaiah Berlin, *The crooked timber of humanity* (New York: Vintage, 1992), p. 32.

Aristotelian doctrine of a human being's monstrous condition if he or she is deprived of, and isolated from, civic life, yet he also insists that activities within the private sphere must be granted their own sanctity and dignity, not simply because they carry over into the public realm, but because they bear the signs of the Christian transvaluation of classic values.

Taylor, presumably, is prepared to grant all of this, showing as he does that our sociality and dignity may be intact whatever our calling in life, yet reminding us that, for medieval Christendom, some callings are more holy, higher than others. Here the Reformation delivers a plenary jolt to medieval doctrines of good works and preferred pieties. The woman in the market is the equal to the saint; the pope is a 'poor stinking sinner' like everybody else in earthly time and space.[17] And, Taylor is quite right, Luther dignifies the everyday, the bodily, the homey verities of mothers, fathers and children, of friends drinking beer and taking sup, of the radical reality of an incarnational doctrine which presents its Saviour entering the world as 'a true Baby, with flesh, blood, hands and legs'.[18] Luther's nativity tale explores the infusion of ordinary events with extraordinary meaning, a down to earth story of the birth in humble surroundings of a vulnerable infant.

What I want to suggest is that the story at this point moves down two tracks, only one of which Taylor has followed in detail. One might tag these the 'story of the self' and the 'story of the state'. For the very era that saw a dramatic re-affirmation of ordinary life also gave birth to a radical new heroic task for politics and political philosophy. The unleashing of sovereign discourse and of the vast, monistic pretensions of sovereignty is a story Taylor doesn't tell – his book, after all, is nearly six hundred pages long as it is! – but it is a story that, I believe, must accompany the story of the self if we are to assess the travail of the present moment in as unblinkered a manner as possible. The great temptation of political thought as a heroic enterprise – the temptation of monism – returns.

Medieval Christendom denied absolute sovereign power to any of the component communities of Christendom, including pope and emperor. The medieval system of rule was, in Perry Anderson's words, 'a patchwork of overlapping and incomplete rights of government . . . inextricably superimposed and tangled' with 'different juridical instances . . . geographically interwoven and stratified . . . plural allegiances, asymmetrical

---

17 I discuss Luther at some length in *Public man, private woman* and in *Meditations on modern political thought: masculine/feminine themes from Luther to Arendt* (University Park, Penn.: Pennsylvania State University Press, 1992 re-issue).

18 Quoted from Hugh T. Kerr, ed., *Readings in Christian thought* (New York: Abingdon Press, 1966), p. 157.

suzerainties and anomalous enclaves'.[19] My claim here is not that monistic striving was unknown to the medieval West – that would be ludicrous when one is talking about a world dominated by a (complicatedly) monotheistic metaphysics – but that this monism never achieved realisation in theory or practice. With the emergence of what I call the Protestant nation state all this was to change, and the changes were not all salutary.

A brief tale of sovereignty to accompany Taylor's story of the self, then. Before Jean Bodin and Thomas Hobbes had penned their very different paeans to sovereign power, the peace of Augsburg (1595) had embedded the principle of *cujus regio ejus religio* in German treaty law. Luther had unleashed more than he knew, helping to set in motion a theory of self-sovereignty that mirrors the sovereignty of the state. (Or is it the other way round?) Luther prepares the way for the political theology that underlies the emergence of the nation state. Its full-blown dimensions become more visible in seventeenth-century calls for holy wars as state-centred enterprises, providentially enjoined, so that tyranny might be banished and the True Godhead worshipped.

Political philosophers did their part to feed notions of sovereignty as a secular mimesis of God as ultimate Law Giver whose commandments must be obeyed and whose power to judge is absolute. Bodin and Hobbes justified sovereign absolutism, each, as I indicated, in his own way. The mark of sovereign power is that it cannot be subject to the commands of another: the power of the sovereign state is, in Bodin's words, 'that absolute and perpetual power vested in a commonwealth which in Latin is termed *majestas*'.[20] Hobbes' views are too well known to repeat here but he is among the most inventive heroicisers of early modern political philosophy, for the choices he presents are either a brutal state of nature or a Leviathan-dominated sovereign polity. Ironically, even as God comes down to earth in celebrations of the blessedness and sanctity of everyday life, in the sphere of political action and the philosophies which accompanied and legitimated this drive to monistic sovereignty, the sovereign God is displaced, taking up residence at a far greater remove than he had for medieval Europeans, for whom God's sovereignty was enjoined as a brake on the king's designs.

The standard narrative, the classical theory and 'story of the state', holds that sovereignty is indivisible and inalienable. Sovereignty shifts from king to state, and this state 'can no more alienate its sovereignty

---

[19] Perry Anderson, *Lineages of the absolute state* (London: New Left Books, 1974), pp. 20, 23.

[20] Jean Bodin, *Six books of the commonwealth* (New York: Macmillan, 1955), p. 25.

than a man can alienate his will and remain a man'.[21] The seeds are here sown for what James Tully calls the reigning juridical conception of modern political thought within and through which the state 'is represented as an independent, territorial monopoly of political power. Political power is the right to kill in order to enforce universal rule of either objective right or subjective rights ... Political power is exercised either directly by some sovereign body ... or indirectly by some representative body.'[22] What rights have become to individuals in the modern West – marks of a sovereign self – sovereignty is to states. Perhaps one might conceptualise it this way or, better, this is one way to clarify the point I am trying to make: the sovereign state is immanentised, thereby constituting a view of citizens, or political subjects, as sovereign selves. But, rather than leading to an affirmation of everyday life, the sovereign individual is tempted to disdain that life as a rather paltry thing *if* it is given over to any measure of luck or chance. Control becomes the password, the key to unlock one contemporaneous version of 'the good life' and that life consists not so much in affirming life's limits as in seeking to overtake them altogether. Sovereignty as task and tale – operating on many levels – invites a disdain for life itself. I will offer two examples of how this works; one seems rather obvious, the other does not. I begin with the latter. I here draw the 'story of the self' and the 'story of the state' together.

II

My example of a threat to the affirmation of everyday life, which may appear initially as a grandiose exaltation of it, is that triumphalist self fed by current technology. Here is a celebration of the dream of radical self-transcendence as envisaged by a feminist theorist who finds hope in pervasive intervention into biological life, creating such possibilities as the following:

[F]or instance, one woman could inseminate another, so that men and non-parturitive women could lactate and so that fertilized ova could be transplanted into women's or even into men's bodies. These developments may seem far-fetched, but in fact, they are already on the technological horizon; however, what is needed much more immediately than technological development is a substantial reduction in the social domination of women by men. Only such a reduc-

---

21 Charles Merriam, 'History of sovereignty since Rousseau', *Columbia Studies in the Social Sciences*, 12, 4 (1900), pp. 33–5.
22 James Tully, 'The pen is a mighty sword: Quentin Skinner's analysis of politics', *Meaning and context: Quentin Skinner and his critics*, ed. James Tully (Princeton: Princeton University Press, 1988), pp. 7, 17–18.

tion can ensure that these or alternative technological possibilities are used to increase women's control over their bodies, and thus over their lives.[23]

The standard of evaluation here is control: what abets it is good, what mutes it is bad. Thus the way is paved for supporting invasive techniques in and upon human bodies as a form of bio-social engineering. Seeing in women's links to the everyday – to birth and nurturance – the vestiges of our animal origins and patriarchal control, anything that breaks those links is, by definition, to be applauded.[24]

This is troubling stuff, as is the constriction of the moral community now under way which specifically targets certain sorts of people (the developmentally disabled, for example) for eugenics efforts. We don't want poor products. We don't want defects. This even extends to sex selection as a basis for abortion. Especially poignant for women is the fact that female foetuses are prime candidates for elimination. The modern technology of sex preselection, by all accounts, will result in a higher proportionate destruction of female foetuses in favour of males – at least for the *first* birth. Writes one commentator: 'In Western countries the prospect is not of a sudden lurch towards an overwhelmingly male population, but of continuing sabotage of women's self-esteem, as they are chosen as younger sisters'.[25] By intervening in, and disrupting, what might be called the 'natural lottery', the fact that no human being can control whether he or she is white or black, male or female, has Down's syndrome or is a musical prodigy, we undermine the basis of human equality: the delicate motifs of the Western story of the self.

Sustaining human equality – the fragile insistence that there is about each and every human being an ontological givenness that human beings themselves did not create and over which no society has or should have total control – requires a generous acceptance of life in many varieties. Once we claim we do in fact have control over the human genome – that we can ensure more males and fewer females, smarter kids by contrast to less intelligent ones, perhaps even manipulate genes to get the musical prodigy – we pave the way for a world of biologically ranked and assessed

[23] Alison M. Jagger, *Feminist politics and human nature* (Totowa, N.J.: Rowman and Allanheld, 1983), p. 132.

[24] There are, of course, radical feminist non-interventionists who eschew any and all forms of bio-social engineering even as they affirm a woman's absolute right to control her own 'reproductive power'. Whether you can do both things simultaneously is, of course, debatable. But the 'antis', in rejecting the feminist interventionist stance, go so far in assimilating women to 'nature' that they, too, lose aspects of the complexity of the modern self Taylor wants to uphold.

[25] Edward Yoken, *Unnatural selection? Coming to terms with the new genetics* (London: Heinemann, 1986), pp. 100–1.

'higher' life. Some will be ontologically inferior, having come lower on the preference list. Others will be disallowed life altogether, and should 'their sort' sneak through, there will be no moral basis to insist on their decent treatment since, if the controls had been working right, they wouldn't be here in the first place.

We are returned to a virulent form of applauding and affirming some human beings (not *callings* or *vocations*) by contrast to others. This is surely an insidious possibility by any standard and far more difficult to combat, if one accepts current stories of the sovereign self, than was the medieval tale of the superiority of spiritual callings by contrast to lives lived in reproducing life itself. For the reformers had access to a meta-physically sanctioned notion of human dignity and we do not; or that notion is very badly battered and cannot be relied upon as a brake against the designs of the bio-engineers and the misguided politics of the party of revolutionary self-transcendence.

Now to a second and more familiar example of how the story of the self and the sovereign intertwine, or conspire, to defeat life itself. I call this the 'will to sacrifice'. Here is a gloss on what I have in mind drawn from one moment in Hegel's theory of the state: another instance of political philosophy as an epic-making and heroic tale. The state is the arena that calls upon and sustains the individual's commitment to universal ethical life, satisfying expansive yearnings through the oppor-tunity to sacrifice 'in behalf of the individuality of the state'. For with the state comes not simply the possibility but the inevitability of war. War transcends material values. The individual reaches for a common end. War-constituted solidarity is immanent within the state form, but the state comes fully to life only with war. Peace poses the specific danger of sanctioning the view that the atomised world of civil society is absolute. In war, however, the state as a collective being is tested, and the citizen comes to recognise the state as the source of all rights. Just as the individual emerges to self-conscious identity only through a struggle, so each state must struggle to attain recognition. The state's proclamation of its own sovereignty is not enough: that sovereignty must be recog-nised. War is the means to attain recognition, to pass, in a sense, the definitive test of political manhood. The state is free that can defend itself, gain the recognition of others, and shore up an acknowledged identity. The freedom of individuals and states is not given as such but must be achieved through conflict. It is in war that the strength of the state is tested, and only through that test can it be shown whether individuals can overcome 'selfishness' and are prepared to work for the whole and to sacrifice in service to the more inclusive good. The man becomes what he in some sense is meant to be by being absorbed in the larger stream of life: war and the state. To preserve the larger civic body, which must be 'as one', particular bodies must be sacrificed.[26]

This is a great and terrible story, a heroic tale in which state politics and political philosophy colluded. To be sure, there isn't the overheated civic blood lust characteristic of classical civic humanists in Hegel's version of the story. As an instance of such, I have in mind Caluccio Salutati's exclamations that the sweetness of one's love for the *patria* is such that one must not cavil at crushing one's brothers or delivering 'from the womb of one's wife the premature child with the sword'.[27] Salutati was extreme, but that sort of extremism has, alas, been the norm in many of the great and horrible events of our own century – events which bespeak a nearly total disdain for the precious dignity of everyday life.

III

Where does this leave us? If anything, our task is even more difficult than Taylor allows – both as citizens and as political philosophers. An affirmation of ordinary life has not been the primary passion of political philosophy: if anything, the opposite is more often preeminent, in the form of temptations to monism and heroicism. But I do have a few final words by way of suggestion and amplification. This is a project not in opposition to Taylor's call for 'retrieval' of the full range and amplitude of our sources of self but, rather, a necessary feature of that retrieval effort. It is a political and philosophical project that requires taming and limiting the demands of sovereignty – both sovereign state and sovereign self. The politics I have in mind shifts the focus of political loyalty and identity from sacrifice and control to responsibility. My target, then, is both images of the sovereign self as a unified, sharply boundaried phenomenon as well as the sovereign state in its full-blown, untrammelled instantiation.

Is a post-sovereign politics possible? What would it look like? How would it forge civic identities in such a way that blood sacrifice is not so pervasive a demand and possibility? Perhaps there will be world enough and time for me to turn to this matter in the future. Here I have space for only fleeting and no doubt ephemeral suggestions. I have in mind the writings of Václav Havel who urges us into a post-sovereign political discourse, a move from sacrifice to responsibility. 'I feel that this arrogant anthropocentrism of modern man, who is convinced he can know everything and bring everything under his control, is somewhere in the back-

[26] See the longer discussion in Elshtain, *Women and war*, pp. 73–5.
[27] Cited in Ernst Kantorowicz, *The king's two bodies: a study in medieval political theology* (Princeton: Princeton University Press, 1957), p. 245.

ground of the present crisis. It seems to me that if the world is to change for the better it must start with a change in human consciousness, in the very humanness of modern man.'[28]

An ethic of responsibility means one is answerable, accountable to another for something; one is liable to be called to account. One is also a being capable of fulfilling an obligation or trust; reliable, trustworthy. This presumes, indeed requires, a particular version of Taylor's modern identity and an ideal of other-regarding, self-responsible freedom. Softening the demands of the iron grip of sovereignty, sacrifice or control does not mean so loosening the bonds of reason that the self flies off in all directions and can find no reason to prefer *this* to *that*, and can hear in such notions as 'responsibility' only a dour and crabby moralism.

Above all, this ethic of responsibility and the affirmation of everyday life which accompanies it demands a recognition of *limits*: limits to what we should do (even or especially if we can do these things). A knowing chastening of projects of self-transcendence. Czeslaw Milosz writes that: 'Man is either a *supported* being, or he dissolves into mist, into a mirage.'[29] In the dark days of World War II, Simone Weil asked: 'What is it a sacrilege to destroy? ... Those relative and mixed blessings (home, country, traditions, culture, etc.) which warm and nourish the soul and without which, short of sainthood, a *human* life is not possible.'[30] Taylor's insistence on our need for a believable framework, we being the sorts of beings we are – finite, mortal, not gods – is, if anything, even more exigent than he claims. We are more and more overwhelmed by 'emptiness, vertigo' in our dizzyingly bustling lives. Taylor offers to political philosophy the not always welcome insistence that without believable frameworks and horizons of intelligibility nothing, finally, makes any sense and no amount of heroic or razzle-dazzle anti-heroic theorising of the sort that calls incessant attention to itself, even as it promotes light-headedness about our collective condition, can disguise that fact.

[28] Václav Havel, *Disturbing the peace* (New York: Knopf, 1990), p. 11.
[29] Czeslaw Milosz, 'Reality', *The Partisan Review* (Winter, 1992), p. 25.
[30] Simone Weil, *The need for roots* (New York: Octagon Books, 1979), p. 129.

Part III

Natural and human sciences

6   The strange estrangement: Taylor and the natural sciences

Clifford Geertz

In the opening paragraphs of the introduction of his *Philosophical papers* Charles Taylor confesses himself to be in the grip of an obsession.[1] He is, he says, a hedgehog, a monomaniac endlessly polemicising against a single idea – 'the ambition to model the study of man on the natural sciences'. He calls this idea many things, most often 'naturalism' or 'the naturalistic world view', and he sees it virtually everywhere in the human sciences. The invasion of those sciences by alien and inappropriate modes of thought has conduced toward the destruction of their distinctiveness, their autonomy, their effectiveness and their relevance. Driven on by the enormous (and 'understandable') prestige of the natural sciences in our culture we have continually been led into a false conception of what it is to explain human behaviour.

The purpose of this polemic, aside from the desire to rid the human sciences of some 'terribly implausible', 'sterile', 'blind', 'half-baked' and 'disastrous', enterprises[2] – Skinnerian behaviourism, computer-engine psychology, truth-conditional semantics, and primacy-of-right political theory – is to clear a space in those sciences for 'hermeneutic' or 'inter-pretivist' approaches to explanation. Interpretation, the 'attempt to make sense of an object of study' in some way 'confused, incomplete, cloudy . . . contradictory . . . unclear',[3] is an irremovable part of any would-be science of human affairs. And it is precisely that which 'the natural science model', with its passion for *Wertfreiheit*, predictability and brute facts – defensible enough in its proper domain – effectively blocks.

Those who, like myself, find the argument that the human sciences are most usefully conceived as efforts to render various matters on their face strange and puzzling (religious beliefs, political practices, self-definitions)

---

[1] The 'Introduction' is repeated, with slightly different pagination, in volume II. The themes in Taylor's work I discuss here run throughout the whole of it, from *The explanation of behaviour* in 1964 to *Sources of the self* in 1989, but for simplicity I shall confine direct citations to *Philosophical papers*, 1985, 2 vols.

[2] Taylor, *Philosophical papers*, I, p. 1; II, p. 21; I, p. 187; I, p. 247; and II, p. 92.

[3] Ibid., II, p.15.

'no longer so, accounted for',[4] to be altogether persuasive, and Taylor's development of it magisterial, may none the less find themselves disturbed to notice after a while that the 'opposing ideal'[5] to which this view is being so resolutely contrasted, 'natural science', is so schematically imagined. We are confronted not with an articulated description of a living institution, one with a great deal of history, a vast amount of internal diversity, and an open future, but with a stereotype and a scarecrow – a Gorgon's head that turns agency, significance, and mind to stone.

Taylor's references to 'natural science', though extremely numerous, appearing in almost every essay in *Philosophical papers*, are, both there and elsewhere in his work, marked by two characteristics: they are virtually never circumstantial, in the sense of describing actual examples of work in physics, chemistry, physiology or whatever in a more than glancing fashion, and they are virtually all to the opening stages of the scientific revolution – Galileo, Bacon, Descartes, Newton, Boyle – not to anything in any way remotely contemporary. Like so many of the 'Others' that we construct these days to haunt us with their sheer alterity, The Japanese, The Muslims, or *L'age classique*, his countercase to the interpretively oriented human sciences is generically characterised and temporally frozen. A foil for all seasons.

One can see the reasons for this. The conception of what it is to be 'truly scientific' in the human sciences has indeed normally been both rigid and anachronistic, as well as deeply uninformed about the realities of the 'real sciences' whose virtues are to be imported into these 'softer', 'weaker', 'less mature' enterprises. Taylor is not wrong to think that the Skinnerian version of behaviourism or the Fodorian version of cognitivism are less extensions of a proven approach to explanation into new fields than parodies of it. Nor is he wrong to think that the rejection of such parodies, and others like them, does not condemn the human sciences to a the-world-is-what-I-say-it-is 'Humpty Dumpty subjectivism',[6] incapable either of framing an honest hypothesis or confronting one with genuine evidence. Yet, it may be that the creation of an out-and-out, fixed and uncrossable gulf between the natural and human sciences is both too high and unnecessary a price to pay to keep such muddlements at bay. It is obstructive at once of either's progress.

The notion of such a gulf, a dichotomy as opposed to a mere difference (which latter no one clothed and in their right mind would want to deny), traces, of course, back to the *Geisteswissenschaften* versus *Naturwissenschaften*, *verstehen* versus *erklären* conceptualisation under which, with Dilthey, modern hermeneutics got definitively under way, and which,

4 Ibid., II, p. 17.   5 Ibid., II, p. 117.   6 Ibid., I, p. 11.

with Heidegger and Gadamer, Ricoeur and Habermas, 'is very strong in the later twentieth century'.[7] And there can be little doubt (at least, I don't have any) that this to-each-its-own view of things did yeoman service in defending the integrity and vitality of the human sciences – sociology, history, anthropology, political science, less so psychology, less so yet economics – under the enormous pressures exerted upon them in the heyday of positivism, logical or otherwise. Without it, Taylor's worst nightmares might well have come true and we would all be socio-biologists, rational-choice theorists or covering law axiomatisers. The issue is whether so radically phrased a distinction is any longer a good idea, now that the point has been made, and made again, that the human sciences, being about humans, pose particular problems and demand particular solutions, and that the idea of a 'social physics' seems a quaint fantasy of times gone by. Are either the human or the natural sciences well served by it? Is the conversation across the *corpus callosum* of our culture inhibited, or prevented, by this sort of commisural surgery? Is such surgery to the disadvantage of both, reductive to half-brained reasoning? Is an eternal methodological civil war, the Hermeneuts versus the Natura-lists, in anyone's interest?

The questions are, of course, rhetorical – not to say, tendentious. The homogenisation of natural science, both over time and across fields, as a constant other, an 'opposing ideal' permanently set off from other forms of thought, as Richard Rorty has put it, 'by a special method [and] a special relation to reality', is extremely difficult to defend when one looks at either its history or its internal variety with any degree of circumstan-tiality.[8] The danger of taking objectivist reductionism as the inevitable outcome of looking to the natural sciences for stimulation in constructing explanations of human behaviour is very great without a richer and more differentiated picture of what they are (and the plural is essential here), have been, and seem on their way toward becoming than Taylor has so far essayed. So also is the possibly even greater danger of isolating those sciences themselves in such an outmoded sense of their aim and essence (as well as an exaggerated sense of their own worth), beyond the reach of

[7] Ibid., I, p. 45; II, p. 15. As Taylor recognises, the genealogy of this notion is both deep and wide in Western thought and in its modern version is perhaps as often dated from Vico as Dilthey, its defining exemplar as often seen to be Weber as Gadamer. For a subtle and detailed tracing of the contrast as it has worked itself out from the ancient world forward, sometimes as a difference, sometimes as a dichotomy, sometimes as a mere unclarity, under the original Greek distinction (they seem to have invented *this* too) of *nomos* and *physis*, see Donald Kelley's important study, *The human measure: social thought in the Western legal tradition* (Cambridge, Mass.: Harvard University Press, 1990).

[8] Richard Rorty, 'Is natural science a natural kind?' *Philosophical papers* (Cambridge: Cambridge University Press, 1991), I, p. 46. Rorty is, of course, as I am, questioning such a view.

hermeneutic self-awareness. The tendency toward oversimplification Taylor so rightly deplores seems to thrive, in both the human and the natural sciences, precisely to the degree that the intellectual traffic between them is obstructed by artificial notions of primordial separateness.

I

Both sorts of schematisation of the natural sciences, that which sees them as being without a history, or anyway as having a history consisting only in the development to greater and greater levels of complexity of an epistemological paradigm laid down in the seventeenth century, and that which sees them as an only pragmatically differentiated mass basically defined by their adherence to that paradigm, are essential to the notion that they form a closed off world, sufficient unto itself. Without either, and certainly without both, such a notion seems distinctly less obvious.

The view that the history of natural science consists in the mere development from a once-and-for-all foundational act ('[The] great shift in cosmology which occurred in the seventeenth century, from a picture of a world-order based on the ideas to one of the universe as mechanism, was the founding objectification, the source and inspiration for the continuing development of a disengaged modern consciousness'[9]) not only neglects both historiographical works, of which Thomas Kuhn's is probably the most famous, stressing ruptures, wanderings and discontinuities in the advance of those sciences and the complications that have been forced on the idea of 'disengaged consciousness' by quantum level theorisations – Heisenberg, Copenhagen and Schrödinger's cat.[10] It more importantly leaves out a fact which Gyorgy Markus, speaking of 'a second scientific revolution' which occurred during the second half of the nineteenth century, has pointed out: the characteristic features of the natural sciences, which Taylor takes to be so destructive when imported into psychology and politics, are not a direct line projection into our times of Renaissance and Enlightenment ideas but a much more recent, and quite

[9] Taylor, *Philosophical papers*, I, p. 5.
[10] Thomas Kuhn, *The structure of scientific revolutions*, 2nd edn. (Chicago: University of Chicago Press, 1977). For an accessible discussion of 'quantum weirdness', see Heinz Pagels, *The cosmic code: quantum physics as the language of nature* (New York: Bantam, 1983). The absence from Taylor's major study of 'the making of the modern identity', *Sources of the self*, of any significant discussion of developments in physical theory as such is, given this tracing of 'modern consciousness' to the mechanical world view, at the very least, odd. Like the Deist's god, 'science' – Descartes and Bacon, Newton and Boyle – got the enterprise going, but doesn't seem to have had much of a hand in it since.

radical, transformation of them. 'Natural science as the cultural genre which *we* know ... is the product of a nineteenth-century development in which [its] cognitive structure, institutional organization, cultural forms of objectivity and ... global social function have changed together.'[11] The world before Maxwell is, in fact, not a very good model of 'naturalism' as now understood. It was a stage in a project (or, more accurately, an assemblage of projects) still going on.

And as it is still going on, and not, so it looks from the outside, becoming all that consensual in its self-understandings, it may transform itself again; unless history really is over, it almost certainly will do so. There are, in fact, more than a few signs that it is already in the process of doing so. The emergence of biology (not just genetics and microbiology, but embryology, immunology and neurophysiology) to the point where it threatens the status of physics as the archetype of scientific enquiry; the epistemological and ontological problems besetting physics itself ('don't ask how it can be that way, it can't be that way'); the increasing difficulty of 'big', that is expensive, science in isolating itself from public scrutiny, as well as the increasing tenuousness of practical spin off arguments for funding much of it; the return of cosmology as a general cultural concern, the appearance of experimental mathematics, the growth of computer-mediated 'sciences of complexity' (negative entropy, fractals and strange attractors) – all these matters, and others, suggest that the withdrawal of the natural sciences over the last hundred-and-twenty years or so from connections with any discourse but their own is not the permanent condition of things.[12]

It may not be the permanent condition of things (to my mind, it almost certainly is not) because, alongside the enormous gains in cognitive power that have accompanied it, there have been considerable costs as well, costs by now severe enough to imperil the gains. The most serious of these is, as Markus points out, precisely the extreme narrowing of the cultural significance of the natural sciences that Taylor, anxious to keep them away from interfering with our conceptualisation of human affairs, seems so determined to reinforce:[13]

[11] Gyorgy Markus, 'Why is there no hermeneutics of natural sciences? Some preliminary theses', *Science in context*, 1 (1987), pp. 5–51; quotations at pp. 42, 43 (emphasis original).
[12] The 'don't ask' quotation has been attributed to Richard Feynman, but I have no citation for it. For discussions of some of the matters mentioned, see, again, Heinz Pagels, *The cosmic code*, see also *The dreams of reason: the computer and the rise of the sciences of complexity* (New York: Simon and Schuster, 1988) and *Perfect symmetry: the search for the beginning of time* (New York: Bantam, 1986).
[13] Markus, 'Why is there no hermeneutics of natural sciences?', pp. 26, 27, 28, 29, references omitted, reparagraphed, emphases original.

Seventeenth-to-eighteenth century 'natural philosophy' still had a markedly mul-
tifunctional character and was in general successfully communicated to socially
and culturally divergent groups of addressees. Even those works which represented the most formidable difficulties of understanding, like Newton's *Principia*,
quickly became not only objects of widely read 'popularizations', but also exercised a deep influence upon ... other, already culturally ... separated forms of
discourse: theological, properly philosophical and even literary ones. In their
turn, these discussions occurring in 'alien' genres seriously influenced that more
narrowly scientific impact of the works concerned, and were usually regarded as
having a direct bearing upon the question of their truth ... It is only with the deep
transformation of the whole organizational framework of natural scientific activities ... that the audience's specialization and professionalization became established during the nineteenth century ... simultaneously with the professionalization of the scientist-author's role itself. It is in this process that the *république
des savants* of the eighteenth century, still loosely uniting scientists, philosophers,
publicists and cultivated amateurs, has been transformed into a multitude of
separated *research communities* comprising the professional specialists in the
given area and now posited as the sole public for the relevant scientific objectifi-
cations.

This historical process in which the monofunctional character of the contemporary natural sciences has first been formed, at the same time meant a progressive *narrowing of their cultural significance* ... When the cultural closure of
natural scientific discourse upon itself becomes a fact ... the divorce of natural
scientific inquiry from general culture and cultivation is also inevitable ... [It]
is now posited as having no significance whatsoever for orienting men's conduct
in the world they live in, or their understanding of this lived world itself. Ten-
bruck aptly formulated it: the view of nature provided by the sciences is no more
a world-view.

This is perhaps a bit overstated, even for the nineteenth century, when
the 'world view' transactions between the sciences technically defined and
the general movement of 'culture and cultivation' were not altogether
attenuated, as witness the 'ringing grooves of change' anxieties of a
Tennyson or the heat death of the universe resonations of a Kelvin. And,
in any case, this image of disconnection again applies rather more to the
physical sciences than it does to the biological; the role that Newton, and
Newtonianism, played in the eighteenth century, Darwin, and Darwin-
ism, played in the nineteenth. But the general drift is clear enough. The
same historical movement that dissolved 'the *république des savants*' into
'a multitude of separated research communities' produced as well the cultural disengagement of the natural sciences, the cultural entrenchment of
the human ones which Taylor opposes to it, and the increasing awkwardness of the relations between them.

If the awkwardness is to be relieved (relieved only, hardly removed)
and the natural sciences re-involved in the self-reflective conversation of
humankind, it cannot be by reversing history. The days of the *république*

des savants, to the extent they ever existed, are over and unrecoverable. The unavailability of the technical interior of particle physics, neurophysiology, statistical mechanics or the mathematics of turbulence (and of whatever succeeds them) to anyone beyond the research communities professionally involved with the matters they address is by now but a fact of life. The whole issue needs to be approached in some other way, one which rather than polarising the intellectual world into a grand disjunction seeks to trace out its obscured dependencies.

II

The beginning of such a reframing would seem to involve taking seriously the image (and the reality) of a loose assemblage of differently focused, rather self-involved, and variously overlapping research communities in *both* the human and the natural sciences – economics, embryology, astronomy, anthropology – and the abandonment therewith of the Taylor–Dilthey conception of two continental enterprises, one driven by the ideal of a disengaged consciousness looking out with cognitive assurance upon an absolute world of ascertainable fact, the other driven by that of an engaged self struggling uncertainly with signs and expressions to make readable sense of intentional action. What one has, it seems, is rather more an archipelago, among the islands of which, large, small and in between, the relations are complex and ramified, the possible orderings very near to endless. Such questions as (to quote Rorty again) '"what method is common to paleontology and particle physics?" or "what relation to reality is shared by topology and entomology?"' are hardly more useful than (my inventions, not Rorty's), 'is sociology closer to physics than to literary criticism?' or 'is political science more hermeneutic than microbiology, chemistry more explanatory than psychology?'[14] We need to set ourselves free to make such connections and disconnections between fields of enquiry as seem appropriate and productive, not to prejudge what may be learned from what, what may traffic with what, or what must always and everywhere inevitably come – 'reductive naturalism' – from attempts to breach supposedly unbreachable methodological lines.

There is indeed some evidence from within the natural sciences themselves that the continental image of them as an undivided bloc, united in their commitment to Galilean procedures, disengaged consciousness and the view from nowhere, is coming under a certain amount of pressure. In a chapter of his *Bright air, brilliant fire: on the matter of mind* called

---

[14] Rorty, 'Is natural science a natural kind?', p. 47.

'Putting the mind back into nature', the neurophysiologist and immuno-
logist Gerald Edelman sounds almost like Taylor in his hedgehog resistance to the domination of such presumptions and preconceptions in his
own field of enquiry, the development and evolution of the human
brain:[15]

[As] Whitehead duly noted, the mind was put back into nature [from which
physics had removed it] with the rise of physiology and physiological psychology
in the latter part of the nineteenth century. We have had an embarrassing time
knowing what to do with it ever since. Just as there is something special about
relativity and quantum mechanics, there is something special about the problems
raised by these physiological developments. Are observers themselves 'things' like
the rest of the objects in their world? How do we account for the curious ability of
observers ... to refer to things of the world when things themselves can never so
refer? When we ourselves observe observers, this property of intentionality is
unavoidable. Keeping in line with physics, should we declare an embargo on all
the psychological traits we talk about in everyday life: consciousness, thought,
beliefs, desires? Should we adopt the elaborate sanitary regimes of behaviourism?
... Either we deny the existence of what we experience before we 'become
scientists' (for example, our own awareness), or we declare that science (read
'physical science') cannot deal with such matters.

Nor is it only *vis-à-vis* 'behaviourism' that Edelman, the natural
scientist, sounds like Taylor, the human scientist, railing against sterile,
blind and disastrous models of analysis drawn from celebrated but
inappropriate places, but with respect to computer-analogy cognitive
psychology – AI and all that – as well. He even uses the same term of
abuse for it:[16]

The term 'objectivism' has been used to characterize a view of the world that
appears at first sight to be both scientifically and commonsensically unexceptiona-
ble ... Objectivism assumes ... that the world has a definite structure made of
entities, properties, and their interrelationships ... The world is arranged in such a
way that it can be completely modelled by ... set-theoretical models ...
Because of the singular and well-defined correspondence between set-theoretical symbols and things as defined by classical categorisation, one can, in this view,
assume that logical relations between things in the world exist *objectively*. Thus,
this system of symbols is supposed to represent reality, and mental representations
must either be true or false insofar as they mirror reality correctly or incorrectly
...

---

[15] Gerald M. Edelman, *Bright air, brilliant fire: on the matter of the mind*, (New York: Basic
Books, 1992), p. 11.
[16] Ibid., pp. 230, 231, 232. For Taylor's very similar animadversions against 'machine
modelled explanations of human performance' see his essay, 'Cognitive psychology',
Philosophical papers, I, pp. 187–212; on 'objectivism', 'Theories of meaning', I,
pp. 248–92. For a related attack on 'objectivism' in neurology, there called 'diagram
making', see Israel Rosenfeld, *The strange, familiar and forgotten: an anatomy of
consciousness* (New York: Knopf, 1992).

The ... development of the computer ... reinforced the ideas of efficiency and rigor and the deductive flavor that ... already characterised much of physical science. The 'neat' deductive formal background of computers, the link with mathematical physics, and the success of the hard sciences looked endlessly extensible ...

The computational or representationalist view is a God's-eye view of nature. It is imposing and it *appears* to permit a lovely-looking map between the mind and nature. Such a map is only lovely, however, as long as one looks away from the issue of how the mind actually reveals itself in human beings with bodies. When applied to the mind *in situ* [that is, in the brain], this [objectivist] view becomes untenable.

It is, no doubt, easier to see the inadequacies of a sheerly oppositionalist 'great divide' formulation of the relations between the 'human' and the 'natural' sciences in work like Edelman's, concerned with the development and functioning of our nervous system, and indeed perhaps in biology, generally, than in work on, say, phase transitions or angular momentum, where God's-eye views would seem less problematical and representationalist mirrorings more in order. But, even if they are (something that itself becomes at least questionable as 'things' like wave functions and non-locality find their way into physical theory), the loss of detail such an overly contrastive view produces obscures other ways of mapping out the landscape of knowledge, other ways of tying together, or separating out, the disciplinary islands of empirical enquiry. 'If you don't know Russian', the mathematical physicist David Ruelle has recently written, 'all books in that language will look very much the same to you.'[17]

Similarly, unless you have the appropriate training, you will notice little difference between the various fields of theoretical physics: in all cases what you see are abstruse texts with pompous Greek words, interspersed with formulas and technical symbols. Yet different areas of physics have very different flavors. Take for instance special relativity. It is a beautiful subject, but it no longer has mystery for us; we feel that we know about it all we ever wanted to know. Statistical mechanics, by contrast, retains its awesome secrets: everything points to the fact that we understand only a small part of what there is to understand.

Leaving aside the particular judgement here (which I am, of course, incompetent to assess, as I am the strengths or weaknesses of Edelman's neurology), the disaggregation of 'the natural sciences' would indeed

---

[17] David Ruelle, *Chance and chaos* (Princeton: Princeton University Press, 1991), p. 122. The notion of 'appropriate training' necessary to appreciate the differences Ruelle, in a book designed after all for an audience that doesn't have it, wishes us to appreciate rather more raises a question, and in a guild-protective form, than answers it. Translation exists, and commentary (Ruelle's being a fine example) too: I don't know Russian, and thus miss much; but Dostoevsky does not look the same to me as Tolstoy.

seem essential to the sort of non-Taylorian, but also non-reductive, non-'naturalistic' vision another mathematical physicist, Richard Feynman, in a passage Edelman uses as an epigraph to his book, has of the general project of human understanding:[18]

Which end is nearer to God; if I may use a religious metaphor. Beauty and hope, or the fundamental laws? I think that ... we have to look at ... the whole structural interconnection of the thing; and that all the sciences, and not just the sciences but all the efforts of intellectual kinds are an endeavour to see the connections of the hierarchies, to connect beauty to history, to connect history to man's psychology, man's psychology to the working of the brain, the brain to the neural impulse, the neural impulse to the chemistry, and so forth, up and down, both ways ... And I do not think either end is nearer to God.

III

But it is not just from the natural science side, indeed it is not even mainly from that side, that the challenges to strongly binary images of 'the whole structural interconnection of the thing' are coming, but precisely from the hermeneutic, intentionalist, agent-centred, language-entranced side that Taylor is, as I am also, so determined to defend against runaway objectivism. The historical, social, cultural and psychological investigation of the sciences as such – what has come to be known in summary as 'science studies' – has not only grown extremely rapidly in the past twenty years or so but has begun to redraw the lines among Markus' 'multitude of separated research communities' in a more various, changeful and particularised way. Looking at 'science' from an interpretivist perspective has in itself begun to displace, or at the very least complicate, the Diltheyan picture that has so long held us captive.[19]

Of all the sorts of work that go on under the general rubric of the human sciences, those that devote themselves to clarifying the forms of life lived out (to take some real examples) in connection with linear accelerators, neuroendocrinological labs, the demonstration rooms of the Royal Society, astronomical observatories, marine biology field stations, or the planning committees of NASA, are the least likely to conceive their task as limited to making out the intersubjective worlds of persons.

---

[18] Cited, Edelman, *Bright air, brilliant fire*, p. vii. The last line suggests that 'hierarchy' may not be the best figure, either, for tracing out such a meshwork of connections.

[19] For a brief general review, see Steve Woolgar, *Science, the very idea* (Chichester: Ellis Horwood, 1988); for a current collection of debates and positions in this creatively disorganised, usefully combative field, Andrew Pickering, ed., *Science as practice and culture* (Chicago: University of Chicago Press, 1992); for a sustained study, crossing the human–natural division with something of a vengeance, Steven Shapin and Simon Schaffer, *Leviathan and the air pump: Hobbes, Boyle, and the experimental life* (Princeton: Princeton University Press, 1985).

Machines, objects, tools, artefacts, instruments are too close at hand to be taken as external to what is going on; so much apparatus, free of meaning. These mere 'things' have to be incorporated into the story, and when they are the story takes on a heteroclite form – human agents and non-human ones bound together in interpretivist narratives.

The construction of such narratives, ones which enfold the supposedly immiscible worlds of culture and nature, human action and physical process, intentionality and mechanism, has been slow in coming, even in science studies, where they would seem unavoidable. ('Où sont les Mounier des machines, les Lévinas des Bêtes, les Ricoeur des faits?' cries perhaps the most strenuous advocate of such enfolding, the anthropologist of science, Bruno Latour.)[20] These issues were avoided, or, more accurately, never arrived at, by the initial sorties in science studies, then called the sociology of science and associated most prominently with the name of Robert Merton, which confined themselves to 'externalist' issues, such as the social setting of science, the reward system driving it, and most especially the cultural norms governing it. 'Internalist' issues, those having to do with the content and practice of science as such, were left beyond the range of enquiry. Later work, more influenced by the sociology of knowledge, attempted to address the operations of science more directly, studying such matters as the evolution of theoretical disputes and the replication of experiments, but in no less objectivist terms – 'standing on social things' (usually summed up rather vaguely as 'interests') 'in order to explain natural things'. It is only quite recently that an interpretivist tack, one that attempts to see science as the consilient interplay of thought and things, has begun to take hold.[21]

As they are quite recent, such interpretivist approaches are both ill

---

[20] Bruno Latour, *Nous n'avons jamais été modernes: essai d'anthropologie symétrique* (Paris: La Découverte, 1991), p. 186. This is Latour's most general, and most provocative, statement of position; for more detailed discussion, see his *Science in action: how to follow scientists and engineers through society* (Cambridge, Mass.: Harvard University Press, 1987); for a specific application, *The pasteurization of France* (Cambridge, Mass.: Harvard University Press, 1988).

[21] The quotation is from H. M. Collins and Steven Yearley, 'Journey into space', a polemic against Latour, in Pickering, *Science as practice and culture*, p. 384. For the Merton approach, see his *The sociology of science: theoretical and empirical investigations* (Chicago: University of Chicago Press, 1973). For the sociology of (scientific) knowledge approach (SSK), sometimes referred to as 'the strong programme', see Barry Barnes, *Interests and the growth of knowledge* (London: Routledge and Kegan Paul, 1977). I borrow the limpid, if antique, term 'consilient' (which seems to me an improvement over, or anyway a useful supplement to, the aesthetical 'coherent' as applied to texts, the formalistic 'consistent' as applied to beliefs, the functionalist 'integrated' as applied to institutions, or the psychologistic 'attuned' as applied to persons) from Ian Hacking, 'The self-vindication of the laboratory sciences', in Pickering, *Science as practice and culture*, pp. 29–64, a searching examination of the course it celebrates. For an extended discussion, cf. his *Representing and intervening* (Cambridge: Cambridge University Press, 1985).

formed and variable, uncertain opening probes in an apparently endless and, at least for the moment, ill-marked enquiry. There are analyses of the rhetoric of scientific discourse, oral and written: there are descriptions of human and non-human agents as coactive nodes in ramifying networks of meaning and power; there are ethnographic, and ethnomethodological, studies of 'fact construction' and 'accounting procedures'; there are investigations of research planning, instrument construction and laboratory practice. But, however undeveloped, they all approach science not as opaque social precipitate but as meaningful social action: 'We have never been interested in giving a social explanation of anything ... we want to explain society, of which ... things, facts and artefacts, are major components.'[22] This hardly seems the objectivist, agentless 'naturalism' of which Taylor is so rightly wary. Different as they are, the natural sciences and the human may not be so radically other, their intellectual congress not so inevitably barren.

IV

Sciences, physical, biological, human or whatever, change not only in their content or their social impact (though they do, of course, do that, and massively), but in their character as a form of life, a way of being in the world, a meaningful system of human action, a particular story about how things stand. Like all such ways, forms, systems, stories – still life, say, or criminal law – they are constructed in time (and, despite their reach for universality, to an important degree in space as well), and thus any image of them that remains stable over their entire course and across their whole range of activities and concerns is bound to turn into an obscuring myth. Such a myth indeed exists, and, as Taylor has demonstrated, has had destructive effects upon attempts by those who have bought into it to explain politics, language, selfhood and mind. But it has also had, as he seems not very clearly to realise, no less baneful effects on, to borrow Woolgar's borrowing of Davidson's slogan, the very idea of science itself.[23]

Taylor's resistance to the intrusion of 'the natural science model' into

---

22 Michel Callon and Bruno Latour, in Pickering, *Science as practice and culture*, p. 348. They continue: 'Our general ... principle is not to alternate between natural realism and social realism but to obtain nature and society as twin results of another activity, one that is more interesting for us. We call it network building, or collective things, or quasi-objects, or trials of force; and others call it skill, forms of life, material practice' (references eliminated).

23 Woolgar, *Science, the very idea*. Cf. Donald Davidson, 'On the very idea of a conceptual scheme', *Proceedings and Addresses of the American Philosophical Association*, 47 (1973–4), pp. 5–20.

the human sciences seems in fact to accept his opponents' view that there is such a model, unitary, well-defined and historically immobile, governing contemporary enquiries into things and materialities in the first place; the problem is, merely, to confine it to its proper sphere, stars, rocks, kidneys and wavicles, and keep it well away from matters where 'mattering' matters.[24] This division of the realm, which reminds one of nothing so much as the way some nineteenth-century divines (and some pious physicists) attempted to 'solve' the religion versus science issue – 'you can have the mechanisms, we will keep the meanings' – is supposed to ensure that ideas will not trespass where they don't belong. What it in fact ensures is symmetrical complacency and the deflection of issues.

There are, as virtually everyone is at least dimly aware, massive transformations now in motion in the studies conventionally grouped under the rather baggy category (does mathematics belong? does psychopharmacology?) of the natural sciences, transformations social, technical and epistemological at once, which make not only the seventeenth-century image of them, but the late nineteenth and early twentieth ones as well, clumsy, thin and inexact. The price of keeping the human sciences radically separated from such studies is keeping such studies radically separated from the human sciences – left to the mercy of their own devices.

Such devices are not enough. The outcome of this artificial and unnecessary estrangement is, at once, the perpetuation within the various natural sciences of outmoded self-conceptions, global stories that falsify their actual practice, the 'sterile', 'half-baked' and 'implausible' imitations that those outmoded conceptions and false stories induce in human scientists ignorant of what in fact, physics, chemistry, physiology and the like come to as meaningful action, and, perhaps worst of all, the production of various sorts of New Age irrationalisms – Zen physics, Maharishi cosmology, parapsychology – supposed to unify everything and anything at some higher, or deeper or wider level.[25]

Fighting off the 'naturalisation' of the human sciences is a necessary enterprise, to which Taylor has powerfully contributed; and we must be grateful to him for the dauntlessness of his efforts in that regard, and for their precision. Possessed himself of some dusty formulas, he has, to our general loss, not so contributed to the no less necessary enterprise of reconnecting the natural sciences to their human roots, and thus of fighting off *their* naturalisation. It is an enormous pity that some of the most consequential developments of contemporary culture are taking place beyond the attention of one of that culture's profoundest students.

[24] Taylor, *Philosophical papers*, I, p. 197.
[25] For some interesting comments on this latter, see Jeremy Bernstein, *Quantum profiles* (Princeton: Princeton University Press, 1991), especially pp. vii–viii, 77–84.

7   Is there an objective spirit?

Vincent Descombes

In his book on Hegel, Charles Taylor presents the Hegelian notion of an objective spirit,[1] and defends it against the objections to which it is commonly subjected.[2] He does not ask us to endorse the concept wholesale. As we know, Hegel's philosophy of spirit, of which the philosophy of objective spirit forms the second part, serves a number of functions in the system. As Taylor points out, the doctrine has become most foreign to us on precisely the point which Hegel would have deemed most important, namely, when it is seen as a theodicy which makes of the human community a kind of *corpus mysticum* through which the divine can achieve its full presence. The concept of objective spirit does, however, possess a certain value if it is taken rather as the descendant of the notion of the 'spirit of the laws' which was elaborated by Montesquieu. The defence of this notion would simply be that a concept of this kind is required in the 'moral' or 'social sciences' (*Geisteswissenschaften*). As Taylor has remarked, however, the objections voiced by our contemporaries to the Hegelian doctrine bear not only on Hegelian theodicy, but also on the very idea of a social thought, or of a social form of thought. As faithful heirs of the Enlightenment project, many of our contemporaries believe that thought can only occur in a personal form. In other words, it is senseless, in their view, to construe thought, or meaning, or representation, etc., without implying that it is *someone's* thought, that of a personal thinking subject. One could speak of social representations or meanings in an indirect and derivative manner only, for instance, to refer to the fact that they belong to the individuals who make up the society in question.

Questions of Hegelian exegesis will be set aside in what follows. I will be

---

[1] The French word *esprit* and the German word *Geist* are quite general: they embrace the meanings of the two English words 'mind' and 'spirit'. Thus, what is called in English 'philosophy of mind' corresponds to *philosophie de l'esprit subjectif* (or psychology), whereas a *philosophie de l'esprit objectif* would be known in English as philosophy of law and social theory.

[2] Taylor, *Hegel*, chapter 14.

focusing not on the Hegelian notion considered for its own sake, but rather on the whole family of sociological conceptions of spirit. This is a family made up of members such as the 'spirit of the laws' (Montesquieu), 'collective consciousness' (Durkheim), 'intentional totality' (Dilthey's *Zweckzusammenhänge*), 'culture' (drawn from American anthropology), 'forms of life' (Wittgenstein), and 'symbolic systems' (Lévi-Strauss).

Generally speaking, Taylor has not undertaken to rehabilitate the Hegelian notion itself, but rather a more positive version of it, freed of its theological baggage, that I will speak of as *sociological*. The term 'sociology' must of course be taken in the strong sense which was given to it by Durkheim and the other members of the French school of sociology. (It goes without saying that many social science researchers would not define the discipline in this way.) For there to be a sociology in the strong sense which I shall be using here, it is not enough to deal with 'social phenomena', or even to attribute great weight to 'social factors'. The sociologist must posit further that social phenomena are intellectual phenomena, and that institutions rest upon representations which are those of the society as such, rather than of associated individuals (whether the association is based upon an explicit social contract or a spontaneous convention). In other words, sociology holds that institutions 'think'.[3] It would be closer to Taylor's own line of thought to express this idea by saying that social life is not reducible to the necessities of common life (utilitarian naturalism), but that it has meaning, and that individuals derive meaning from it. Meaning is not locked up within individuals' inner realm; public and collective forms of existence and action are its natural element. In a philosophy of objective spirit redefined as sociology, the study of social life takes its bearings from a study of the *spirit* of these institutions.

It must be acknowledged from the outset that the very notion of an 'objective spirit' is rendered singularly obscure by its embeddedness within a cumbersome metaphysics which conceives of everything in terms of the opposition between a subject and an object. Even those who have taken up the notion anew have a great deal of trouble making use of it adequately. They speak of the opposition between the objective and the subjective as an opposition between two ways in which a thing can be present to an intelligence, the first public (for anyone), and the second private (for a single subject, for me). But they slide from there to another opposition which contrasts the material and the spiritual, the inert and the living. Thus, according to Merleau-Ponty, objective spirit simply involves the presence around us of material objects which bear witness to a human presence. For example, he writes that: '[N]ot only do I live in the

---

[3] See Mary Douglas, *How institutions think* (Syracuse: Syracuse University Press, 1986).

midst of earth, air and water, I have around me roads, plantations, villages, streets, churches, implements, a bell, a spoon, a pipe. Each of these objects is moulded to the human action which it serves . . . [A]n Objective Spirit dwells in the remains and the scenery.'[4] 'Objective' spirit is thus nothing more than what remains of a civilisation once its 'subjects' have departed: roads without travellers, churches without the faithful, traces of a dwelling. In the examples just given, 'objectivity' construed as the physical reality of material objects prevails over the kind of 'objectivity' that one could ascribe to spirit, an objectivity which is located in the social practices to which the objects cited above bear witness. Lévi-Strauss also sometimes speaks of a material spirit in a manner similar to Merleau-Ponty's 'culturalist' sense. In response to a question concerning his definition of ethnology as 'psychology' or study of spirit,[5] for example, Lévi-Strauss argued that the definition ceased to appear paradoxical if one thought of the objects collected by the ethnographer as 'thought somehow made concrete'.[6] Here again, spirit only becomes 'objective' once it is fossilised. In the texts where Lévi-Strauss characterises anthropology as the science of the spirit, however, he understands matters differently. Structuralist science must deal not only with things which bear the marks of intelligent activity, but rather also with an objective spirit conceived of as a *thinking thing*. In a striking yet original phrase, for example, he writes 'as the mind too is a thing, the functioning of this thing teaches us something about the nature of things: even pure reflection is in the last analysis an internalisation of the cosmos'.[7] This is in his view the principal teaching of structuralist linguistics: 'Linguistics thus presents us with a dialectical and totalizing entity, but one outside (or beneath) consciousness and will. Language, an unreflecting totalization, is human reason which has its reasons and of which man knows nothing.'[8]

In short, there is an equivocation between three different conceptions of objective spirit: it can be thought of as a spirit which resides within things themselves (rather than being situated, as our common sense would indicate, in our heads); alternatively, it can be construed on the model of a material system operating mentally (in the sense that the system could adequately combine meanings or construct finalised programmes); finally, it could be seen as akin to a sharable 'state of mind' or a rule to follow, as a condition for the exercise of intelligent activity, a condition to which

4 Maurice Merleau-Ponty, *Phenomenology of perception*, trans. Colin Smith (London: Routledge and Kegan Paul, 1962), pp. 247–8.
5 Claude Lévi-Strauss, *The savage mind* (Chicago: University of Chicago Press, 1967), p. 131.
6 Claude Lévi-Strauss and Didier Eribon, *Conversations with Claude Lévi-Strauss*, trans. Paula Wissing (Chicago: University of Chicago Press, 1991), p. 109.
7 Lévi-Strauss, *The savage mind*, p. 248 fn.   8 Ibid., p. 252.

individuals would be subject in a manner not requiring their consent (and which would in this sense be 'objective').

One could say that a library or a collection of folkloric objects represents an objective spirit in the first sense, and that a computer, defined as a 'thinking machine', is an objective spirit in the second sense. It must be pointed out that one could give full expression to these two construals within the conceptual apparatus of Cartesian and post-Cartesian philosophies (whether they involve a mind–body dualism or a subject–object dualism). This is not the case for the third sense, which is of particular importance to a sociological theory of spirit. Kinship systems, religions, or more directly, languages, would be examples of objective spirit in this third sense. It is the possession of what Humboldt called *die innere Sprachform*, of an internal form (as opposed to the mere 'external form' which is the sole object of study of behaviourist linguistics), that confers a 'spirit' upon a language. This internal form allows us to envisage a typological (and therefore structural) classification of languages, in addition to an historical (genealogical) one.[9] An objective spirit of this kind is made up of rules and established uses, which transcend the free agency of individuals and their mutual conventions. The problem is to define an ontological status for these rules and conventions. They are neither material objects (such as churches or pipes), nor mental acts. In other words, to take up the terms of nineteenth-century philosophy, they are neither 'things', nor 'representations'. From a philosophical point of view, the importance of the question of objective or collective spirit is to force us to recognise the limits of classical philosophy of mind, which can only acknowledge two positions: the neo-Cartesian mentalism of *mental acts* and the materialism of *brain-states*. Neither of these positions permits us to make room for those realities of which language is perhaps the least controvertible example, and which we may want to term *institutions*. What is required is a metaphysics different from that of the *cogito*.

In order to avoid the drawbacks associated with the post-Kantian terminology of subject and object, I will not be speaking of an objective spirit, but rather, in a manner similar to Montesquieu, of a *general spirit*. In his notebooks, Montesquieu writes that: 'There are principal as well as secondary laws, and in each country is constituted a kind of generation of laws. Nations, like individuals, think along certain distinctive lines, and their total way of thinking, like that of each individual, has a beginning, a middle and an end.'[10] Since my task is to elucidate a concept which has often appeared unintelligible, (and thus to make a case for a purely

[9] See Lucien Tesniere, *Eléments de syntaxe structurale*, 2nd edn. (Paris: Klincksieck, 1988), chapters 12–15.

[10] Baron de Montesquieu, *Oeuvres complètes* (Paris: Les Editions du Seuil, 1964), p. 895.

philosophical line of enquiry), I will first try to ascertain whether the notion of a collective spirit is meaningful (that is, whether or not it is incoherent); I will then discuss whether it is legitimate (that is, whether it is possible to dispense with it in the description of human affairs).

I

Theories which attempt to make room for a social dimension of thought are often perceived as dangerous as well as aberrant. It is worth enquiring into the reasons behind this assessment. As Taylor has remarked, two debates seem to be run together here. In debates in the area of political philosophy, we find discussions of the proper definition of the public good (individualism versus collectivism). Debates in social metaphysics moot the possibility of reducing society to the individuals which constitute it (atomism versus holism). A proponent of moral individualism (a liberal) is not in theory forced to represent society in the terms provided by an atomist model. In fact, it can be observed that the motives driving an atomist metaphysics of society are most often moral: the possibility of the self-realisation of the individual is supposed to be better secured by this kind of atomism.

To posit a social being inevitably suggests a downgrading of the individual. Why is this?

I believe that this suggestion stems from the fact that the whole debate is expressed in the terms of one of the metaphysical positions in question, namely the atomist position. The argument underpinning the atomist (or atomist-individualist) objection to any social conception of spirit seems to run as follows: to posit a social being on the intellectual, rather than simply on the material level amounts to downgrading the individual by raising doubts about her freedom of conscience and of judgement. But relative to whom, if not to other individuals, would this downgrading occur? Collectivists tell us that we must defer to the superior interests of the collectivity. In fact, a particular individual is invited to defer relative to other individuals who are in positions of power, who have claimed for themselves the status of *representatives* of the superior interests of all, by means of some name or other (Committee, Bureau, Office, Party). The individuals who occupy these dominant positions succeed in representing their own goals as legitimately requiring the collaboration of all. Ontologically, however, the committee or bureau which requires this submission is simply a collection of other individuals. From an atomist point of view, there can never be anything else but a confrontation among individuals seeking to modify the balance of power.

It must be acknowledged that the objection just cited, which is shared by moderate as well as by radical (often Nietzschean) liberals, is not without some force. It expresses the perception of a remarkable fact: indeed, it is a stunning irony that the exaltation of the historical role of the masses has coincided with the 'cult of personality' of tyrants. It has also been possible to observe in a more 'worldly' context that the recent proclamation by literary critics of the 'death of the author' has had the paradoxical effect of promoting these very critics to the rank of writer, in the name of an 'active' and 'plural' doctrine of interpretative reading. More generally, the positing of any reality as lying beyond individuals is justifiably perceived as oppressive, because it expresses itself through the same atomist metaphysics as that which is used by the defenders of the individual against the State and the Collective.

In France, a 'debate over the subject' has opposed defenders of the philosophical tradition of the *cogito* (Sartre, for example) and critics of that tradition, for a time united under the banner of structuralism. The conflict ought in principle to have been centred on the point with which we have been concerned here, namely whether all thought must be construed, defined and studied in relation to an individual thinking subject, or whether there are not such things as collective representations and ideas. But in fact, the discussion has been drawn into the magnetic field of individualism. The question has thus been cast as a competition between two candidate conceptions concerning the subject of individual thoughts: 'me' or someone other than me. Thus Lévi-Strauss, after having usefully opposed his point of departure to that of the 'philosophy of the Cogito', appears tempted to substitute for it a surrealist philosophy which posits 'something which thinks in me' rather than a philosophy of thought without a thinker. He sets up an opposition between Rousseau and Descartes, and writes that the former discovered, in opposition to the latter, a truth which psychologists and ethnographers would later redis-cover: '[T]here exists a "he" who "thinks" through me and who first causes me to doubt whether it is I who am thinking.'[11] The conclusion is clear: critics of the subject are not necessarily adversaries of individual-ism. That which is opposed to a personal individual is still an individual.

This whole discussion can be summed up by a single observation: critics of sociological notions have legitimate worries concerning several ver-sions of the social theory of spirit. Indeed, they observe that the social being they are asked to acknowledge 'above and beyond' the individual itself resembles an individual. But since it is being posited above and beyond individuals, it is presented as a *superior* individual, as a 'collective

---

[11] Claude Lévi-Strauss, *Structural anthropology*, II, trans. Monique Layton (New York: Basic Books, 1976), p. 37.

individual', which is named and treated as an individual and to which all the attributes of a person are naively ascribed. It seems to them as if they are being offered an 'organicist' doctrine of the social (society as a large organism made up of smaller organisms). And since the background to the debate is moral, they cannot quite understand how a union of a number of individual organisms into a supra-personal system (the collective individual) can confer upon the latter any moral value and authority over its members.

We therefore have an answer to our *first* question. The sociological (holist) conception of human spirit is obviously incoherent if it is formulated in the terms of a metaphysics which rules it out. If only the existence of individuals is acknowledged, then collective spirit must be the spirit of some collective individual. There therefore immediately arises an inevitable conflict between collective and individual spirit, because the notion of a collective individual does double duty, from an ontological standpoint, with the individuals who constitute it.

But this response also points to the *limits* of the atomist objection. It only has force *within* the atomist perspective. It prevents the atomist from speaking of collective spirit. It becomes clear that sociology properly understood has no place within an atomist conception of reality. An effort is therefore required on the part of sociologists to clarify the content of the notion of a general spirit in ontological terms.

II

In fact, a consistent atomist will not refuse to *speak* of a 'supra-individual spirit': great advantages flow for him from the use of notions which would seem to belong to a more holistic conception of things. The nominalist does not balk from 'objectifying' spirit, that is, from hypostatising it *in representation*, making it into an object of description. She concedes that it is often useful to speak as if there existed such entities as states, culture, the spirit of the times, etc., but this is simply a *façon de parler* which (like the notion of the 'average Frenchman' in a statistical description of the country) is not to be taken seriously. It is nothing more than a tool used to represent facts. What the nominalist will not do, however, is to hypostatise the collective *in reality*, to commit herself to it ontologically. It can legitimately be claimed that the market ensures the best distribution of existing resources as a function of demand and of commercial actors' reason. But this does not entail the conclusion that there exists an entity, the market, which is capable of efficiently calculating the best division of labour. Everyone understands that the market is an *ens rationis*, a figure of speech, a way of referring in an abbreviated manner to the myriad of decisions which are taken by independent agents without coordination or consultation. Similarly, the 'invisible hand' which directs the global economy is in fact not an invisible hand. Conversely, in the case of the analysis of 'perverse effects', it is as if a stupid organiser, afflicted with cretinism, had planned things in a catastrophic manner. It is as if he had scheduled the workday to end at the same time for everyone, forced everyone to take their holidays at the same time, asked everyone to attend the same show, etc. Collective spirit is no longer seen as brilliant, no longer surprises us with its 'cunning of reason'. Instead, we are confronted with 'errors of ineptitude', the manifestations of a collective incompetence, of an idiot having usurped the functions of Providence.

The real objection against all social theories of spirit focuses not on a figure of speech but on the hypostasis of social reality. When it is represented in the form of a great collective individual, the community is, so to speak, in competition with the individuals which make it up. But it is precisely the conception of the community as a great individual which indicates how difficult it is, even for thinkers whose intention is sociological, to escape from the spontaneous atomism of modern common sense.

Thus, we find in Durkheim that the very expression of 'collective consciousness' is constituted by adding the incongruous predicate 'collective' to a term taken from the most classical philosophical vocabulary. In this manner, classical philosophy of mind in its entirety is re-affirmed. To think is above all *to have representations*, (and, according to some philosophers, to combine them according to principles of reason). The representationalism inherited by Durkheim from his philosophy teachers as it were forces him to locate collective thoughts *within* a collective subject. The theory which accounts for the genesis of collective representations in times of effervescence (such as primitive religious festivals) still has Cartesian traits; this collective thought is construed as a vast *cogitamus*. And a supra-personal subject is obviously required in order to account for these collective thoughts and lived experiences, just as, according to Descartes, the *cogito* revealed itself as the act of thinking of the personal subject.

How might we avoid this pitfall? Let us take as our premiss that sociological description is not concerned with the actual lived experience of people, but with their *general* ways of life, their customs and practices, what would in classical parlance have been called their mores and manners. Thus, in *The spirit of the laws*, Montesquieu focuses not only upon laws, but also upon the mores of peoples (that is, upon their 'ways of life', such as with respect to frugality and luxury) and upon their manners (in the sense of 'good manners', the way in which people conduct themselves with their peers). Here, for example, are his observations on jealousy, which in his view exists in two forms, the 'jealousy of passion' (an individual phenomenon) and the 'jealousy of custom' (a social phenomenon, a trait of the spirit of institutions): 'With respect to nations, we ought to distinguish between the passion of jealousy and a jealousy arising from customs, manners and laws ... The one, an abuse of love, derives its source from love itself. The other depends only on manners, on the customs of a nation, on the laws of the country, and sometimes even on religion.'[12] Political philosophers have most often been concerned with laws, and have tended to disregard mores and manners. It is because he considers that laws are in fact subordinate to mores (and thus, independent of the arbitrariness of the individual) that Montesquieu (and, following him, Rousseau) can be claimed as a precursor of sociology: 'We have said that the laws were the particular and precise institutions of a legislator, and manners and customs the institutions of a nation in general. Hence it follows that when these manners and customs are to be changed, it ought not to be done by laws; this would have too much the air of tyranny; it would be better to change them by introducing other manners and other customs.'[13] But to speak of 'mores,' 'manners', 'habitual practices', and 'customs' is not to suppose that a certain intellectual content is simultaneously present in the minds of individuals (as the theory of collective consciousness as *cogitamus* would have it). Mores cannot be reduced to representations, to ideas which are actually present to the consciousnesses of people. All of these terms of Montesquieu's are, as it were, 'dispositional'; they denote habitual ways of doing things, tendencies and inclinations, habits, 'bodily techniques' (Marcel Mauss), in short, a certain style of conduct.

Like most of the philosophies of the nineteenth century, sociological theory uses the term 'consciousness' as a synonym for 'spirit'. Transposing the debate between empiricists and rationalists, Durkheim wrote that: 'It is doubtless a self-evident truth that there is nothing in social life that is not in the consciousness of individuals. Yet everything to be found in the latter comes from society.'[14] Fundamentally, the question is whether, for example, the jealousy which a person feels is for her a 'jealousy of passion' or a 'jealousy of custom'. But Durkheim expresses his thought in a manner which requires that he see such jealousy as a 'state of consciousness'. He continues: 'Most of our states of consciousness

---

12 Baron de Montesquieu, *The spirit of the laws*, trans. Thomas Nugent (New York: Hafner Press, 1949), p. 259 (book XVI, chapter 13).
13 Ibid., p. 298 (book XIX, chapter 14).
14 Emile Durkheim, *The division of labor in society*, trans. W. D. Halls (New York: The Free Press, 1984), p. 287.

would not have occurred among men isolated from one another and would have occurred completely differently among people grouped together in different way.'[15] We must dissociate the sociological thesis concerning the contents of spirit (is this content in essence social or individual?) from the metaphysical thesis according to which the *presence in the spirit* (of a content) must always be an actual *presence to spirit* (of an object of representation). For the presence of the social is best construed as an *habitual* presence: it is not a 'state of consciousness', but rather consists of that which in the individual is already determined as far as his future reactions to a given situation are concerned. What would the subject in a state where jealousy is 'customary' do if his personal honour seemed to him to be under threat?

Contemporary philosophy of language, above all Wittgenstein's, has provided the occasion for a radical critique of the 'actualism' of the classical doctrines of spirit. To understand the meaning of something does not involve having a representation present to the mind. If 'explication of meaning is explication of usage', it follows that understanding, in turn, does not involve the actual possession of a 'state of consciousness', but rather the possession of a capacity. We can impose a 'linguistic turn' on Durkheim's thesis, by substituting for it the slogan put forward by Rom Harré to summarise the 'constructivist' theory of the mind: 'nothing is in the mind that was not first in the conversation.'[16] In so doing, we exchange the theoretical idiom of representation (which belongs to the philosophy of consciousness) for the idiom of meaning.

It is precisely by appealing to the privileged model of language that Taylor rehabilitates something like an 'objective spirit' in a formulation which is deemed necessary by sociologists, though it might not have been acceptable to Hegel. Is the place occupied by language in the mental life of an individual sufficient to establish that he can only think within a social context? This last point is not in dispute, but everything turns on what is meant by 'to think in language' or 'to think with others in society'. What has, in a very general manner, been termed the 'linguistic turn' of contemporary philosophies, consisting in emphasising the link between thought and language, has inspired a number of attempts to construe human reason in terms of communication, of dialogical exchange, as opposed to classical theories (collected by Habermas under the rubric of 'philosophies of consciousness') according to which reason is the individual faculty permitting the individual solitary access to necessary truths. It is possible, however, that we are still short of the sociological

[15] Ibid.   [16] Rom Harré, *Personal being* (Oxford: Basil Blackwell, 1983), p. 116.

thesis of spirit as part of society. The *public space* of communication only establishes intersubjectivity. At least, this is what must now be established.

Taylor's strategy involves two claims:[17] he shows how any social practice presupposes *common*, as opposed to merely *shared* meanings; and he shows that these ideas and meanings, which resemble the Hegelian 'objective spirit', are 'expressed' by institutions, which can therefore themselves be compared to a language.

I will take up these two points in turn, in order to address the question of the sort of model we might find in language to advance our elucidation of the ontological status of general spirit.

At the basis of all institutionalised practices lie common meanings

We will use the term 'personal meanings' to denote the explanations which a given individual could provide for the meaning of his conduct. In order to follow Taylor's own analysis, let us take up the example of the meaning of a person's vote in an election. Two persons can without a doubt vote for the same candidate while doing so for different reasons. Their objectives might even be opposed. We can thus take our bearings from these meanings to identify those which are shared. We will say that the members of a group must share a significant proportion of their conceptions and tastes, without which collective life would be impossible. These meanings, which it must be possible for people to share (although it is not possible to say of any of them that they *will* be shared), are illustrated by the 'judgements of taste' of Kant's aesthetics, with their legitimate presupposition of a *common sense* as the condition of the public's being able to emit such judgements. A number of contemporary philosophers, from Arendt to Lyotard, and including Habermas, have tried to derive a political philosophy from Kant's *Critique of judgement*. But this is to suppose that the social can be reduced to the *public space*, and, thus, to what might be termed an intersubjective space (that is, a space where subjects discover that they can and must come into contact with one another freely). Personal meanings, necessarily including intersubjective ones, are produced by individuals as a function of their experiences. A great number of these personal experiences, however, concern events and facts which presuppose meanings of another type, which Taylor calls 'common'. To return to the example of voting, it might happen that a number of voters have no understanding of what they are doing when they cast their ballot. In principle, only citizens who under-

17 Taylor, *Hegel*, pp. 380–2.

stand the meaning of the practice can take part in the vote. In fact, it is assumed that, as of the moment he or she reaches legal adulthood, any citizen defeasibly satisfies this condition. There is therefore a *meaning* to the practice; the institution of elections rests upon a conception. To whom does this conception belong? It belongs neither to each individual (who is not free to ascribe a personal meaning to the electoral institution), nor to all individuals united in a consensus emerging from a free debate (for there can be exceptions or lacunae to this consensus). The collective conception of things is thus in a sense external to individual conscious-nesses. As Taylor writes: 'The meanings and norms implicit in these practices are not just in the minds of the actors but are out there in the practices themselves, practices which cannot be conceived as a set of individual actions, but which are essentially modes of social relation, of mutual action.'[18] If the common meanings are not simply in the heads of actors (even when considered 'simultaneously'), it is in the first instance because they are meanings and not *cogitationes* (they are nowhere present in the mode of actuality), and second, because they are constitutive, in the manner of the rules of a game, of the practice in which the actors are engaged. The meaning of a social practice outruns each individual mind, in that individual participation in a practice expresses not only the way in which a given person sees things (which makes him vote for X or Y), but also the way in which society considers that things ought to be done (for example, that certain officials must be elected, and that an election must be conducted according to a given procedure). A practice therefore contains *more* than what individuals themselves put into it.

The meanings which make up the general spirit of institutions are comparable to a language

Having compared the general spirit with *meanings*, we must now take sides in a methodological debate. This debate does not really oppose 'positivists' and 'non-positivists'. Rather, it has to do with that in virtue of which we are entitled to speak of *human* sciences (of a non-arbitrary description of human affairs) when we cannot avail ourselves of a posi-tivist epistemology.

If the social presents itself mainly in the form of the meanings that constitute social practices, we can legitimately compare the general spirit to a language. On this subject, Taylor has observed that:

In this sense we can think of the institutions and practices of a society as a kind of language in which its fundamental ideas are expressed. But what is 'said' in this

[18] Taylor, 'Interpretation and the sciences of man', *Philosophical papers*, II, p. 36.

language is not ideas which could be in the minds of certain individuals only, they are rather common to a society, because embedded in its collective life, in practices and institutions which are of the society indivisibly. In these the spirit of the society is in a sense objectified. They are, to use Hegel's term 'objective spirit'.[19]

It is here that the oft-repeated slogan, the 'linguistic turn', finds its limits. Indeed, the comparison of social institutions and language does not restrict us to a single methodological orientation. A number of positions can be made sense of: that institutions are a language in that they say something – that, like a text, they are bearers of a message (this is the hermeneutical thesis, suggested by Taylor in the passage just quoted); or that institutions are like a language in that they function as a *code of communication* allowing people to express themselves, and which permits us to see social life as a vast network of communication among individuals; or finally, that institutions are not so much a language (a semiological thesis) as they are 'structured like a language' (a structuralist thesis), that is, that they are 'symbolic systems' organised around an 'internal form'.

It remains to be seen how the linguistic model helps us to understand more clearly what is meant by a general spirit. Since this model can be that of *parole* – in this case, of *parole* transmitted through writing – or that of *langue*, we must in brief consider the two great theories which have traced their lineages back to these two models: hermeneutics and structuralism (the latter comprising two distinct and independent versions, the semiological and the anthropological).

III

The linguistic model of the text: concerning textualism

Taylor opposes a traditional vision of the world – the world conceived as a text – to the modern one, according to which the world is not the incarnation of meanings or of ideas, but the place of contingent correlations.[20] But this is a bit too quick. For contemporary French *textualism*, inspired largely by Mallarmean speculations, teaches us that the figure of the text is eminently suited to transmit a modern vision of things, that is, to produce a typically modern discourse on the question of meaning. This modern discourse is clearly expressed by what Claudel says of Mallarmé in 'La catastrophe d'Igitur': 'Mallarmé is the first to have placed himself before the external world, not as if before a spectacle, or the subject for a

---

[19] *Hegel*, p. 382.   [20] Ibid., pp. 4–5 and 12–13.

schoolboy's essay, but rather as if before a text, with this question: "But what does this mean?" '[21] The central point brought out by this portrait of Mallarmé as a modern poet is that the poet finds himself placed before an *external* world (though not before a spectacle to relish, but before a text). The poet is therefore not inside anything whatsoever; he does not see himself as part of what he is to interpret. In other words, textualism expresses quite precisely the dualism of human and world which Taylor, following others, rightly sees as a philosophical characteristic of modernity. To the extent that the poet is part of the 'text', it is to its material body rather than to its thought that he belongs. Granted, Claudel in the same article opposes Mallarmé's nihilist reading of the text-world to the symbolic reading offered by the Church fathers and by Dante; he is none the less 'resolutely modern', since this figure of the world as text leaves him but one rather untraditional and quite contemporary alternative. Indeed, like any good Cartesian, he writes: 'We know that we are made to dominate the world, rather than the world being made to dominate us.'[22] This amounts to saying that the figure of the text allows for the introduction of a notion of a non-organic totality, whose parts constantly refer back to one another. However, the reader of this text is by definition on the outside, either to be crushed by the 'bounteous machine of appearances' (Mallarmé, according to Claudel) or to be referred from the text back to its transcendent author.

What is the value of the linguistic model of the text?

The hermeneutically inspired human sciences invite us to compare the study of institutions to the philological study of texts. On this view, the sciences of man are sciences of interpretation. I think that this thesis is, on a certain reading, justified, but quite indefensible on another. The hermeneutical conception of the social sciences can be read in an anti-naturalist sense, and would thus basically amount to Evans-Pritchard's argument against functionalism. Social science is unlike the study of a chemical or even a biological phenomenon, for its object is a symbolic rather than a natural system.[23] Evans-Pritchard himself spoke of interpretation, of translation, of that which situates us within a linguistic, or even a textual paradigm. But no particular method is advocated, which means that the problem of the metaphysical status of the general spirit remains whole.

[21] Paul Claudel, 'La catastrophe d'Igitur', *Oeuvres complètes*, Bibliothèque de la Pléiade (Paris: Gallimard, 1965), p. 511.
[22] Ibid., p. 512.
[23] E. Evans-Pritchard, 'Social anthropology, past and present', *Essays in social anthropology* (London: Faber and Faber, 1962), pp. 3–38.

It is possible in the light of this to employ the analogy between a text and a civilisation more ambitiously. Indeed, ethnology would on this view be an explication of texts which would apply itself to 'quasi-texts', that is, to the intentional actions of the members of the society under study.[24] But it is here that our difficulties begin. First, we are threatened by the return of a conception of society as a 'collective individual'. If culture is a text, and if we must decipher the message it bears, it is difficult not to arrive at the question: 'Who is speaking?' It is then necessary to find an *author* of the text.

Taylor has, it seems to me, decisively rebutted the idea that social science ought to interpret its objects, that is, that it ought to treat them like texts: 'The text is replaced in the interpretation by another text, one which is clearer. The text-analogue of behaviour is not replaced by another such text-analogue . . . [I]n science the text analogue is replaced by a text, an account.'[25] The social scientist does not replace a ritual ceremony by another, more intelligible one. She simply writes a book about the ceremonies of a given people. To say that she is *translating* the ceremony would be to place the object under study (a particular practice) and the enquirer's discourse within the same category of things.

If this is the case, then it seems that the textual model of ethnographic enquiry cannot possibly be that of an *explication de texte*. It should rather be seen as a somewhat special type of translation. The use of the term 'translation' underscores that the social fact which must be described, for example a certain ceremony, must be described in a theoretical language, in a system of categories. We must be able to determine whether the ceremony in question is a religious rite, a solemn political event, a public game, etc. In our own societies, *we* distinguish between the realms of the religious, of the political, and that set aside for games. The 'theoretical language' of the enquirer will, at least at the outset, necessarily be her own. We have until now simply found what the hermeneuticist has told us all along: there can be no descriptions that do not presuppose an interpretation, that do not put prejudices into play, that do not constitute appropriations. However, the same object of enquiry can also be described in the terms of the 'native theoretical language', understood not as denoting the theories which the native thinkers may have elaborated, but rather the system of categories which is theirs and by virtue of which they represent their customs and practices to themselves. What is the real meaning of the practice? As long as the enquirer remains at the level of her initial answer, formulated in the common-sense categories of her own society, it is clear that she has still not *understood* anything. We can say

---

[24] Taylor, 'Interpretation and the sciences of man', p. 15.   [25] Ibid., p. 25.

that she has *interpreted*, but only in the sense of interpretation, which means translating a text too quickly from one language to another, without *rethinking* it each time according to the structure, the 'interior form' of the language used. But what the enquirer studying different forms of life must do is to discover the native categories. We might say that this enterprise is as much an *exercice de thème* (moving from one's own language to a foreign one) as it is an *exercice de version* (going from a foreign language to one's own). She must renounce thinking about the ceremony according to her own categories (just as Latin *thème* consists of a rethinking of the text given in French in Latin terms in order to avoid gallicisms). It is as if, in correcting her first attempt at description, she had to reconstitute an original which, in a sense, has never existed (since natives do not normally practise anthropological description of themselves). The enquiry does not therefore go from a 'foreign' text to a clearer 'interpretation'. If we insist on speaking of texts, it would rather move from a faulty translation of a text to a more adequate original, in order then to be able to return to a more satisfactory translation.

The original in question is not, however, the ceremony itself, but rather the way in which the actors in the ceremony understand what they are doing. It is not the object itself, but rather the first faulty interpretation offered by the enquirer, that can be compared to a text, and that we can thus correct as we would an awkward translation.

Finally, the aim is to *understand* the ceremony in question. It is not to simply reproduce the 'original' constituted by the native ideology. The enquirer must take her bearings from this ideology, and translate it into more universal categories. What should be learned from this analogy between culture and text is thus that a translation always establishes a contrast between two languages. Apart from that, the philological model is best construed as a comparative syntax aiming to establish a typology of languages.

Man is a self-interpreting animal

It is true that Taylor himself responds to the objection which he has just made to himself, and maintains that the two objects, that is the object under study and the enquirer's texts, are not as heterogeneous as might have appeared at first. The enquirer's text is an interpretation. But the object under study is also itself an interpretation: it is, or at least it presupposes, a 'self-interpretation'. The two objects are sufficiently homogeneous for it to be possible to represent them as analogous to a page of text accompanied by an opposite page of glosses, as in the scholarly edition of a text.

The notion of self-interpretation has also been employed by a number of Heidegger's American commentators. It appears to raise the same difficulties as does the existentialist notion of a radical choice of oneself. Thus, Hubert Dreyfus, in underscoring that human beings do not have a natural instinct pushing them to build houses, writes that, in certain cultures, it happens that one will 'interpret oneself as being a hermit and live outdoors on a mountainside'.[26] Similarly, he writes that to pursue the career of a professor involves interpreting oneself as a professor. One is tempted to ask: is the hermit a hermit or not? If so, where is the *interpretation*? If, in order to explain his withdrawn life, a fringe-dweller from a large Western city were to describe himself as a recluse, we could say that he indeed 'interprets himself' as a hermit. In such a case, we would indeed here have the sketch of an activity of interpretation, an attempt at construction which mobilises analogies in order to fill an initial shortfall of meaning.

Pursuing this example, however, the notion of 'self-interpretation' only corresponds to half of the phenomenon of eremetism, to wit, its *individual* aspect. The description of what is in fact a perfect example of a 'radical choice of oneself' lacks any account of the other aspect of choice, namely that it is made in the terms of a social institution. Eremitism is possible in some traditional societies, but not, for example, in a large modern metropolis. Contrary to what one might think at first glance, it is impossible to be a hermit *alone*. The hermit has doubtless chosen a solitary life. However, if he can in this manner marginalise himself without seeming like a madman or a parasite, it is because this possibility for individualisation is provided for and, therefore, intelligible within the system. As Louis Dumont indicates in the chapter he devotes to Indian renouncers, the practice of renouncing is precisely 'a social institution which transcends the society'.[27] In what sense is it social? Dumont appeals to the complementarity of the opposing statuses to highlight that a solitary life has a meaning from the point of view of a traditional society such as India.

Now, if we bring together the society on the one hand and the renouncer on the other, we have a whole containing an equilibrium between quite different things: on the one hand a world of strict interdependence, in which the individual is ignored, and, on the other hand, an institution which puts an end to interdependence and inaugurates the individual. In the last analysis, the overall system does not neglect the individual, as the description of the caste system alone would

---

26 Hubert Dreyfus, *Being-in-the-world: a commentary on Heidegger's Being and time, division I* (Cambridge, Mass.: MIT Press, 1991), p. 95.
27 Louis Dumont, *Homo hierarchicus: an essay on the caste system*, trans. Mark Sainsbury (Chicago: University of Chicago Press, 1970), p. 184.

lead one to believe. It may be doubted whether the caste system could have existed and endured independently of its contradictory, renunciation.[28]

It seems that a hermeneutic built around the notion of humans as self-interpreting beings is too existentialist, and that it has remained within an excessively atomistic vision of human institutions. To represent an action as a text does not lead us to try to discover the place which the action occupies within a *system* in which opposed meanings (statuses, positions, etc.) stand in a relation of necessary complementarity to one another. Rather than comparing the meaning of the action to that of a text, it would be necessary to look for this meaning in the *texture* of actions, in their interrelations governed by principles that endow them with meaning.

IV

Is the model of language which will allow us to conceptualise the status of the general spirit as in structuralism that of *langue*? The answer to this question hinges on the version of structuralism involved. But the paradigm of the so-called national *langue* recommends itself for one reason: it is that Humboldt himself, that great representative of the expressivism whose ambition and richness were restored by Taylor in his *Hegel*, found in language the means to reconcile what at first had seemed opposed, to wit, a sense of the individual act and a sense of the signifying totality. A remark made by Louis Dumont in his study of Humboldt's development might shed some light here. Humboldt had tried to define a programme of comparative anthropology, but had not been able to carry it forward to any great degree because, according to Dumont, he had not thought to focus his comparisons upon cultures. He had remained at the level of the individual human essence, bearer of social 'particularities' most often held to be contingent and thus, insignificant. It is only on the linguistic terrain that Humboldt succeeded in drawing a comparison between languages (that is, between totalities not referred back to the individual), and thus in taking up a *holistic* point of view on human beings.[29] During a trip to the Basque country, he discovered with enthusiasm a linguistic community, which allowed him to conceive of a given social whole.

What, for our purposes, are the lessons which must be retained from structural anthropology? The problem posed by Lévi-Strauss seems to be the following: how to account for human institutions and customs if one refuses the choice between the two models of explanation proposed by

[28] Ibid., pp. 185–6.
[29] Louis Dumont, *L'idéologie allemande* (Paris: Gallimard, 1992), p. 234.

Enlightenment philosophy: *conscious and deliberate origin* (self-interested calculation) or *fortuitous origin* through a concatenation of historical circumstances (chance). Either there exists a rationality of traditional institutions which must be attributed to the intention of an author; or there is no author, and the explanation must be 'historical', in the sense of an apparition stemming from encounters and influences, which subsequently find their extensions in routine and superstition.[30] In other words, Lévi-Strauss takes his bearings from the *sociological principle*: in contrast with what is claimed by the political economists and by the 'critical theory' of the Weberian Marxists, there is meaning in social life, and human practices (even exotic ones) are endowed with 'rationality'. The *structural* solution involves the holistic notion of a *system*. From this point of view, human institutions are

structures whose whole – in other words the regulating principle – can be given before the parts, that is, that complex union which makes up the institution, its terminology, consequences and implications, the customs through which it is expressed and the beliefs to which it gives rise. This regulating principle can have a rational value without being rationally conceived. It can be expressed in arbitrary formulas without being itself devoid of meaning.[31]

Let us therefore keep this in mind: institutions have meaning in virtue of their structural properties. There is a rationality to tried and true practices. This rationality cannot be found in the *motives* of a legislator or of a utilitarian agent, but rather in the *fact of the system*, whose parts only exist in function of one another. To adopt the terms of the post-Kantians, this is an 'objective' rather than a 'subjective' rationality. Structural anthropology is therefore a theory of objective spirit. This 'objective spirit' is now called a 'symbolic system'.

Durkheim had indeed been guilty of viciously circular reasoning in his sociology of religious life:[32] when he undertakes to explain the symbolic in terms of the social, he presupposes that it is possible to have a society (in the sense of a mere concatenation of human beings) and to witness therefrom the birth of the symbolic (of the 'collective representations'). But this amounts to separating morphology from ideology. Strict structuralism therefore consists in searching for a 'regulative principle' which could be given *before* the parts. But in order to be given before them it

---

30 Claude Lévi-Strauss, *The elementary structures of kinship*, trans. James Harle Bell, John Richard von Sturmer and Rodney Needham (London: Eyre and Spottiswoode, 1969), p. 100.
31 Ibid., pp. 100–1.
32 On this point, see Claude Lévi-Strauss, 'Introduction à l'oeuvre de Mauss', in Marcel Mauss, *Sociologie et anthropologie* (Paris: Les Presses Universitaires de France, 1950), p. xxii.

must be the principle which permits us to distinguish among these parts, and to define them in a given domain: this principle is thus necessarily that of *distinctive opposition* (in virtue of which two terms are related to one another as complementaries).

It seems appropriate to reserve the title of 'structuralism' to this idea of a virtual preexistence of the whole in relation to its parts, in the form of a principle of distinction. This idea has rarely been grasped on its own merits in the general culture, so that structural analysis has been confused with other doctrines which have been held by Lévi-Strauss at one time or another. These doctrines must be set aside, as they are inhospitable to the notion of a general spirit of institutions which has been introduced here. One need only cite the *semiological* dogma according to which institutions constitute a code which individuals use in order to communicate with one another. This dogma, which was advanced at a time when cybernetic theory was being developed, belongs to an individualist social theory, as institutions only appear as tools which individuals can use for their own ends, just as an individual commuter might use the Parisian metro. The phonologist dogma, which is that language could be reconstructed on the basis of its phonological infrastructure, could also be cited. Strangely enough, this kind of reconstruction was supposed to shed some light on the relation between mental life and the brain.

Generally speaking, the concept of structure equivocates in Lévi-Strauss' work between three metaphysical statuses. Structures are at times presented as *natural causes*, as mechanisms which generate phenomena. The hope here is of reducing the social sciences to the natural sciences. They are also at times presented as *laws of spirit*, as constants which the observation of cultural phenomena allows us to discern. Finally, they are sometimes defined as *ideal rules*, as intellectual models which agents could not follow if they did not have some understanding of them.[33] Structuralist theory has been guilty of not siding decisively among these metaphysical options. The structural principles invoked to account for 'symbolic systems' can obviously not both be principles of *operation* (in the sense of the principles of thermodynamics) and principles of *justification*. It is certainly this latter construal which is of interest for a sociological theory of spirit.

We are perhaps in a better position than researchers of entirely Cartesian or Kantian training to differentiate between the *actualism* of representationalist theories of spirit and a conception which we can now draw from Peirce's pragmatism or from Wittgenstein's philosophical grammar, which places the individual acts of human beings and the rules to which

---

[33] See for example, Lévi-Strauss, *The savage mind*, pp. 251–2.

these acts must be referred in distinct ontological classes, either because the rules are 'constitutive' of the acts (the classic example is that of the game constituted by its rules), or because they determine the conformity of the acts to the normative standards posited by the group (rules of justice, for example).

To bring my argument to a close, I would like to underscore the affinities between a sociological theory of spirit and a 'pragmatic' conception of language (as opposed to a 'psychological' conception, centred on the speaker, who is viewed as possessing a personal spirit, which some would want to 'reduce' to a brain-state).

I will take my cue from Sir Alan Gardiner, a writer influenced by Saussure.[34] He invokes the classic distinction between *langue* and *parole*. *Langue*, according to the Saussurian doctrine, is an institution, and therefore a collective fact. What then is the status of the act of *parole*? Is it a purely individual phenomenon? Yes and no, answers Gardiner: *the act of speech is at once social and individual*. The supposed difficulty raised by doctrines positing an individual–society dualism is thus lifted by the most ordinary fact of conversation. The act of *parole* is by definition a social act, since it necessarily involves two people. (We must obviously accept a definition of soliloquy and of inner speech as complex, derivative performances, in which a single agent takes on two roles.) But the act of *parole* is not a collective act, since it is highly personal, in its undertaking as well, very often, as in its subject matter. It unquestionably happens that one has to speak at the same time as others, but we will in such cases have to treat their words as noises which must be muffled. Outside of certain rites, it is rare that one has intentionally to speak the same words as someone else. It is therefore not the social and the individual which must be opposed, but rather the collective and the individual. With what must the social be contrasted? With the *independent* and the *inner*, with what the philosophers have called the absolute, which is ontologically indifferent to what happens outside of itself, to the state of the 'external world'. Gardiner indicates this by noting that the act of *parole* is but one example among many of an activity which is indistinguishably individual and social. He cites as evidence the relations of master and servant and of buyer and seller. Defined in this manner, Gardiner's *social* corresponds to the 'communities' of which Aristotle spoke in book I of the *Politics*: the *koinonia* of husband and wife, that of parent and child or of master and servants. All these relations are defined by the fact that a 'community', a

---

[34] Alan Gardiner, *The theory of speech and language*, 2nd edn. (Oxford: Oxford University Press, 1951).

'whole' is constituted by them, not by an assembly of individuals (as in a collectivity, in which individuals are taken into account according to their resemblances with others), but rather by an *opposition* of roles (listening is the inverse of speaking, selling is the inverse of buying) which renders them complementary. The social therefore only exists in the form of a *dyadic unity* (real in the case of a conversation, fictional in the case of a soliloquy). In these examples, each individual, no matter how independent he may be ontologically, takes part in an activity which calls for a partner. Uttering a sentence in order to say something to someone and saying it to oneself, oblivious to others, for example as part of a private exercise geared at improving one's pronunciation of a language, are distinct activities. In terms of the classic distinction, there is an *external relation* between the individual and the person who takes on the role of her partner; but there is an *internal relation* between the activity which one of them undertakes (speaking to someone, selling a product, ordering) and another activity which is thereby necessarily called for on the part of someone else (listening, buying the product, obeying). Unless the second activity is carried out by someone, the first simply does not occur. The relation of the two is conceptual rather than physical (it is not enough to speak in order to create an audience). It is therefore an internal relation.

Let us return to the question of the subject: *who is speaking*? At each stage of an elementary conversation between two people, one or the other is speaking (the occasions where both speak at the same time are rather episodes of confusion). The subject of the emitted *parole* is thus individual: it must be either A or B who is speaking. But we must be able to represent the difference between the activity of someone speaking to someone else and that of someone uttering exactly the same words in order to practise enunciation in a new language. It should be noted that from a 'physicalist' point of view, and perhaps from a neuronal point of view as well, these two types of activity are indistinguishable. Behind the question 'who is speaking?' there must therefore be the question 'who is speaking with whom?', a question which requires as an answer a dyad or a polyad rather than a monad. The individual A is speaking to the individual B, but A and B are speaking with one another, which is to say, if we want to identify the subject of the act of 'speaking with one another' (understood as an activity in which the complementary roles can be taken up successively by both participants), that the subject of attribution of this 'speaking with one another' (or more simply of this conversation) is the dyadic entity AB. But we must insist on the fact that this collective entity is not simply the conjunction of A and B (and thus of a set corresponding to the predicate ' ... speaks to ... '). The dyadic being capable of having a conversation is not reducible to a simple collective being as a logician might define it. It must have a social structure, which means that A and B must speak with one another in the mode of conversation (and thus by taking up the complementary and reversible roles of speaker and audience), and not on the mode of cacophony (by speaking to one another without listening, which would satisfy a purely collective conception of the act of speaking with one another, as everyone would be speaking to everyone, in such a way that the members of the collectivity would be speaking together, but without trying to establish understanding).

I announced at the outset that the question of the general spirit of a society was a metaphysical one. It is therefore appropriate that my conclusion be metaphysical.

From a metaphysical point of view, the sociological thesis in the philosophy of mind requires the primacy of the *dyad* over the *monad* (if I may be permitted a recourse to this Platonic vocabulary). Let us admit, on the empirical rather than the conceptual level, the primacy of general conversation (of what Heidegger contemptuously called the 'idle talk' of the 'they') over the speech initiatives of individual subjects. This is not all, as, more fundamentally, there must be, as Peirce saw it, a primacy of the *polyad* over the *dyad*. In the social activity which the slightest interchange between two people constitutes, the exchange supposes a dyadic relation (A and B are speaking with one another). But analysis requires that we conceive this exchange as polyadic, and that we not view its polyadicity as reducible to the sum of several dyads. This polyadic relation must indeed be defined in terms which refer back to distinct ontological categories. In order to be able to say of two people that they are speaking with one another (rather than both simply speaking at one another), there must be a *langue*, in the sense of a normative rule authoritative for the meaning of the words uttered, in terms of which their 'speaking with one another' occurs. With Michael Dummett, we can say of theories which cannot find room for *langue* as a distinct reality that they refute themselves by this very fact.[35] The fact that interlocutors can understand one another necessarily presupposes the collective institution of a common *langue* realised outside the partners to the conversation, one which is not to be understood on the model of an individual *tertium quid*, which would be as useless a mediator as the 'third man' of the *Parmenides*.

---

[35] In particular, see Michael Dummett, 'The social character of meaning', *Truth and other enigmas* (Cambridge, Mass.: Harvard University Press, 1978), p. 428; and '"A nice derangement of epitaphs": some comments on Davidson and Hacking', *Truth and interpretation: perspectives on the philosophy of Donald Davidson*, ed. E. Lepore (Oxford: Oxford University Press, 1986), pp. 472–6.

Part IV

Philosophy in practice

8   Literature: Romantic expression or strategic interaction?

Mette Hjort

Charles Taylor's philosophical anthropology has much to offer literary critics, and his most recent major study, *Sources of the self: the making of the modern identity*, is quite rightly receiving a good deal of attention in literary contexts. The curiosity of literary audiences is clearly piqued by the social and political philosopher's claim that literary discourse somehow helps articulate the moral sources that are constitutive of the modern identity. Taylor thus joins a select group of Anglo-American philosophers (including Stanley Cavell, Alexander Nehamas, Martha Nussbaum and Richard Rorty) whose distinctive voices are gradually changing the terms and direction of on-going literary debates.[1]

The literary tribe is always flattered by the favourable attentions of outsiders, and the relevant emotion is all the more intensely felt when the recognition stems from a member of a group that typically exhibits little patience with the literati's characteristic goals and less-than-rigorous interpretive approaches. Yet the appeal of Taylor's work cannot simply be explained in terms of the dynamics of academics' interaction, and clearly has to do with the particular view of modernity being proposed. The key issue, I believe, is signalled by the term 'philosophical anthropology', which Taylor characterises, in the introduction to his *Philosophical papers*, as a certain understanding of human life and action.[2] Questions of agency have long been central to Taylor's philosophical project, and in this sense a common focus unites his technical refutation of behaviourism, *The explanation of behaviour*, his study of a central philosophical figure, *Hegel*, and his ambitious intellectual history, *Sources of the self*. In my mind it is precisely Taylor's complex narrative of what it means to be a

---

[1] See Stanley Cavell, *Disowning knowledge in six plays of Shakespeare* (New York: Cambridge University Press, 1987); *In quest of the ordinary: lines of skepticism and romanticism* (Chicago: University of Chicago Press, 1988); Alexander Nehamas, *Nietzsche: life as literature* (Cambridge, Mass.: Harvard University Press, 1985); Martha Nussbaum, *The fragility of goodness: luck and ethics in Greek tragedy and philosophy* (New York: Cambridge University Press, 1986); Richard Rorty, *Contingency, irony, solidarity* (New York: Cambridge University Press, 1989).

[2] Taylor, *Philosophical papers*, I, pp. 1–12.

being capable of self-interpretation and purposive behaviour (or action) that strikes a deep chord with literary critics. If I am right, then Taylor's current salience in literary contexts is particularly noteworthy, for it is symptomatic of the failure of postmodernist and poststructuralist attempts to do entirely without concepts of agency.

What is equally striking is that it is not in fact what Taylor has to say about *literature* in *Sources of the self* that has placed this text on the literary critic's list of obligatory philosophical readings. Indeed, Taylor's views on literature sit uncomfortably with many critics, for his claims are at odds with the widespread tendency to foreground the political dimensions of literary culture. What is more, the very phenomenon that supports Taylor's appeal – agency – is barely outlined in his picture of literature, which is largely informed by Romantic doctrines of aesthetic autonomy, the very doctrines, it should be noted, that are associated with formalism and that have been under heavy fire for some time now in literary–critical circles.

Although Taylor's approach to literature is fruitful in many respects, it by no means amounts to a comprehensive account of literary phenomena. More specifically, Taylor makes no mention of literature as a form of action and interaction, thereby overlooking the many important, pragmatic dimensions of literary discourse. It would be absurd to expect Taylor to provide an exhaustive theory of literature, but the proposed generalisations do have to grasp the salient features of the relevant phenomena in order to be wholly persuasive. And in my mind literary agency, understood as the pragmatics of literary interaction, is precisely one of the crucial features that requires, but fails to get, close scrutiny in *Sources of the self*. What is more, Taylor's tendency to embrace a Romantic aesthetics has a number of unappealing consequences, including a normative conception of literature and a highly pejorative view of popular culture. Although Taylor's examples are drawn from a selective tradition of high art, they are made to support a series of general claims about literature, and the result, whether intended or not, is that 'literature' becomes synonymous with 'good literature'. The implication is that the popular novels that some critics would call 'bad literature' simply do not qualify as literature.

Certain omissions are clearly more troubling than others. In some cases, for example, it is simply a matter of completing an otherwise accurate picture. But my suspicion is that the lacunae identified here are of the more vexing variety, for it is not clear that Taylor's account, as it currently stands, can comfortably accommodate a fully developed pragmatics of literature. Although it is by no means impossible to imagine a view of art that would be at once expressivist and pragmatic, the fact remains that the Romantic conception of expression largely rules out the idea of agents catering strategically to particular publics. I would like to begin, then, by focusing on features of the current literary landscape that make it such fertile ground for Taylor's philosophical views on agency. I then want to go on to reconstruct briefly the claims that Taylor makes about art and literature in *Sources of the self*, paying particular attention to his deep-seated sympathies for Romantic thought. Finally, I shall discuss some of the pragmatic and strategic phenomena that, in my opinion, pose a problem for Taylor's account.

I

To say that poststructuralist thought has profoundly changed the nature of literary values, institutions and research is to make an uncontroversial claim. Poststructuralism, we know, is either heralded or condemned as a form of relativism, and it is certainly true that this doctrine has serious epistemological and ethical implications. What is of particular interest here, however, is the poststructuralist's attempt to unsettle a number of influential understandings of the subject or self. It is helpful to recall that poststructuralism was a response, not only to the scientism of structuralism, but to the subject-centred outlook of German idealism, existentialism and humanism. Taking issue with philosophers such as Kant, Hegel and Sartre, poststructuralists proposed a decentred conception of subjectivity in which the alleged fiction of autonomous agency was replaced by a series of discursive effects. On the poststructuralist account, the discrete entities that we in everyday interaction refer to as 'individuals' do not in any meaningful way shape the course of their lives. Instead, their characteristic modes of behaviour are entirely determined by a cluster of irreducibly social entities, of which language is the most important.[3] The implications for theories of agency are devastating, for if actions ultimately cannot be undertaken by selves or agents, but can only be produced by discourse, then the theories in question clearly have no purchase on reality. Poststructuralists, it would appear, would have us believe that the beings we commonly call 'agents' in fact are merely patients passively registering the effects of discursive events.

This rejection of concepts of agency makes possible a specifically poststructuralist view of literature, and of textuality more generally. For example, literary texts are no longer seen as the medium through which

[3] See, for example, Alice A. Jardine's claim, in *Genesis: configurations of woman and modernity* (Ithaca, N.Y.: Cornell University Press, 1985), that 'the notion of the 'self' – so intrinsic to Anglo-American thought – becomes absurd. It is not something called the self that speaks, but language, the unconscious, the textuality of the text', p. 58.

unusually gifted individuals give voice to some inner, outer, shared or higher reality. Indeed, in poststructuralist contexts the efficacy traditionally associated with authors and readers is attributed largely to the literary text itself. It is not uncommon, then, to find a language of intentions, goals and desires mobilised in relation to texts, as opposed to particular individuals. In affirming textual agency, literary critics implicitly celebrate the power of literature to constitute, rather than simply to reflect, reality. To acknowledge the efficacy of texts is thus somehow to enhance the significance of literary discourse. What is more, by calling attention to the constitutive role played by textual processes, poststructuralist critics clearly hope indirectly to legitimate a profession that in many quarters is regarded as somewhat superfluous.

Although the celebration of textuality and accompanying denial of subjective efficacy may have been exciting at one point, critics are slowly awakening to the problems entailed by the outlined approach. To insist on the impossibility of lucid and self-determining agents is in many cases to become entangled in what Karl-Otto Apel, in his critique of relativism, has referred to as a performative self-contradiction.[4] Thus, for example, the relativist inevitably acknowledges the existence of truth as he or she attempts to persuade the realist of the virtues of relativism. An analogous situation arises when poststructuralists insist on the impossibility of agency, for the very idea of a self-determining agent would seem to be presupposed by the critic's rather vehement denunciation of rival perspectives.[5] The more general point is quite simply that the discourse of non-agency, or of exclusively textual agency, in fact is unlivable; it paints a picture that even its advocates cannot live by. In spite of much talk about disappearing or non-existent subjects, most literary critics continue to think of themselves as beings with intensely personal trajectories, defining traits and projects.

The fact is that many critics are moved by issues that cannot be adequately dealt with, or even made sense of, without concepts of agency. In this regard it is interesting to note that what makes recent challenges to deconstruction, such as multiculturalism and identity politics, so compelling is the underlying recognition of the reality and complexity of political agency. On-going attempts to transform universities into inclusive institutions capable of reflecting accurately the racial, class and gender com-

---

[4] Karl Otto-Apel, 'Das Apriori der Kommunkationsgemeinschaft und die Grundlagen der Ethik: zum Problem einer rationalen Begründung der Ethik im Zeitalter der Wissenschaft', *Transformation der Philosophie: das Apriori der Kommunikationsgemeinschaft* (Frankfurt am Main: Suhrkamp, 1973), pp. 358–435.

[5] I discuss the self-defeating nature of certain poststructuralist arguments in 'Strategic action and performative self-contradiction', *Proceedings of 'Self, democracy, and practical reason'*, ed. Lukas Sose (Paris: Vrin-Bellarmin, 1993).

position of society at large in no way commit multiculturalists to some idealist fiction of total lucidity and autonomy. Yet, such goals do require a modest or minimal notion of agency, for it is considered desirable to be able to identify, and perhaps even change, the self-concepts of at least some of the included and excluded parties. What is striking is that although many critics at this point recognise the need for a renewed discourse of agency, they are unclear on what this discourse ought to look like. The identified need is clearly reflected, not only in the successes of multiculturalism, but also in the titles of recent conferences, such as the 1992 'Passions, persons, powers' conference, organised by Anthony Cascardi at Berkeley. Yet, exactly *how* this need is to be met remains largely an open question.

Given the current situation in literary studies, critics have every reason to turn to Taylor's work, for this philosopher has over the years developed a persuasive alternative to transcendental-idealist, radically decentred, and eliminative conceptions of agency. Although questions of agency lie at the heart of much recent work in psychology, philosophy and cognitive science, Taylor's views, basic intuitions and philosophical style have a particular appeal for literary critics. In support of this claim, three issues may usefully be examined: naturalism or reductionism; values and monologism.

A recurrent feature of much literary culture is the assumption that natural science ultimately is reducible to a form of textual practice. On this view, science, much like literature, relies heavily on rhetoric and on the persuasive power of a set of favoured tropes. These tropes, it is claimed, produce a scientific world picture that has no referential relation to a mind-independent reality.[6] Given that Taylor is an unswerving scientific realist, he would be strongly inclined to reject this kind of reasoning. Yet, inasmuch as Taylor is an articulate spokesperson for methodological dualism, he does speak directly to at least some of the concerns motivating literary critics' relativism. That is, Taylor would readily agree that scientific methods cannot legitimately be extended into the domain of the humanities, for action cannot adequately be explained in terms of brute physical processes or concepts framed within the context of natural-scientific research. Taylor's rejection of what he calls 'naturalism' makes him a ready ally for literary critics, for his theory of agency eschews the reductive methods and ideas that are deemed, not only wrong-headed, but ideologically suspect in most literary contexts. Although Taylor's critique of naturalism fits neatly with the intuitions of

[6] For examples of this position, see George Levine, ed., *Realism and representation: essays on the problem of realism in relation to science, literature and culture* (Madison: University of Wisconsin Press, 1993).

many literary critics, the latters' virulent rejections of scientific culture do stand corrected before the philosopher's more nuanced account. Taylor, I would suggest, offers a more generous view of naturalism, for he shows that this outlook, too, is motivated by moral sources and that, inasmuch as we are shaped at all by the project of modernity, at least some of our ethical intuitions draw on these very same sources.

A second crucial feature of Taylor's theory of agency comes to the fore in his on-going debate with cognitive scientists and philosophers of mind for whom computer models of the brain are convincing. What emerges from Taylor's engagement with such thinkers is the importance he attributes to the question of value, meaning or significance. Taylor argues that what ultimately distinguishes agents from machines is that situations and events matter to the former, and not the latter.[7] It is not simply a question of pointing out that agents imbue their surrounding world with meaning, but of recognising the extent to which agents care about the *kind* of beings they are. Agents, that is, articulate for themselves an understanding of what it means to live up to a higher sense of self, and of what it means to fail to realise the relevant aspirations, and it is this process that Taylor wishes to describe by means of the concept of strong evaluation.[8]

Inasmuch as such evaluations go to the heart of what it means to be an agent, the issue of value figures centrally in any adequate theory of agency. It is precisely the importance that Taylor attributes to the question of value that separates his views from those of action theorists who ultimately believe that agency is reducible to a set of purely instrumental calculations. And, what distances Taylor from these philosophical colleagues is also what affords him a warm welcome from the tribe whose specialised task has been to grasp the ways in which certain texts lend meaning and value to human life.

In Taylor's view action theorists, such as Donald Davidson, follow directly in the footsteps of Descartes and Locke, who laid the foundations of the 'modern epistemological tradition'. Now, although Taylor recognises the positive contributions of this tradition, in the form of a set of distinctively modern moral sources, he also believes that it is responsible for a number of influential, but essentially impoverished conceptions of the self. What makes these theories 'monological', and hence inadequate, is their definition of the subject as first and foremost a vehicle of representations.[9]

---

[7] See the complementary works by Hubert L. Dreyfus, *What computers can't do: a critique of artificial intelligence* (New York: Harper and Row, 1972), and Albert Borgmann, *Technology and the character of contemporary life* (Chicago: University of Chicago Press, 1984).

[8] See Taylor, 'What is human agency?', *Philosophical papers*, I, pp. 15–44.

[9] Taylor, 'To follow a rule', in Mette Hjort, ed., *Rules and conventions: literature, philosophy, social theory* (Baltimore, Md.: Johns Hopkins University Press, 1992).

Agents, that is, are assumed to be characterised by their capacity to frame, and properly order, clear and distinct representations of a separate and external reality. Taylor has argued persuasively that this privileging of representation, clarity and lucidity entails a number of undesirable consequences. For example, monological theories repeatedly fail to reflect the ways in which intentional actions and conscious deliberations are embedded in a set of background conditions that remain largely beyond the purview of the agent in question. Although the body cannot be fully thematised in a set of explicit representations, it does play an essential role in determining the specific nature of human agency. Monological theories have, however, typically construed the body as nothing more than an obstacle to properly human and rational forms of behaviour.

Taylor further takes members of the epistemological tradition to task for neglecting the intersubjective or dialogic dimensions of agency. Thus, for example, in the same article, Taylor draws heavily on Pierre Bourdieu's concept of *habitus* in order to argue that we are agents inasmuch as we have been inducted into a community and its practices. Action presupposes certain *dispositions* that are acquired, not through processes of explicit explanation and understanding, but through observation and imitation. It is important, then, to recognise that shared entities, such as language and culture, provide the enabling conditions of individual agency, and that our ability to think and act in large part is a function of our early and continued *interaction* with other agents.

What is interesting about Taylor's critique of the modern epistemological tradition is that it is motivated by intuitions that come remarkably close to those underwriting literary critics' attempts to 'deconstruct' the Subject. What is more, Taylor's own positive conception of agency gives pride of place to dialogue and the body, two phenomena that have been explored at great length by critics of a poststructuralist bent. Having identified what I take to be the main reasons for Taylor's current prominence in literary circles, I shall now proceed to isolate some of the key elements in his account of literature as articulated in *Sources of the self.* My main point is that Taylor fails to recognise the ways in which literary practices are shaped by self-interest, social conflict and power. Although my task here is to identify problems with Taylor's approach to literature, it is worth noting in passing that these issues are similarly overlooked in his theory of agency, as well as in his genealogy of the modern self.

II

Art, and especially literature, occupies a central place in Taylor's careful retrieval of the multiple strands making up the modern identity. Indeed, most of Taylor's claims about art are based on his understanding of important literary texts and authors. Taylor is quite right to point out that we moderns in many ways construe artists as sacred figures and that art currently assumes some of religion's former roles. That writers, for example, are believed to be moved by what is spiritually elevated and inherently valuable is clearly reflected in the longing, experienced by many bankers, lawyers, doctors and other professionals, some day to write a great novel. Although personal ambition no doubt is a factor here, it is clearly not the whole story. Think also of the extraordinary sums of money paid for famous paintings that are good investments precisely because they mysteriously partake of the aura of sacred relics.

Taylor's claim is that creativity becomes increasingly important in the modern age as the idea of an essential, or normative, human nature loses its force. Inasmuch as many moderns believe that selves are to be fashioned in a process of on-going articulation, the artist becomes a powerful model and source of inspiration. It is Taylor's ability to identify the ways in which literature and art embody moral sources that makes his perspective so interesting and unique. Indeed, most literary texts may even be fruitfully read as helping to make manifest a number of the moral sources that are believed by Taylor initially to have emerged in *non-literary* contexts. Thus, for example, Enlightenment playwrights, such as Brecht and Arthur Miller, clearly engage in what Taylor calls the 'affirmation of ordinary life', just as counter-Enlightenment figures, such as Jean Genet and Antonin Artaud, affirm the body and a particularly modern understanding of freedom. In order to do full justice to Taylor's account of literature, it would be necessary to explore the relation between literature and moral sources at greater length. Unfortunately I can only point here to what I take to be a promising avenue of research, as I also want to raise a number of critical points.

It is important to note that Taylor begins his discussion of literature by focusing on Romantic doctrines of art. He then goes on to trace the transformation of these Romantic views in a series of modernist shifts and partial negations. In Taylor's mind, the specific contribution of Romantic aesthetics and related conceptions is to have called attention to the creative, expressive and transformative capacities of artists, and by extension, agents. What emerges in the modern period, says Taylor, is a view of art as epiphanic, that is, 'as the locus of a manifestation which brings us into the presence of something which is otherwise inaccessible, and which is of the highest moral significance; a manifestation, moreover, which also *defines* or *completes something*, even as it reveals'.[10] Following Taylor,

---

[10] Taylor, *Sources of the self*, p. 419.

Romantic poets (Schiller, Wordsworth and Coleridge), modernists (Mallarmé and Baudelaire), and neo-Nietzscheans (Genet, Strindberg) can thus all be seen as expressing their essential modernity as they variously celebrate the power somehow to transform reality through art.

What is noteworthy, and ultimately questionable here, is Taylor's decision to read the entire tradition of modern art and literature in terms of an originally Romantic conception. The suspicion that no single conception can do justice to a tradition so complex comes readily to mind, and it is difficult to dispel. The same is true of the fear that Taylor's account may be crippled by some of the failings characteristic of the doctrines of aesthetic autonomy that constitute the backbone of Romantic aesthetics. Indeed, what may ultimately be the limited or exclusionary nature of Taylor's analysis is itself a recurrent feature of such doctrines, for they start from the assumption that it is only what corresponds to the proposed aesthetic categories that counts as art. Practices that fall short of the relevant standards allegedly require no discussion since they fail to qualify as aesthetic in the specified sense.

Although there are many different versions of aesthetic autonomy, they do tend to converge on the following theses: (1) the maker of a properly aesthetic artefact is a special being, a genius whose gift is natural, rather than social; (2) works of art are non-mimetic, that is, they have no referential dimension; (3) art is untouched by means–end calculations; (4) art is an end in itself; (5) the world of art is autonomous and is governed exclusively by a set of specifically aesthetic norms and conventions.[11]

In his discussion of Mallarmé and Baudelaire, Taylor accurately identifies the Romantic origins of the idea that art is autotelic. Yet, Taylor clearly feels that the dictum 'art for art's sake' sells art short, and as a result he seeks to pinpoint a number of alternative perspectives *within* the Romantic tradition. Wordsworth and Yeats are thus praised for having 'produced works which are not "auto-telic" in this stringent Mallarmean sense, but which strive towards an epiphany'.[12] What Taylor neglects to make clear is that these softer views none the less uphold some of the other theses identified above. Insofar, then, as art of the modern period is viewed through the lens of Romantic aesthetics, it is inevitably judged by the norms articulated by proponents of aesthetic autonomy.

Taylor's tendency to construe art as high art, and his related commitment to some version of the first, third and fifth theses, can be discerned in his isolated remarks on nineteenth- and twentieth-century popular

[11] See Göran Hermerén, *Aspects of aesthetics* (Lund: Gleerup, 1983); Siegfried Schmidt, 'Conventions and literary systems', and Richard Schusterman, 'Challenging conventions in the fine art of rap', both in Hjort, *Rules and conventions*.
[12] Taylor, *Sources of the self*, p. 420.

culture. An analysis of the artist as marginal figure leads Taylor to oppose the world of art, with its specifically aesthetic values, to the domain of crass means–end calculation: 'The opposition of the visionary artist and the blind, or "philistine", "bourgeois" society brings together this vision of an exceptional fate and the hostility to commercial capitalist civilization.'[13] What begins as an attempt to articulate the alienated artist's self-understandings gradually becomes a condemnation of art forms that cater to values and interests that are non-aesthetic. To put it a little more polemically, Taylor finds fault with, and ultimately discounts, a class-specific taste culture that involves little or no appreciation of works of high art. Murger and Puccini are cited as examples of artists who play up to members of the middle class 'who operate fully within commercial civilization, who run their lives by disengaged, instrumental reason, [and who nonetheless] want to have some part in the epiphanies of the creative imagination.'[14] Taylor's rejection of art contaminated by interest and poor taste becomes all the more forceful when he turns his attention to the products of contemporary mass culture:[15]

The ambivalent relationship continues up to our day, and has become in the context of the contemporary mass media and art market an almost open collusion between supposedly revolutionary artists or performers and the mass public. The decent distance in the nineteenth-century relation between bourgeois and Bohemia depended on each side preserving its integrity; it required that the bourgeois world stand by its values and that the genuine avant-garde stay clear of the Murger–Puccini game of playing up to the bourgeois world. But now that free self-expression and polymorphous perversity offer ideas for advertising slogans and thus help to turn the wheels of commerce, and the media, as the late Andy Warhol put it, can make anyone a celebrity for an hour [sic], the distance is hard to maintain. When the collusion becomes so close, a certain corruption has set in.

Taylor is right to point out that advertising slogans now commonly incorporate phrases from well-known films and literary texts. Yet, this recent form of intertextuality is only an instance of corruption if we are seriously invested in what was probably always a fiction: the autonomy of the aesthetic sphere. Instead of seeing the identified borrowings as a symptom of decline, it may ultimately be more fruitful to explore, as Siegfried Schmidt and his colleagues are currently doing, the implications of advertisers' seeing themselves as artists, and their products as works of art.

What interests me here, however, is not the question of advertising and its serious flirtations with art. Rather, I wish to determine what constitutes an adequate response to the popular, non-canonical culture that gets

---

13 Ibid., p. 424.   14 Ibid., p. 424.   15 Ibid., p. 425.

short shrift in Taylor's discussion of art. Indeed, when it comes to popular culture, Taylor is what he refers to in *The malaise of modernity* as a 'knocker'.[16] This is unusual for Taylor, who tends to correct the excesses of the 'knockers' by articulating what is valuable in new, and hence disturbing, cultural forms and modes of behaviour. The reason Taylor dismisses popular culture is that he fails to recognise the extent to which aesthetic products and responses vary as a function of the class-specific nature of taste cultures. By universalising the standards of a particular taste culture, Taylor denies much of modern culture the value and status of art, just as he effectively negates the self-understandings of many agents who would be artists. It is my belief, then, that Taylor's failure to deal adequately with popular culture is symptomatic of deeper problems inherent in his proposed theory of literature and art. As I suggested earlier, the identified lacunae may also be related to the largely communitarian and dialogic nature of Taylor's account of agency.

III

Drawing on Pierre Bourdieu's increasingly influential theory of art, as well as on my own work, *The strategy of letters*,[17] I want to propose a view of popular culture that has the merit, not only of potentially giving horror films, rap music and other departures from high culture a hearing, but of revealing the pragmatic and strategic underpinnings of doctrines of aesthetic autonomy. The point is to show that, in sustaining a certain taste culture through the production and reception of art, agents engage in social interactions involving motivations and interests that can be considered neither wholly benign nor specifically aesthetic. In short, if a theory of art is to be comprehensive, then it must call attention to art's social conditions and consequences, as well as to what agents actually *do* with art.

According to Bourdieu there are no universal and necessary standards defining great art and good taste. Indeed, what constitutes art and taste, in the honorific sense of these terms, is itself a matter of *power*, and the sociologist of art should thus seek to identify those agents whose social position allows them to determine what genuinely counts as art. Now, it is true that Bourdieu's sociological approach easily supports a certain kind of relativism. Yet, it is important to note that we can learn from Bourd-

---

[16] Taylor, *The malaise of modernity*, pp. 11, 22.
[17] Pierre Bourdieu, *Distinction: a critique of the judgement of taste*, trans. Richard Nice (Cambridge, Mass.: Harvard University Press, 1984); Mette Hjort, *The strategy of letters* (Cambridge, Mass.: Harvard University Press, 1993).

ieu's intuitions concerning self-interest, social conflict and power without adopting the relativist's uncomfortable posture.

Compelling empirical evidence for Bourdieu's claims about the divisive nature of art may be found in Richard Shusterman's 'Challenging conventions in the fine art of rap'.[18] More specifically, Shusterman argues that members of the group Stetsasonic reveal an acute awareness of the relation between power and art, for they refuse to allow dominant social groups to discount rap on the grounds that it conflates knowledge, politics and art, and thus fails to instantiate the allegedly timeless conventions of true art.

Now, it would be a mistake to assume that although social conflict can be discerned beneath white, middle-class rejections of rap, this conflict merely is the exception that proves the rule making art a means of expression, rather than of interaction. A realistic picture emerges when one instead acknowledges that rivalry and other kinds of *conflictual* attitudes are recurrent and fundamental features of the art world. What is construed as aesthetically valuable is not, in other words, a simple given, but itself a social construction involving social interests and conflict. And if literature is marked by conflict, then literary interaction is strategic in crucial respects.

Now, according to the great theorist of strategy, Carl von Clausewitz, strategic action in the military sphere is motivated primarily by emotions of enmity and hatred leading to physical violence.[19] What I would like to suggest here is that literary interaction is strategic insofar as similar emotions are expressed primarily, but not exclusively, by symbolic means. Given that many literary institutions construe originality or genius as the basis for inclusion in a highly exclusive canon, strategic thinking emerges quite naturally as an integral part of literary life. Indeed, there is an intimate connection between strategic dispositions and what is commonly defined as one of the goals of literary production, the pursuit of glory, or 'symbolic capital', to use Bourdieu's provocative term.

Literary success frequently hinges on an agent's ability to realise goals and objectives that are divisive because they are systematically understood in terms of some notion of exclusivity. Thus, for example, in the course of the *querelle du Cid* (involving Richelieu, the newly founded Académie and a number of rivalrous playwrights), Corneille clearly emphasised the *singular* nature of his literary achievement, while pointing to its far more *general* desirability.[20] And, in one of his pamphlets,

---

[18] In Hjort, *Rules and conventions*.
[19] Carl von Clausewitz, *Vom Kriege* (Bonn: Ferdinand Dümmlers, 1973).
[20] See Armand Gasté, ed., *La querelle du Cid: pièces et pamphlets* (Paris: H. Welter, 1899) for the texts of the *querelle*.

Georges de Scudéry quite rightly accused Corneille of preferring a situation in which personal success contrasts vividly with the mediocre success of others, to a situation in which literary glory is distributed equally. The literary strategist's pursuit of distinction would thus seem to be accompanied by an unmistakable desire to witness the failure of rival figures.

If, as Bourdieu believes, taste is one of the ways in which the deep-seated divisions of literary culture are articulated, then aesthetic judgements involve a properly strategic and metacommunicative dimension. Such judgements do not simply convey information about an individual's response to a given film, literary text or musical composition. The judgements also convey information about the individual's relation to other individuals and groups. Taste, then, is in some sense a strategy for communicating about *social relations*.

Individuals express their *inclusion* within a given social group – and their *distance* from other social groups – through cultural practices involving taste. It is for this reason that Bourdieu sees taste as a 'marker of "class"'.[21] The person who is moved by classical music does not typically belong to the same social class as the individual who prefers rap, heavy metal or country and western. This point is compellingly made in Bob Rafelson's film, *Five Easy Pieces*, in which Karen Black and Jack Nicholson play characters desperately seeking to bridge the great divide caused by class and taste. Their attempts are doomed to failure, for Bobby and Rayette are ultimately as unlikely a combination as the composer he appreciates and the singer she admires: Chopin and Tammy Wynette. It is important to note that differences in taste do not simply reflect class differences, but also the related hierarchical relations. Think, for example, of the sense of social discomfort that may be deliberately provoked by the suggestion that an expressed preference for Tammy Wynette over Chopin is an indication of 'poor' taste.

Taste may be said to involve *distinction* in at least two senses of the word. First, to appreciate a given work of art is by the same token to reject others, for it is always a matter of singling out some object as special, unique, outstanding or unusually appealing: *this*, unlike *that*, is pleasing. Second, taste may at times be a privileged means of distinguishing *oneself* from others. In that case what is affirmed as outstanding and special in the act of judgement is the agent herself: *I*, unlike the individuals at the institution down the road, have *good taste*.

Although in Bourdieu's mind there are no legitimate grounds for insisting on the superior nature of any one taste culture, relatively stable hierarchies are none the less created and upheld. Thus, a given taste

---

[21] Bourdieu, *Distinction*, p. 2.

culture may or may not be a source of symbolic capital – of distinction in the second sense – depending on its relative position within a given hierarchy. Now, in his study of the modern European art world, Bourdieu uses the terms 'legitimate', 'middle-brow', and 'popular' to identify three substantially different taste cultures. In Bourdieu's mind members of the elite, legitimate culture largely define the terms and rules of the game called art. That is, they decide what is included in the canon of properly aesthetic works, just as they determine what the appropriate response to these works should be. These agents appreciate canonical works with the kind of facility that has every appearance of a natural gift, but in fact is deeply social. Given that the social basis of the favoured responses goes largely unrecognised, a failure to produce the appropriate response becomes a stigma, an indication that an agent naturally belongs to one of the two inferior cultures. What is more, high-handed gestures of exclusion may be internalised to the point where agents consider their own popular tastes inferior to the attitudes of the elite.

For the purposes of the present discussion, it suffices to consider the defining features of legitimate and popular taste. Legitimate taste is what is valorised by doctrines of aesthetic autonomy. Agents who are part of the cultural elite privilege form over function, for they do not enquire after the purpose of the work. Indeed, they consider such questions irrelevant and inappropriate. Instead, these agents focus on the specific techniques (formal innovations, properly cinematic codes and literary allusions) mobilised by the artist in question. The attitudes of such agents are largely *disinterested*. Thus, for example, when Geneviève Bujold is subjected to a violent gynaecological examination in David Cronenberg's *Dead Ringers*, female viewers with legitimate tastes somehow manage to abstract from their own situation as women and to appreciate the scene simply 'as art', focusing once again on the purely formal or aesthetic features of the work. Such disinterested attitudes are reserved for the privileged, for only they have the luxury of setting aside questions of utility, function and truth/falsehood. The exploration of fictional worlds for their own sake makes little sense in situations in which basic needs have yet to be met. Legitimate taste favours what is conceptual, abstract and formal. In this regard the highly stylised modes of behaviour deemed appropriate at classical concerts come to mind.

In contrast, agents with popular tastes privilege function over form. In the course of a series of empirical studies, Bourdieu discovered that manual workers tend to reject photography for photography's sake. A photograph of pebbles, for example, generated the following responses: '"A waste of film," "They must have film to throw away", "I tell you, there are some people who don't know what to do with their time",

"Haven't they got anything better to do with their time than photograph things like that?" [22] The underlying assumption throughout is that unless the photograph serves a purpose – conveys information or records a scene worth remembering – it is pretentious and absurd. Think also of the reactions to the 'meat dress' displayed recently in the National Gallery in Ottawa. Whereas members of the cultural establishment considered the carefully arranged slabs of meat a brilliant piece of avant-garde art, others saw the dress as an expensive and insulting hoax.

Agents with popular tastes adopt a wholly interested stance toward art, forging links between the works and their own lived experiences. What is thus emphasised is the continuity between art and life, as well as the thrill of intense participation. Such agents also attribute an important role to bodily sensations, as is clearly evidenced by the frenetic dancing and intense interaction engaged in at rock concerts.

If we now in conclusion compare Taylor's account of literature and art to the pragmatic view outlined above, it becomes clear that Taylor's sympathies for Romantic thought lead him to focus primarily on the works and attitudes associated with legitimate taste, which are thus held largely to exhaust the world of modern art. The result is that terms such as 'literature' and 'art' are reserved for the products of what is but one taste culture among many. Although this may ultimately be the position that Taylor wishes to adopt, he cannot do so without argument, which is essentially what happens in *Sources of the self*. As it stands, Taylor runs the risk of being perceived as an apologist for high culture. My own hope is that Taylor will expand his account to make room for popular culture, rather than bolster with arguments what would appear to be his current conception of 'art'. What needs to be acknowledged is that art is not only a matter of elevated activities and noble or virtuous intentions. Bourdieu's perspective is undoubtedly one-sided in that it ultimately reduces art to a form of social warfare. Yet, the fact remains that art does involve at least as much conflict as it does communion.

I have been arguing that Taylor needs to revise his conception of art in ways that allow pragmatic considerations to be taken seriously. As I suggested above, Taylor may ultimately need to modify his largely expressivist account of agency in order to do justice to the strategic dimensions of the art world. Taylor's approach to agency remains fruitful within the context of literary studies where thinking about agents tends to be impoverished. However, what literary critics ultimately need is a view of agency that does justice to the strategic, as well as the expressivist, dimensions of culture.

[22] Ibid., p. 41.

9   The role of articulation in understanding
     practice and experience as sources of
     knowledge in clinical nursing

Patricia Benner

Both the manner and content of Charles Taylor's writings and lectures
have shaped my research in nursing.[1] Taylor's effective critique of the
narrow theory-bound nature of the social sciences and his explication
and defence of interpretive phenomenology for the human sciences
provide the content that guides my examination of the knowledge
embedded in nursing practice, and the experiences of suffering and
comfort as central to that practice.[2] His writings and lectures provide a
dialogical manner imbued with an ethic of listening, and respectful
articulation of self and other. His view of practical reasoning as involving
the enabling transition toward increasingly perspicuous interpretive
stances, and his phenomenological understanding of the experience of
gain, and of liberation from impediments to action to which such transitions give rise, provide an accurate account of a practice-based ground
for knowing similar to the practical, engaged reasoning characteristic of
clinical nursing practice:[3]

Practical reasoning ... is a reasoning in transitions. It aims to establish, not that
some position is correct absolutely, but rather that some position is superior to
some other. It is concerned, covertly or openly, implicitly or explicitly, with comparative propositions. We show one of these comparative claims to be well
founded when we can show that the move from A to B constitutes a gain episte-
mically. This is something we do when we show, for instance, that we get from A
to B by identifying and resolving a contradiction in A or a confusion which A
screened out, or something of the sort. The argument fixes on the nature of the
transition from A to B. The nerve of the rational proof consists in showing this
transition is an error-reducing one. The argument turns on rival interpretations of
possible transitions from A to B, or B to A.
  The form of the argument has its source in biographical narrative. We are convinced that a certain view is superior because we have lived a transition which we
understand as error-reducing and hence as epistemic gain.

[1] See in particular Taylor, *The ethics of authenticity*.
[2] See the papers in Taylor, *Philosophical papers*, I, II.
[3] Taylor, *Sources of the self*, p. 72.

The influence of Taylor's work is evident in my efforts at articulating the nature of nursing expertise, ethical comportment in nursing and stress and coping in illness and health.[4]

A practice differs from discrete behaviours in that it is a culturally constituted, meaningful action. In a critique of behavioural psychology Taylor contrasts atomistic behaviours and socially constituted meaningful practices.[5] He makes the distinction between the discrete behaviour of raising the arm and the culturally constructed public human action of raising the hand in a voting practice. A practice is located within a tradition and is continually being worked out in history and through the on-going development of the practice. A practice has a referential context of meanings, skills and equipment, and has the capacity to be worked out in contexts that allow actualisation of the notions of good embedded in a practice. A practice has the capacity for being worked out in new situations. In *Sources of the self*, Taylor offers a broad definition of cultural practices that I am drawing on, with the distinction that these practices get further articulation and elaboration in a formally organised caring practice such as nursing.[6]

By 'practice', I mean something extremely vague and general: more or less any stable configuration of shared activity, whose shape is defined by a certain pattern of dos and don'ts, can be a practice for my purpose. The way we discipline our children, greet each other in the street, determine group decisions through voting in elections, and exchange things through markets are all practices. And there are practices at all levels of human social life: family, village, national politics, rituals of religious communities and so on.

The clinical and caring practices of nurses are socially embedded in formal schooling and health care institutions and informally in communities of practitioners. This is similar to MacIntyre's definition of a practice as socially coherent and as always possessing an internal good.[7]

Taylor's career-long project of articulating the notions of good in our social and political practices and traditions is masterful in showing

---

[4] See Patricia Benner, *From novice to expert: excellence and power in clinical nursing practice* (Reading, Mass.: Addison–Wesley, 1984), *Stress and satisfaction on the job: work meanings and coping of mid-career men* (New York: Praeger Scientific Press, 1984); Patricia Benner and J. Wrubel, *The primacy of caring: stress and coping in health and illness* (Reading, Mass.: Addison–Wesley, 1989); Patricia Benner, 'The role of experience, narrative, and community in skilled ethical comportment', *Advances in Nursing Science*, 14, 2 (1991), pp. 1–21; P. Benner, C. Tanner and C. Chesla, 'From beginner to expert: gaining a differentiated world in critical care nursing', in *Advances in Nursing Science*, 14, 3 (1992), pp. 13–28.

[5] Taylor, 'Interpretation and the sciences of man', *Philosophical papers*, II, pp. 15–57.

[6] Taylor, *Sources of the self*, p. 204.

[7] Alasdair MacIntyre, *After virtue: a study in moral theory* (Notre Dame: University of Notre Dame Press, 1981).

sources and remnants of social practices in the fabric of our everyday lives. For example, his articulation of the valuation of the ordinary life can lend much understanding to Florence Nightingale's extension of domestic caring practices to public institutions.[8] Both practical clinical knowledge and caring practices have been marginalised in modern health care, and yet health care institutions are dependent on them for their own survival. By articulating the nature of these marginalised practices, I hope to create more public institutional space and legitimacy for them. Modern commodified health care highly values what can be made into scientific and technical procedures and assumes that what has not yet yielded to means-ends analysis, objectification and procedural accounts is under-developed and only awaits scientific and technical formalisation. And until this scientific, procedural articulation occurs, all other aspects of our knowledge are considered private, inarticulate and of lesser epistemic warrant. Thus, caring practices are further marginalised because tradi-tionally they have been practices of the domestic or private sphere and have lacked adequate public language. Taylor's view that articulating notions of the good embedded in practices and broad institutional and cultural frameworks of self-understanding, along with Heidegger's writings on the role of meaning and concerns, provide the vision and theoretical underpinnings for my project of articulating major areas of socially embedded knowledge and notions of the good in nursing prac-tice.[9] I have examined narratives from nursing practice and observations of actual nursing practice in research, in the classroom and in many workshops with practising nurses in hospitals and community health settings. Nursing is a particularly interesting case of the role of articulat-ing practical knowledge and notions of the good embedded in everyday clinical practice, because nursing encompasses a broad base of scientific and technical knowledge that is formal and publicly accessible through technical procedural descriptions. But in addition to the formalisable knowledge, nursing presents three areas of implicit knowledge that yield them selves to the kinds of articulation that Taylor undertakes in his writings on cultural and political experience. In this chapter I will take up a portion of a larger project of articulating clinical knowhow; caring practices; uncovering moral sources of caring practices, and examining notions of good embedded in caring practices.

---

[8] Taylor, 'Legitimation crisis?', in *Philosophical papers*, II, p. 265; Florence Nightingale, *Notes on nursing: what it is and what it is not* (Philadelphia: J. B. Lippincott, 1969).

[9] Martin Heidegger, *Being and time*, trans. J. Macquarrie and E. Robinson (New York: Harper and Row, 1962); H. L. Dreyfus, *Being-in-the-world: a commentary on Heidegger's Being and time, Division I* (Cambridge, Mass.: Harvard University Press, 1991); Benner, *From novice to expert*; Benner, *Stress and satisfaction on the job*; Benner and Wrubel, *The primacy of caring*.

I

Nursing, like medicine, involves a rich, socially embedded clinical knowhow that encompasses perceptual skills, transitional understandings across time, and understanding of the particular in relation to the general. Clinical knowledge is a form of engaged reasoning that follows *modus operandi* thinking, in relation to patients' and clinical populations' particular manifestations of disease, dysfunction, response to treatment and recovery trajectories.[10] Clinical knowledge is necessarily configurational, historical (by historical, I mean the immediate and long-term histories of particular patients and clinical populations), contextual, perceptual, and based upon knowledge gained in transitions.[11] Clinical knowledge exists in communities of practice and progresses in those communities through dialogue, and often becomes manifest through emotional reactions elicited when things do not go as the clinicians expect, or when the course of events appears dangerous. One might say that every clinician engages in articulation analogous to that described in Taylor's project, so that clinical understanding becomes increasingly articulate and translatable at least by clinical examples, narratives and puzzles encountered in practice. This everyday articulation project is illustrated in the following research interview by the pejorative phrase 'practicing anecdotal medicine':

NURSE: I took care of a 900 gram baby who was about 26 or 27 weeks many years ago who had been doing well for about two weeks. He had an open ductus [ductus arteriosus] that day. The difference between the way he looked at 9.00 a.m. and the way he looked at 11.00 a.m. was very dramatic. I was at that point really concerned about what was going to happen next. There are a lot of complications of the patent ductus, not just in itself, but the fact that it causes a lot of other things. I was really concerned that the baby was starting to show symptoms of all of them.

INTERVIEWER: Just in that two hours?

NURSE: You look at this kid because you know this kid and you know what he looked like two hours ago. It is a dramatic difference to you but it's hard to describe that to someone in words. You go to the resident and say: 'Look, I'm really worried about X, Y, Z' and they go: 'OK.' Then you wait one half hour to 40 minutes, then you go to the Fellow (the teaching physician supervising the resident) and say: 'You know, I am really worried about X, Y, Z.' They say: 'We'll talk about it on rounds.'

INTERVIEWER: What is the X, Y, Z, you are worried about?

NURSE: The fact that the kid is more lethargic, paler, his stomach is bigger, that he is not tolerating his feedings, that his chem strip (blood test) might be a little strange. All these kinds of things. I can't remember the exact details of this

---

[10] See Pierre Bourdieu, *The logic of practice* (Stanford: Stanford University Press, 1990).
[11] See Taylor, *Sources of the self*, pp. 72–5.

case, there are clusters of things that go wrong. The baby's urine output goes down. They sound like they are in failure. This kind of stuff. Their pulses go bad, their blood pressure changes. There are a million things that go on. At this time, I had been in the unit a couple or three years. I was really starting to feel like I knew what was going on but I wasn't as good at throwing my weight in a situation like that. And I talked to a nurse who has more experience and I said: 'Look at this kid', and I told her my story, and she goes: 'OK.' rounds started shortly after that and she walks up to the Attending [Physician in charge of patient] very quietly, sidles up and says: 'You know, this kid, Jane is really worried about this kid.' She told him the story, and said: 'He reminds me about this kid, Jimmie, we had three weeks ago', and he said: 'Oh'. Everything stops. He gets out the stethoscope and listens to the kid, examines the kid and he says: 'Call the surgeons.' (Laughter) It's that kind of thing where we knew also what had to be done. There was no time to be waiting around. He is the only one that can make that decision. It was a case we had presented to other physicians who should have made the case, but didn't. We are able in just two sentences to make that case to the Attending because we knew exactly what we were talking about.

INTERVIEWER: That's a very interesting form of persuasion. You might want to talk more about that. You talked earlier about anecdotal medicine. By being able to point out that this kid was indeed like this other kid. Was that the clinching argument?

Nurse: Absolutely, because this physician is one who does rely not so much as some of them, but at least half the time on anecdotal medicine. So that was one thing, the other thing was that this particular nurse really knew what she was doing. He knew that she knew what she was doing and she also practiced a lot of anecdotal medicine. She knew exactly what button to push with him and how to do it. So between the two of them, there had to be very little argument about what was occurring and what needed to be done. I learned a lot from that exchange, a great deal: that you can tell the same story to a lot of people and you are not going to get the right reaction. And that you have to keep telling it until you find someone who listens, who really hears what you are saying.

This potentially dangerous clinical situation turned out well. The infant did well after surgery. It illustrates that clinical knowledge is socially embedded and dialogical. It also demonstrates that perceptual acuity and skill are taught experientially and conveyed 'anecdotally'. For the practitioner, science and technology must be augmented by actual experiential learning complete with dialogue. This is how practice communities develop shared distinctions and meanings that are carried forward in living traditions. I take this to be a practical example of Charles Taylor's explication of reasoning in transition in that practitioners arrive at increasingly perspicuous and accurate articulations of their experience through the dialogical enterprise of trying to understand that experience.

II

Articulating caring practices has all the challenges described for clinical knowledge (i.e. they are transitional, contextual, dialogical, particularistic, etc.). However, caring practices have added new articulation challenges, since nurses have even less public language for talking about their intents, meanings, notions of the good and relational aspects of their caring practices. Caring, as defined from a phenomenological perspective, is the most basic mode of being and is central to all helping professions. Caring means that people, interpersonal concerns and things, matter. Caring shapes language and determines what can show up as an issue of public debate in the culture. Caring sets up the possibility for and is integral to knowing. In health care, caring sets up the possibility for cure.

Caring practices are central to nursing. What it is to be a nurse cannot be separated from what it is to care about others. Nursing has earned the right to understand itself as a caring profession, along with the right to determine how and under what circumstances caring practices can thrive, though this right is often undermined by status inequities and sexism. Nursing cannot claim to be the *only* caring profession but it may rightfully claim to be the paradigmatic public caring practice in Western cultures, while parenting, particularly mothering, is the paradigmatic caring practice in the private sphere.

Caring and caring practices have become problematised for the modern for a number of reasons. When the word 'care' or 'caring' is used, most often it is thought of in psychological, individualistic terms – as a sentiment or attitude possessed by a private individual. Care or caring is thought of as a 'private feeling' and most often is thought of as a radically free choice – a self-possessed choice to care or not to care. Bureaucracies that set stringent limits to the timing and control of caring practices create additional barriers for doing highly contingent, relational caring work, thus reinforcing the individualism in terms of which caring is construed in our culture.[12]

When caring is studied in traditional social scientific ways, it is decontextualised, operationalised and turned into delimited behaviours or factors with the implied technical promise that performing these discrete caring behaviours will be perceived by a second private individual as caring and result in specifiable physiological, psychological and social outcomes.[13]

[12] S. Reverby, in 'A caring dilemma: womanhood and nursing in historical perspective', in *Nursing Research*, 36 (1987), pp. 5–11.
[13] J. M. Morse, J. Bottorff, W. Neander and S. Solberg, 'Comparative analysis of conceptualisations and theories of caring', *Image*, 23 (1991), pp. 119–26.

For Morse et al., the stakes for describing and caring in discrete behavioural terms associated with specific outcomes are high:[14]

If the relevance of caring to practice and to the patient cannot be clearly explicated, or *if* it is claimed that caring cannot be reduced to behavioural tasks, *and* if caring is the essence of nursing, then nursing no longer will be a practice discipline.

In this traditional scientific approach, the context and relationship between the persons can be overlooked. Caring, in this traditional scientific view, is one more therapeutic technique. These modern understandings of care and caring are based on the assumptions that persons are atomistic, utilitarian individuals related to one another at best by an enlightened self-interest. On this view each autonomous, 'self-possessed' individual freely chooses to care in order to fulfill some psychological need, or in order to further his or her own self-interests, or develop desirable character traits (views of the person espoused by Locke and Hobbes.)[15]

But since caring is relational and must be dictated by the concerns, needs and personhood of the one cared for, focusing on the self-based sources of caring will objectify, if not devalue or pity, the one cared for. Fortunately, the wisdom and the moral sources of caring as they are revealed in the actual practices of nurses are richer than those which the picture of the atomistic, disconnected, punctual self would lead us to expect. I will return to this issue after making some distinctions between public and private caring practices and illustrating actual caring practices as a way of providing evidence for the possibility of non-objectifying and non-exchange based caring practices.

Since caring is shaped by context and intent, distinctions between public and private caring practices matter. Caring as a public practice does not have the same burdens as caring in one's private life since the growth, vulnerability and suffering of the one cared for does not threaten or damage the personal world of the care-giver. The nurse or physician goes home to whatever personal world she has. Though memories and feelings linger, they do not signal the level or kind of loss incurred in the care-giver's inner circle. As a public practice, caring practices are done without exchange in mind. In fact they are structured institutionally so that those cared for do not have to feel indebted or personally encumbered by the care giving rendered. While public caring practices do attend

---

[14] Ibid., p. 26.
[15] Taylor, 'The concept of a person', *Philosophical papers*, I, pp. 97–114; Taylor, *Sources of the self*, pp. 159–76; Michael Sandel, *Liberalism and the limits of justice* (Cambridge: Cambridge University Press, 1982).

to mutuality and reciprocity, the reciprocity is almost always formalised by payments and often is symbolic, and graduated by the ability of the one cared for to reciprocate. In order to be appropriate in public caring practices, any reciprocity must serve the ability, dignity and independence of the one cared for. Reciprocity is managed largely by institutionalisation since nurses, physicians, social workers, teachers and physicians are paid to engage in caring practices. Furthermore, the caring practices are understood as a societal good required at times by all human beings. Thus, participating in public caring practices is an expression of a common good. One can feel good in caring for another in authentic and skilful ways that actually respond to the needs of the other. The skilful care-giver feels disappointed or sad when caring fails to be attuned or the one cared for cannot respond. Caring, to qualify as truly caring, cannot dictate the response of the other or usurp the other's standing *as* other, rather than mere projection or pure idealisation. Thus caring practices are limited and bounded by the notions of the good which are internal to them.

The ways in which emotions are tied to public meanings and to embodied learning and knowing in this view are overlooked in the Cartesian vision of a private subject standing outside and apart from an objective world, and for whom meanings and feelings are private and individualistic, only dimly intelligible to others. Furthermore, emotions are considered as something to be managed so that they do not interfere with learning and knowing. Taylor's view of the emotions as socially constituted and meaningful opens up the possibility of attuned, skilful care guided by an emotion-based understanding of the situation.[16]

One of Taylor's pervasive themes is that human beings who grow up in a similar culture and share the same languages and practices, share common meanings. Common or shared meanings do not mean that everyone agrees with one another or even that they always get the correct understanding of the situation. But common meanings, concerns, habits, skills and practices do make it possible for one embodied human being to understand another's situation and plight. Common meanings and practices are what make things show up even in situations of disagreement.[17] Without a common understanding of issues or meanings, disagreement and/or dialogue are inconceivable.[18]

The claim here is that caring and caring practices must be located in a

[16] Taylor, 'Self-interpreting animals', *Philosophical Papers*, I, p. 61.
[17] See Heidegger, *Being and time*.
[18] Thomas Kuhn, *The structure of scientific revolutions*, 2nd edn. (Chicago: University of Chicago Press, 1970); H. G. Gadamer, *Truth and method*, trans. G. Barden and J. Cumming (New York: Seabury Press, 1975).

community, in a shared world of members and participants. I take this to be the communitarian stance articulated by Taylor. Caring and caring practices are not limited to a 'private feeling' or psychological state. They are grounded in the shared public, historical world of being related to one another in social groupings, common meanings, mores, practices and skills. The ethic of care and responsibility dares not exclude the role of the therapeutic and the ethic of rights and justice in challenging oppressive, distorted community relations. The private individual or self-contained community cannot always be the final arbiter, as is illustrated in the cases of mass suicide in Jonestown, or where children have been abused and have come to accept and expect terror, or where intimate pairs have developed hurtful relationships.

Articulation allows for uncovering innovation in practice and the positive notions of good, and in this respect it is constructive and conserving. But articulation also can uncover breakdown, injustice and oppression, and thus can serve a critical function. Once practices are given language and narrative descriptions they can be scrutinised and debated. However, rules (universal, or otherwise) or formal explanatory models will not be sufficient to judge the quality of human caring, because prior to the 'rules' one must have caring practices situated or enframed in a community where dignity, justice, interdependence and equality are valued.[19] In other words, rules are meaningless unless they are embedded in actual caring practices.

In nursing, caring encompasses many specific practices such as supporting life functions, promoting health, care of the body, focused attention, systematic listening, coaching, fostering a healing relationship and/or a healing environment and healing community, and decreasing the sense of alienation and restriction of world that often accompanies illness. Caring practices also encompass bearing witness to human experiences that range from everyday activities of living to suffering, recovery and death. Because caring practices are integral to everyday actions of nurses and because they are being extended and developed in everyday practice, an exhaustive list of caring practices cannot be compiled. However, caring practices can be described and exemplified and this is the scope of the articulation project described and illustrated here. As has been shown by Taylor's work, articulation is distinct from the creation of a formal or total systems account of a human activity.

Even though caring practices cannot be made completely explicit, i.e. spelled out in an exhaustive list or formalised by rules, procedures or

---

[19] Taylor, 'Response to crisis in care conference', in *The crisis in care*, ed. S. Philips and P. Benner (Washington, DC: Georgetown University Press, in press).

techniques, they can be described and interpreted as they exist in the public world of nursing practice. This is illustrated in earlier studies and in examples from an in-progress study of nurses practising in intensive care units.[20] These examples illustrate that caring practices can exist even in highly technical, crisis-ridden areas. A critical care nurse states:

I think in a critical care setting that we have to help repersonalise a patient because a family comes in and they see alarms, tubes, teams, and beds and all this paraphernalia and this body that does not look like their loved one. They are not used to seeing them laid flat out with a blue gown over them. I think that if you repersonalise the patient through talking to the family that it helps us to under-stand the human being who is in the bed . . . One of the biggest things that you deal with in that situation is, what would he want or what would she want, or what are they like? I always ask questions about my patients because often we greet them when they have totally succumbed to anaesthesia. And when they become more long term, I ask the family to bring pictures that *we* can see. It doesn't only help the patient . . . [a bit later, referring to pictures of a patient with dogs] When he woke up and I asked him about his dogs, it did make him feel good to see them again, and it made me know a little bit about him.

This nurse echoes a common theme in this study of expert clinical nursing practice in intensive care units. The nurse works with the patients' and families' world, humanising the technology and domesticating the alien environment. I see these as central caring practices in nursing. These nurses actively try to preserve the dignity and personhood of their patients:

We look at the monitors and look at the drips and figure everything out, but their appearance makes a big difference to families and how this person is.

The core practice of mutual realisation and empowerment are evident in these nurses' discourse. For example, in weaning an extremely debili-tated person with a stroke, an ICU nurse states:

But it was over a period of days making him comfortable with his weaning (from the respirator) and making him psychologically comfortable, that he began showing improvement. Then his personality started to come out and he was now willing to fight for his rehabilitation, willing to participate in his care . . . Really, our main thing is to psychologically keep him boosted enough so he can go through the weaning process.

Another nurse illustrates the common practice of giving patients a say and empowering them through their caring practices. The patient's every-day activities become meaningful signals of hope, and of self-control:

[20] Patricia Benner, *From novice to expert: a phenomenological study of clinical nursing expertise in intensive care units*, sponsored by the Helene Fuld Foundation. Co-investiga-tors: Patricia Benner, Christine Tanner, Hubert L. Dreyfus, Stuart E. Dreyfus, Jane Rubin. Project Director: Catherine Chesla (manuscript in progress for Springer, New York).

I always let them have even the smallest decisions, everything. 'How do you like to be positioned? Would you rather me not do this?' Don't take things away from them. Sometimes it's faster for you to do things for them, but if you have the time, let them do that. It makes them feel like a human being. They think: 'If I can still brush my own teeth, I must not be dying, or it couldn't be that bad.' Sometimes when we get the chronic patients, the problem is the other way around, it's making them take *back* control because they get so passive and so withdrawn. It's like forcing them to open their eyes and look at you, and nod and answer a question.

For these nurses the work-place technology is tempered by the centrality of their caring practices, though they are experts in intensive care technology and though the technical aspects of care take up much of their time. For example one nurse stated (and others in the small group interview agreed):

I think you get a lot more satisfaction out of achieving some kind of family interaction or getting a real good rapport and trust with the patient. That's more satisfying than noticing this patient has a gastric PH of one and initiating antacids. That does make a difference because nobody else does it except for the nurse. So it could go on for weeks. He could possibly have had an ulcer and bleeding there, but because you caught it before, sure there is no problem. We'll give him antacids, something simple like that. It does make a difference, but we don't see it as making a real big difference, not like the psychological barriers that we deal with sometimes.

This nurse gives priority to coaching the patient/family through the illness and engaging them in the recovery process. The following nurse also illustrates the primacy of caring practices in the neonatal intensive care unit. Her voice easily slips into the voice of the parents as she identifies with their plight:

I think of new parents, first-time parents who have a baby who is severely ill, that they think might die, have a great dilemma about whether or not to bond with that child. It's not a natural thing, when the child has been taken away from you, without your ever having been able to touch the child, or sometimes even see the child. Then the first time you see the child it's paralysed, its eyes are closed, and it can't respond to you physically. You have no idea how to respond with all these other people in control of your child. You have no control. I think some of the most valuable things that I've done with parents is to take them, in that situation, and put their hands on the baby and be physically comforting, because they can't do it on their own. And it's that thing I like about the nursery too, that you can be physically comforting in situations that are outrageous ... I directly say: 'I know this must be awful for you to feel like other people are in control of your baby but you're the baby's parent, you're the only person who is the baby's parent.' And I try to tell them about things that they alone can do.

This nurse goes on to describe her practice of encouraging breast feeding, comforting touch, and explaining the value of the familiar parental voices to the infant's developing sense of world. These nurses have a strong sense that caring practices, particularly comforting practices, are not rule based, and require more than an intellectual understanding:

Ten years ago I probably never thought that much about a baby's comfort. You get into this high tech taking care of critical patients mode. But now even with a really critical baby, I still find myself thinking a lot about the comfort throughout. The critical care aspects get to be second nature after a while, and you don't have to think about them so much, and you have more time to think about other things ... I think a lot of people know about the importance of comfort care with premature infants intellectually, but they don't do it. It isn't a part of their practice.

This interview excerpt follows a discussion of the complications which follow from disruptive and painful procedures for premature infants which have not been supplemented by adequate comfort measures. The possibility is put forward of substituting comfort measures for sedation in instances where the carer has expert ability in comforting and handling the baby. It is clear from this excerpt that the ethic of comfort care can only be located in the activity itself, and that the capacity to comfort deftly is hard won in an intensive care setting. The excerpt also illustrates that the caring practice is shaped by the possibilities inherent in the situation and in the sensitivities and skill levels of the nurses.

The responsibility side of the ethic of care is also expressed as a sense of respect for another human being's body:

I have always been awed and still am that I can adjust a little machine and with the flick of my finger somebody's body does some horrendous thing. Their blood pressure will go up and down by what I say. It's just awesome. It's such a respectful thing that if you can't have respect for what you're impinging on this other human body, then I don't see how you can do it. I am not saying that everyone has to have a religious belief, it's just respecting the human body and realizing that you really do determine how this body will respond ... You have the ability and responsibility to manipulate the finest portions of this person's body and it should be scary.

Neonatal ICU nurse (responding to above CCU nurse):

There are also other dimensions. You know that you are also going to influence how this child grows up. What kind of person they're going to be by how many brain cells you leave them with in the end. Whether you respond quickly or not may mean the difference between an A student and a B student, or worse ... And they can never tell you ... you have to be constantly so observant.

These nurses discuss personal and professional safeguards to their vigilance and sense of responsibility. Examples of the centrality of caring practices to counter, cushion and humanise highly technical, intrusive and instantaneous intensive care unit therapies are pervasive, in this study of 130 critical care nurses in eight different hospitals.

These nurses link advanced clinical knowledge with highly evolved caring practices. It is evident that they evaluate the ethics of heroic care from a perspective of caring practices. They place themselves inside the patient-family's community, as advocate, seeing themselves as persons who stand along side, empowering patient-families to have a voice when they are weak and vulnerable. They talk about their commitment to be vigilant in ensuring that adequate care is given, that early warnings of patient change are given, that instantaneous therapies are given with an understanding of the particular patient's responses. And they describe themselves as persons who ensure that the health team and patient/family have a congruent understanding of the intent of care.

Over the past seventeen years I have been collecting exemplars of caring practices that recognise the other and bear witness to his or her plight. In these narratives the nurse takes on a significant role in coaching the patient and family through a long illness or convalescence. I am amazed at how often this includes home visits (unpaid, if the nurse is not a community health or home care nurse) and visits to other institutions (e.g. hospitals and rehabilitation centres) to coach the patient-family through transitions in care. This coaching function of the nurse involves both a coaching role and a 'bearing witness'. It requires standing alongside patients and families during a difficult illness. In this way, the nurse becomes an effective community member, one who understands and knows what the patient-family has been through over time. In the case of exemplars from oncology nurses, the nurse becomes the one who has witnessed the recovery from a past crisis, and now reminds the patient-family simply by his/her presence of the past struggles and successes. The nurse bears witness and affirms the patient's and family's experience. As 'outsider–insider' he/she has become a kind of respondent to an often difficult to absorb experience of an other. A story that Linda Smith submitted to *American Journal of Nursing* illustrates this. I consider it a paradigm case or 'strong instance' of this caring practice. Notice that Linda Smith begins her account with the assumption that 'any nurse' will understand. Here she refers to common meanings embedded in the caring practices of nurses and I am sure that she is right; any nurse will understand.

Baby T's Story

Nursing is a profession that requires a mastery of skilled knowledge. However an oft overlooked, yet integral, part of our profession is the role of compassion. I am sure the following situation will be understandable to any nurse reader.

I was employed as a staff nurse in a small intensive care nursery. After approaching my head nurse about a difficult family and the lack of continuity of care, I asked her if I could be Baby T's primary nurse. Baby T was 26 weeks gestation at birth and was five months old when I began as his primary nurse. He was ventilator dependent because of severe bronchopulmonary dysplasia. Given the challenges of this case, I saw in it an opportunity to explore new facets of nursing care.

My motivation skyrocketed as I planned various activities for his daily routines. Our unit did not allow ventilated infants to lie on their stomachs, but I believed that this intervention would allow him a new position of comfort so we placed him on his stomach with a stockinette securing his head. I found an infant seat and placed him upright so he could begin to make eye contact and look at his environment sitting up. I encouraged his mom to hold him several times a week, so he would become adjusted to being held. One evening, a fellow nurse told me I had turned Baby T every way but on his head! Like all cribs of chronic babies, T's was full of signs made with tender loving care. The philosophy of this approach focused on his developmental, as well as his physical needs.

T's parents had been involved with many staff members during his lengthy stay and like all chronic families, confrontations occurred. Between the family's need to have some control in T's care and the staff's responsibilities, I found myself serving the role of the mediator. What a challenge to interpret the family's needs to several of these physicians and nurses, though I was saddened by the fact that the family viewed the staff as adversaries.

One evening, I had cared for Baby T as usual. The next morning I received a call at home stating Baby T had just died. The nurse said there had been problems with reintubation. I drove to the hospital and found the curtain pulled with Baby T lying, wrapped in blankets, on his bed. How many times could I endure the helpless, out of control feelings that occur when we can't improve the situation? I gazed at T's bed covered with the signs I had made with loving care, all his toys, clothes. Could I be strong again? Tears flowed down my face as I held T for the last time. Baby T died at six months of age.

T's physicians belonged to a paediatric clinic and Dr A was on call that morning. I had remembered that T's parents had experienced difficulties with Dr A in the past, but I was stunned when I learned that he had called the mom at home and calmly stated that T had died and that they would need to come to the hospital as soon as possible. Did he ever stop to consider that she was alone with her six year old daughter and that she might have needed support around her to hear this news? It took the family three hours to arrive at the hospital when their normal commute time was one hour.

In the period of time we were waiting for the family, I went to look for Dr A to discuss a supportive action for the family. He was alone, eating breakfast in the hospital cafeteria. I asked him to call Dr B, a paediatrician the parents liked and had found supportive in the past. He was very opposed to the idea, stating that Dr B was busy with morning office appointments. Perhaps his ego could not let him acknowledge that Dr B might be more supportive for this family. Sensing this, I laid out my feelings by telling him that they needed someone else, someone they trusted, because at this point the welfare of the family should be our only concern. I strongly encouraged him to call Dr B. Well, Dr B arrived before the family and was there to greet them with arms full of love and support.

Several months after Baby T's death, I went to dinner at the parent's home. Baby T's six year old sister grabbed my hand because she wanted me to see which room would have been T's. It had been turned back into a guest room, but she described where his bed had been and where his clothes were kept. His sister asked me questions like: 'Do all babies that live in the hospital die? and 'Did T die because he was a bad boy?' My role as his primary nurse had been multifaceted. Even months after his death, I could still make a difference. T's sister had been scared to discuss her baby brother's death because she said her mommy might cry.

It had been six years since this event occurred in my career. I believe my role as a nurse has been enriched by my experience with Baby T and his family. I receive Christmas cards from his family annually. I had thought my most important role as his primary nurse was the day to day care I had given him. Now I feel the most important function I performed was simply caring.

Of course, her caring was not simple nor could she have carried it out without adequate knowledge and preparation. Her discovery is that caring is a good in itself. Losses are made bearable by a community who cares and understands. In this case, Linda Smith was the only other human being who knew Baby T as intimately as the family. Friends and extended family had stopped visiting the hospital after the first few weeks. She had borne witness to Baby T's existence. Dr B also played a key supportive role but did not take up this aspect of understanding the lived meanings and everyday practices involved in the care of Baby T. The family's memories of Baby T as a baby and family member are bound up with Linda Smith's humanising and personalising caring practices for Baby T and his family. The Christmas cards are perhaps in part a memorial to Baby T.

I have chosen narrative exemplars with interpretive commentary as a primary strategy for articulating clinical knowledge and caring practices because narratives show the transitions, the gains in understanding in first person experiential terms. The narratives can depict timing, attunement, context, relationship and the particular. Stories allow for meanings and emotional responses to be understood. Finally, narratives are suited for demonstrating understanding and responses.

III

If morality can only be powered negatively, where there can be no such thing as beneficence powered by an affirmation of the recipient as a being of value, then pity is destructive to the giver and degrading to the receiver, and the ethic of benevolence may indeed be indefensible. [This is] Nietzsche's challenge on the deepest level, because he is looking precisely for what can release such an affirmation of being. His unsettling conclusion is that it is the ethic of benevolence which stands in the way of it. Only if there is such a thing as *agapē*, or one of the secular claimants to its succession, is Nietzsche wrong.[21]

In this passage, Taylor articulates a deep question for nursing practice. Can nurses take up a public caring practice in authentic ways that do not degrade or make dependent the ones cared for? The question is further complicated by the marginal status of caring practices in highly technical curative modes of health care administered in bureaucratic settings with the impersonal forces of commodification and economism driving the structures and institutional realities of nurses' practice. Practising authentic care is a particularly challenging project for nurses because they care for people in a full range of health, vulnerability and dependency.

In narrative and observational accounts of expert caring practices of nurses my colleagues and I are encouraged to find that nurses talk about knowing the patient and that in the knowing is embedded mutuality and genuine care.[22] We also find degraded variants of objectification, pity and rejection. However, these are either told or heard as instances of breakdown, demonstrating that there is still a quest for authentic care embedded in actual nursing practice. For example, when nurses are asked how they came to connect with the patient-family, they describe concrete episodes and aspects of the person-family that allowed for connection, respect and mutual realisation. Sometimes the connection was based upon respect for the person's anger, sense of humour, courage. In any case, coming to know and respect the actual person-family is central to the exemplary or excellent care-giving relationship. Nurses do not typically attribute the excellence of their care giving to their traits and talents nor to personal intents to develop themselves as care-givers. They do not give self-conscious accounts of developing their character, or performing their duty by exercising benevolence. While, from an 'outside in' vantage point one might attribute particular traits and talents, the nurses engaged in the care-giving experience typically describe their response and knowledge-based actions in relation to particular patients and families. In these specific narratives, the nurse typically describes specific ways of connecting and learning from the person-family. This is illustrated in the following narrative account given by Pamela Minarik, a clinical nurse specialist, who cared for a patient who underwent multiple surgeries to repair the damage done to his body by an attempted suicide from drinking a caustic chemical:

He would say: 'Don't talk to me. Don't hassle me. I don't want to talk about that. Don't talk that psychiatric stuff.' Then if I talked anything that he considered

[21] Taylor, *Sources of the self*, p. 516.
[22] C. Tanner, P. Benner, C. Chelsa and D. Gordon, 'The phenomenology of knowing a patient', *Image* 25 (1993), pp. 273–80.

psychiatric stuff, he would refuse to have anything to do with me. Interviewer: What did he consider psychiatric stuff?

'Psychiatric stuff' was anything that had to do with how he felt. Anything that was going on inside him. Any attempt to explore anything that was going on inside him was psychiatric talk. Some days I would get half an answer to a question and that would be it. Other days for days on end I wouldn't get anything. And we would just have these general conversations. Also because of his wariness, he didn't want to talk about his family, his sisters. It was a real struggle for me. I thought, how am I going to build a relationship with this man? I was looking for anything that he could care about in his life. I don't know what engaged me, but I got very engaged. I think that I got engaged by his struggle to be independent. His determination not to be dependent even in the face of these terrible surgeries, and constantly having to be tube fed, being afraid of being killed, and all this other stuff tied up with survival. He was just determined to be strong and independent. I think that it was characteristic of the way he coped with his life. He wasn't someone who had been cared for a lot in his life. He had pretty much been on his own.

Pamela Minarik goes on to describe a year of working with this patient and long-term follow up through correspondence and Christmas cards. He shares his milestones of recovery and she clearly responds with appreciation and respect for his triumphs. He teaches her much about the power of anger, fierce independence and his own brand of dignity that was related to resisting therapeutic labels and demands.

Caring practices are a way of knowing and respecting specific individuals that artfully go beyond mere techniques of behavioural change or other objectifying discourses. Clearly not every nurse achieves this level of caring practices with every patient, where recognition of the concrete other and respect is accorded through daily practices of listening and care of the body, but nurses recognise this kind of engagement as authentic and what they value most in their caring practices. Recognition and response to the other are pervasive as nurses tell stories that depict their notions of excellence in care giving. I take this to be evidence that caring practices in nursing have not been completely colonised by an objectifying devotion to a duty to be benevolent or a technological self-understanding where the recipient of care becomes an objectified behavioural change project except in situations that nurses themselves acknowledge as breakdown and failure.[23]

Or must benevolence ultimately come to be conceived as a duty we owe ourselves, somehow required by our dignity as rational, emancipated moderns, regardless of the (un)worth of the recipients? And to the extent that this is so, how close will we

[23] Taylor, *Sources of the self*, p. 517. See also Benner, *From novice to expert*, 'The role of experience, narrative, and community in skilled ethical comportment'; and Benner et al., 'From beginner to expert'.

have come to the world Dostoyevsky portrays, in which acts of seeming benefi-cence are in fact expressions of contempt, even hatred.

The dangers of disengaged reasoning, and of viewing benevolence simply as a manifestation of the care-giver's capacity for choice are avoided and countered by these nurses' accounts of the best of their practices.

A pervasive notion of good expressed in expert nursing practice involves limiting the encroachment of technology by following the body's lead. One nurse captured this sentiment in the common ICU maximum: 'If you're not helping you're almost immediately doing harm with ventilat-ing.' The other nurses in the same small group interview pointed out that the same maxim holds for all technology. Technical interventions should be limited to the necessary, moving the patient toward the recovery of the body's own powers of recovery. The same nurse goes on to say: 'That's what I think nursing is all about, nudging this kid towards normal.' The notion of good at play here requires leaving behind intrusive, unwarranted hindrances to the body's own recuperative powers as soon as possible. These nurses are caught in the cultural dialogue of sanctioning and legitimising the necessary intrusive technology, rendering it less frighten-ing, and recognising when the technology use has become excessive. Nurses talked about being vigilant about preventing unnecessary and unwarranted technological interventions:

She had a trach and we were actively weaning her. She was fine. We put her on a mask for about ten hours during the day and then she would be back on the ventilator at night. But they had an arterial line in her for about 50 days. They kept putting A-lines in her. I said: 'Why are you putting A-lines in her?' 'Well she is vented and needs to have one.' I said, 'No, she doesn't need to have one. One machine does not give you the criteria to put in an A-line. We know what her gasses are . . . We know when she gets into trouble. She tells us by other parameters . . . ' She was also having hematocrit problems because they had been taking such frequent blood gas samples for the past 50 days.

Nurses describe the problem of technological proliferation and escala-tion. This shows a critical assessment of technology in relation to patient needs and responses to the diagnostic procedures. This critical assessment of technology is a small, but important triumph of person over body-machine and thoughtless use of technology.

There are many ways the body-person can become objectified to become body-machine. In the following example, the nurse refuses to use the patient's anxiety and agitation as a way to maintain his blood pressure:

I refused to take him off sedation just to keep his blood pressure up. That's the other thing I fought for. It is not fair. He is also somebody. I knew him. He is somebody that is just so agitated. He is going to work himself up to another M.I. if he is not kept restful.

This seems to be an obvious stance once the nurse voices it, but there is subtle pressure to instrumentalise and subjugate the body so that the body as person is overlooked. Neonatal intensive care nurses do an amazing recovery of body as person and following the body's lead in their work:

In the ICU, the babies tell you what to do. You don't say, 'Oh, it's 9:00 and I have to take vital signs because I'm supposed to.' No, if the baby is asleep, let him, that's why the monitors are there so you do not have to disturb the baby.

Another neonatal nurse talks about following the baby instead of imposing their own agenda in a harmful way:

When we think we know what the course ought to be and the baby says: 'No, we're not going to do it that way, you know, I can only eat so much, or I can only tolerate so much.' We find out that when we actually go with what the baby seems to want to do ... I know that sounds strange, but letting them sort of guide their care a little bit more directly instead of enforcing them into a mould that we think they ought to follow.

She and other nurses talk about attending to and following the body's lead. This is a dialogue with the particular that depends on knowing the embodied patient, and proceeding with care that sets limits on dominance and control of the body that ignores bodily responses and needs. The person's bodily capacities and responses are given moral worth and considered a form of personhood and intentionality that require attention, respect and response. This ethical comportment preserves the status of the other as one who makes ethical claims for consideration when using therapies and care that alter the body's own adaptive and recuperative powers.

Charles Taylor's work provides the vision and example for examining notions of the good embedded in narratives and observations of actual practice. Practice is a way of knowing and a source of knowledge and innovation. His view of practice as socially embedded and dialogical allows the observer-participant to uncover the notions of the good inherent in the skills of involvement, responsibility and the skills of preserving the world and personhood of extremely ill persons. There is a limit to what language can convey about clinical knowhow and caring practices since the knowledge will always point to understanding gained experientially by moving from one articulation to another. As Polanyi notes, 'clinicians always know more than they can tell'.[24] But here Taylor is right about articulation; clinicians must keep trying to give language to what they know in their practice and that articulation will have to include

---

[24] Michael Polanyi, *Personal knowledge* (London: Routledge and Kegan Paul, 1958).

narrative accounts of transitions.[25] Capturing this understanding narratively in transitions takes us beyond mere explanation and outside in procedural accounts. Exemplars give a vision of the good and open up the possibility of taking up the skilled practices in new ways.

[25] Taylor, *Sources of the self*, pp. 72–5.

Part V

Ethics, politics and pluralism

10 Rights and pluralism

Richard Tuck

The modern rights-bearing subject has been one of the principal examples for Charles Taylor of the modern self, the exploration of which has preoccupied him for the last fifteen years. In section 1.3 of *Sources of the self*, a section which contains in many ways the germ of the whole book, he observed that the modern moral world is significantly different from that of previous civilisations: all cultures have had some sense that human beings command our respect, but 'what is peculiar to the modern West among each higher civilization is that its favoured formulation for this principle of respect has come to be in terms of rights'.[1] But section 1.3 provides merely a brief sketch of what Taylor takes rights theories in general to be claiming; in many ways, the *Vorarbeiten* of the book, and in particular the articles which he published at the beginning of the last decade, give us a clearer idea of the assumptions governing *Sources of the self*. So in what follows, I shall draw as much on those articles (where relevant) as on the book.

His 1979 article on 'Atomism' set out the account of rights theories which was to remain at least implicit throughout his later work:[2]

Theories which assert the primacy of rights are those which take as the fundamental, or at least a fundamental, principle of their political theory the ascription of certain rights to individuals and which deny the same status to a principle of belonging or obligation, that is a principle which states our obligation as men to belong to or sustain society, or a society of a certain type, or to obey authority or an authority of a certain type. Primacy-of-right theories in other words accept a principle ascribing rights to men as binding unconditionally, binding, that is, on men as such. But they do not accept as similarly unconditional a principle of belonging or obligation. Rather our obligation to belong to or sustain a society, or obey its authorities, is seen as derivative, as laid on us conditionally, through our consent, or through its being to our advantage. The obligation to belong is derived in certain conditions from the more fundamental principle which ascribes rights.

The picture sketched by this passage is of a moral world in which there is, first, an overriding drive for unification and simplification – rights are

[1] Taylor, *Sources of the self*, p. 11.   [2] Taylor, *Philosophical papers*, II, p. 188.

'fundamental', and other principles 'derive' from them – and, second, the foundational moral properties are supposed to inhere in individuals rather than in any other entities. Although 'Atomism' is principally devoted to the second feature, many of the important elements of rights theories (as Taylor describes them) are in fact the consequence of the first feature. As we shall see, a rights theory which does not suppose that all other moral principles derive from individual rights looks very different from Taylor's sketch, even if it does continue to give some special status to rights. Moreover, as we shall also see, it was the phenomenon of moral variety which arguably lay behind the first and most influential rights theories.

Taylor has always been both fascinated and appalled by programmes of moral or cultural unification. In another essay of about the same period, 'The diversity of goods' (1982), he argued that the drive to radical simplification has been the characteristic modern response to moral diversity. He envisaged this diversity as involving the full recognition of the *moral* difference between ways of life, and their incommensurability when viewed from within any particular one of the ways of life, together with the impossibility of standing outside all of them in a straightforward manner. For example, we might respect or hanker after the austere life of the rational, goal-directed agent, or the emotionally richer life of Christian *agape* in which we strive to become a channel for God's love towards humans. But if we take on the commitments of either of these ways of living, it necessarily involves us in seeing what Taylor terms a 'qualitative contrast' between them – that is, in seeing that 'one way of acting or living is higher than others, or in other cases that a certain way of living is higher than others, or in other cases that a certain way of living is debased. It is essential to the kind of moral view just exemplified that this kind of contrast be made.'[3]

We cannot, as committed ethical beings, believe in the morality of Christianity, without *ipso facto* feeling that an atheistical morality is fundamentally unacceptable in some way; and if we manage mentally to slip out of our theism into the atheist's viewpoint, we will find the same phenomenon in reverse. Trying to stand outside both of the moral visions in order to bring them into a comparative perspective, on the other hand, merely means that we fail properly to understand either one of them.[4]

---

[3] Ibid., p. 236.

[4] It is interesting that a very similar view was expressed by the greatest of the nineteenth-century English critics of utilitarianism, *à propos* the interpersonal comparison of 'pleasurers': 'As a matter of fact we do not look upon pleasures as independent things to be thus compared with each other, but as interwoven with the rest of life, as having their history and their reasons, as involving different kinds of enjoyment in such a manner that our being able to enter into one kind is accompanied with a horror of another kind, which

It should be stressed that this does not mean, in Taylor's eyes, that no relationship between different moral visions is possible. In 'The diversity of goods' he accepted that keeping a genuine plurality of goods in focus is extremely difficult psychologically, and may not be a plausible goal for human beings:[5]

The habit of treating the moral as a single domain is not just gratuitous or based on a mere mistake. The domain of ultimately important goods has a sort of prescriptive unity. Each of us has to answer all these demands in the course of a single life, and this means that we have to find some way of assessing their relative validity, or putting them in an order of priority. A single coherent order of goods is rather like an idea of reason in the Kantian sense, something we always try to define without ever managing to achieve it definitively.

Moreover, the language of 'qualitative contrast' in this paper links up with the use of the same language in his discussions of ethnocentricity (e.g. 'Understanding and ethnocentricity' (1981)), in which he argued that we can understand another society's way of life through,[6]

what one could call a language of perspicuous contrast. This would be a language in which we could formulate both their way of life and ours as alternative possibilities in relation to some human constants at work in both. It would be a language in which the possible human variations would be so formulated that both our form of life and their could be perspicuously described as alternative such variations. Such a language of contrast might show their language of understanding to be distorted or inadequate in some respects, or it might show ours to be (in which case, we might find that understanding them leads to an alteration of our self-understanding, and hence our form of life – a far from unknown process in history); or it might show both to be so.

He gave as examples of 'perspicuous contrast', Gadamer and Montesquieu. Elsewhere, he has asked himself the questions 'what are the capacities of practical reason? Is it quite helpless before such basic differences in spiritual outlook, like that between the disengaged identity and its opponents? Or is there, at least in principle, a way in which this kind of question can be rationally arbitrated?', and has answered himself in the following terms. 'I am fiercely committed to the latter view,

would entirely prevent the comparison of the one with the other as pleasures, besides this, it must be remembered that, in the interval between the one pleasure and the other, the mind is changed: you have no permanent touchstone, no currency to be the medium of comparison. Suppose a man whose youth has been grossly vicious, whose mature age is most deeply devout; according to disposition, the view as to past life in this case will probably much differ: but most commonly I think the man will wonder that he was ever able to find pleasure at all in what he once found pleasure in. Earnestness in the later frame of mind, whatever it is, would only preclude the possibility of a cool comparison of it, as to pleasure, with the earlier one ...' (John Grote, *An Examination of the Utilitarian Philosophy* (Cambridge: Cambridge University Press, 1870) p. 54).

[5] Taylor, *Philosophical papers*, II, p. 244.   [6] Ibid., pp. 125–6.

and I recognize that the onus is on me to come up with a good argument. I am working on it, and I hope at not too remote a date to be able to publish something convincing (as least to some) on this.'[7] So it is important to recognise that although Taylor is very hostile to the traditional means of comparing ways of life by standing outside them, he is not (at least *in posse*) a conventional sceptic; though his own solution to this problem must remain difficult to understand until he has delivered on his promise to provide a full account of it.

However, a prime characteristic of modernity, on Taylor's account, has been a restlessness about living with this contrastive language, and an unhappiness about the impossibility of standing completely outside evaluative schemes. As moderns, he claims, we have an epistemological commitment to reducing this plurality of goods and of moral visions to a single ordering based on one fundamental good. Utilitarianism, here as well as in many of Taylor's other works, is the prime example of this modern reductivism, but a rights theory of the kind outlined above would also count. Indeed, in many ways (historically speaking) it fits the general thesis even better. As we shall see presently, the seventeenth-century rights theories were substantially motivated by a desire to cope in some way with ethical relativism, and to isolate men's natural rights as transcultural universals, leaving other moral properties prey to scepticism; at the same time, they fitted in some imaginatively plausible way into the new naturalist account of man. These are precisely the features which, in a striking couple of pages, Taylor pointed out as the considerations underlying the modern reductivist approach to qualitative contrast.[8]

No one seems very ready to challenge the view that, other things being equal, it is better that men's desires be fulfilled than that they be frustrated, that they be happy rather than miserable ... Again, as we saw, formalistic theories [e.g. Kantianism] get their plausibility from the fact that they are grounded on certain moral intuitions which are almost unchallenged in modern society, based as they are in certain preconditions of moral discourse itself combined with a thesis about the racial homogeneity of humanity which it is pretty hard to challenge in a scientific, de-parochialized and historically sensitive contemporary culture.

The premises of these forms of moral reasoning can therefore easily appear to be of a quite different provenance from those that deal with qualitative contrast. Against these latter, we can allow ourselves to slip into ethical scepticism while exempting the former, either on the grounds that they are somehow self-evident, or even that they are not based on ethical insight at all but on something firmer, like the logic of our language.

But, in fact, these claims to firmer foundation are illusory. What is really going on is that some forms of ethical reasoning are being privileged over others because in our civilization they come less into dispute or look easier to defend.

---

[7] Ibid., p. 12.   [8] Ibid., pp. 241–2.

In a similar way, we have been manoeuvred into a restrictive definition of ethics, which takes account of some of the goods we seek, for example utility, and universal respect for moral personality, while excluding others, viz. the virtues and goals like those mentioned above, largely on the grounds that the former are subject to less embarrassing dispute.

In addition, Taylor continues, naturalism treats the language *of contrast in a similar* manner, as referring to 'subjective factors', and thus leading to 'ethical scepticism'.

So, rather than assert (as an honourable ancient might have done) the clear truth of compelling quality of his own moral vision, and attempt to work out 'rationally' some *modus vivendi* between this vision and that of other people, the modern employs the evasive technique of discrediting all views but his own by the employment of allegedly extra-moral consider-ations, thereby transferring the moral debate to a new arena where he can be assured of victory.

Reductivism of this sort may have been the consequence of the appear-ance of rights theories in our culture, but I am far from sure that it is a reasonable way of characterising the great rights theories themselves. Moreover, an account of this sort has the demerit that it obscures the historical origins of the theories, and their actual point (a clear weakness of *Sources of the self*).[9] What I want to do here is to suggest an alternative reading of those theories which provides at least some kind of explanation for their appeal to moderns and which implies that Taylor has (in a sense) been asking the wrong questions of them. I should say at the outset that it is an idealised reading and that many other currents cut across the stream I shall be talking about; but the interpretation I shall put forward engages with most of Taylor's central preoccupations.

I

My view can be put quite simply. It is that the extraordinary burst of moral and political theorising in terms of natural rights which marks the seventeenth century, and which is associated particularly with the names of Grotius, Hobbes, Pufendorf and Locke, was primarily an attempt by European theorists to deal with the problem of deep cultural differences, both within their own community (following the wars of religion) and between Europe and the rest of the world (particularly the world of the various pre-agricultural peoples encountered around the globe). Taylor's hunch that the problem of moral disparity is at the heat of modernity is especially true of these theorists, even though Taylor perhaps did not fully

[9] As Taylor himself acknowledges in his historical digression in *Sources of the self*, pp. 202–7.

realise it. But the theorists were not properly reductive, in Taylor's sense, for they did not believe either that rights are the *only* form in which a moral language can be cast, or that they are (properly speaking) *foundational* to other values. Instead, they present natural rights as the only means whereby in practice different cultures can negotiate a *modus vivendi* which allows their *other* values to be preserved or respected – that is, their overall aim was much closer to Taylor's own programme than he has allowed (and, correspondingly, Taylor is much more of a traditional liberal than he might be willing to acknowledge).[10]

The key writer here is Grotius, for it was he who in effect invented the natural rights tradition. He did so as an answer to late-Renaissance scepticism, voiced by authors such as Montaigne and Charron, who had expressed pessimism about the possibility of ever finding a universal *criterion* (the technical term of ancient scepticism) to adjudicate between differing moral or religious views – pessimism, in other words, about the ability of an Aristotelian-style practical reason to solve these puzzles. Both Grotius' principal works on ethics and politics (his *De iure praedae* or *De indis* of 1604–5 and his *De iure belli ac pacis* of 1625) were, as their names suggest, devoted to the moral dilemmas thrown up by international relations: the issue of how to negotiate a common ground in practice between cultures with very different views about how to conduct oneself in the world was therefore central to his enterprise. What Grotius argued was, essentially, that *whatever else* one believed, one must accept the force of two propositions. One was that everyone has (all other things being equal) a right to defend themselves, and the other was that (again, all other things being equal) no one is entitled *wantonly* or *unnecessarily* to injure another human being – that is, to do so for reasons other than (ultimately) self-defence. Notoriously, he presented these two propositions as having force for us because all men agree on them – 'What the common consent of mankind has shown to be the will of all, that is law,'[11] Grotius took common consent of this kind to be the solution to the sceptical problem, for upon it could be built the 'intermediate' type of justice of which he spoke in the following passage:[12]

The foregoing observations show how erroneously the Academics [i.e. the sceptics] – those masters of ignorance – have argued in refutation of justice, that the

---

[10] Some of the following draws on what I have already set out in 'The "modern" theory of natural law' in *The languages of political theory in early-modern Europe*, ed. A. Pagden (Cambridge: Cambridge University Press, 1987), pp. 99–122, and in my 1991 Oxford University Carlyle Lectures on *Political thought and the international order from Grotius to Kant* (to be published shortly).

[11] Hugo Grotius, *De iure praedae commentarius*, I, trans. G. I. Williams (Oxford: Clarendon Press, 1950), p. 12.

[12] Ibid., p. 13.

kind derived from nature looks solely to personal advantage, while civil justice is based not upon nature but merely upon opinion [this is a reference to Carneades' famous argument that natural justice is really self-interest, as altruism would be *stultitia*]; for they have overlooked that intermediate aspect of justice which is characteristic of humankind.

Intermediate justice, for Grotius, was the core of moral beliefs which *as a matter of fact* all societies had in common, and which could therefore be used as a basis for negotiation between them. He was (to a modern reader) astonishingly uninterested in the basis for these beliefs, or why they should be common to all societies, though his writings often imply a pretty pure functionalist argument: one could not imagine any possible society which denied either of these two principles, since if it refused its members the right to defend themselves, a single psychopath could destroy it, while if it allowed its members to treat other human beings as if they were trees or lower animals, to be destroyed for relatively trivial needs, it would also quickly disappear. But this lack of interest was compatible with the general post-sceptical framework in which he was operating. From the point of view of a sceptic, there was an indefinite set of reasons for anyone to hold the moral beliefs which they did hold, a set which included the particular history of their life or their culture. The sceptic did not necessarily deny the validity of these reasons; indeed, he might be able to give some higher-order argument in favour, for example, of living according to the laws and customs (including the moral beliefs) of one's country. But he did deny that enough of these beliefs could cross the various cultural barriers in which we live to make a universal ethics possible.

For Grotius, on the other hand, it was as if cultures were Venn diagrams which happened to overlap at a particular, minimal spot. From the point of view of the moral agent in each culture, the belief in the right to self-preservation was the same kind of thing as (for example) the belief in the virtue of magnanimity (a classic object of derision for anti-Aristotelians); but a Grotian observer could see that the first belief was shared with other cultures while the second was not. The fact that they were shared in this way did not mean, however, that this common set of moral beliefs was foundational to all the agent's other beliefs, nor that the common beliefs were to be understood as a different *kind* of belief from the others. Rather, it was simply that there were some human needs which were so universal that all societies would have to recognise them in some fashion, and others which were not.

Properly to understand this position, we have to remember that there are two different things which we might label 'foundationalism'. One supposes that there can be (in principle) a systematic hierarchy of reasons for moral beliefs, analogous to the system of a particular mathematics, in which a set of fundamental propositions are both necessary and sufficient for the deduction of the superstructural propositions. Thomist scholasticism is an ideal type of this kind of foundationalism, and on Taylor's account so are utilitarianism and Kantianism. His complaint about these modern foundationalisms is that their buildings are erected on absurdly constrained footings. Foundationalism of the kind encountered in Grotius and his followers, however, supposes that there are primary and secondary human needs, but that our ethical attitudes to the secondary ones are not straightforwardly determined by the primary ones. The universal human need for food and shelter is obviously foundational, in this sense, to our moral life, however rich and complex that life may be, and the moral values attached to these preconditions of life may therefore be regarded as fundamental; but Aristotelian magnanimity, as Aztec warrior virtue, are not derivable from these foundations, however hard or perceptively we think.

Isolating the common core of universal beliefs will be foundationalist in the first sense only if we already believe, independently, in the existence of a hierarchy of beliefs in which a suitably primitive segment will determine the rest (rather like cloning an entire creature from a scrap of DNA). If we are deeply anti-hierarchical, as the Renaissance sceptics were, then we will not suppose that finding a common set of moral beliefs commits us to a particular reductivism; and in this respect it is a matter of the first importance that the seventeenth-century rights theorists were intellectual heirs of the sceptics and not (as has sometimes been supposed) of the scholastics.

A good analogy with this approach comes from the characteristic theology of these seventeenth-century writers, with, again, Grotius himself leading the way. Both in his *De iure belli ac pacis* and in his *De veritate religionis christianae*, he argued that there is a universal or natural theology consisting of the idea that there is 'at least one God' who has made the Earth and who cares for it, rewarding and punishing men in some appropriate fashion. This is the equivalent of the universal human need for survival, and every society (Grotius believed) must build this theology into its religious and ethical doctrines. But clearly, no actually existing religion, at least in the first half of the seventeenth century, left this natural theology unelaborated, and equally clearly the elaborations were not *derivable* from this minimal principle. The elaborations had a value of their own, and it was not an easy matter to put them into a 'contrastive' focus (though it should be said that Grotius did try doing so, as far as Christianity, Judaism and Islam were concerned, in his *De veritate*. I shall have something to say about the implications of this attempt at the end of this essay.).

A universal, natural ethics of the Grotian type, therefore, was not intended to be a comprehensive account of man's moral life. As its location in the context of international relations illustrates, it was intended to be the basis for inter-national or inter-cultural negotiation, by providing the common ground upon which the rival and conflicting cultures could meet. This meeting was not necessarily to be benevolent or mutually respectful in any very full sense: a dramatic instance of this is provided by the collision of European and aboriginal in North America, the clear subject of some of Grotius' discussion of property in *De iure belli ac pacis*. Here, Grotius in effect started the seventeenth- and eighteenth-century Anglo-Dutch practice of justifying the seizure of aboriginal land on the grounds that the native peoples were not using it properly – that is, that their hunter-gatherer or minimally agricultural economy left land waste which could (under a European agrarian régime) be used to feed people.[13]

The essential piece of this argument was the claim that people must be entitled to preserve themselves (including above all providing themselves with food) if they can do so without injuring other people (i.e. by depriving them of life or the necessities of life). On this view, farming automatically trumps hunting as a way of using land, since it provides far more food and therefore enables far more people to survive. Grotius and his successors put this argument forward as one which ought to compel the agreement of the Indians themselves, since the Indians (like all men) would recognise the force of the minimal moral principles. If we leave aside the obvious point that this looks very much like an ideological justification of a pretty disreputable process of conquest, we are left with the disconcerting fact that there was in principle a real and tragic moral dilemma in this conflict; the minimalist universal ethic as the basis for negotiation was not absurd, and there is no reason to suppose that the native peoples would have denied the force of the principle of self-preservation.

A similar dilemma confronts us today in the arguments of those who say that the forests of Amazonia must give way to farmland to feed the poor of Brazil. Our usual, and obviously reasonable, first response is to deny the character of the need – there must in the modern world be ways of feeding the poor without destroying Amazonia. But suppose that the facts were not as morally convenient as that, and that there were good grounds for supposing that men would die unless more food could be grown on the waste lands of the globe. Then, I think, one begins to get a sense of the real issue which these seventeenth-century writers thought

---

[13] For this, see *De iure belli ac pacis* II.2.6–17 (especially 17), and my forthcoming Carlyle Lectures.

they were confronting, and how intercultural negotiation will not necessarily be a pleasing process.

Our understanding of the *negotiatory* character of these early rights
theories, and of their refusal to provide a comprehensive account of man's
moral life, has been clouded to some extent by a careless reading of
Grotius' first major follower, Hobbes. As I have now argued in a number
of places, Hobbes essentially took the Grotian argument about intercultural negotiation and applied it to *individuals*.[14] Hobbes was not committed
to the idea that our whole moral life can be understood in terms of natural
rights; like the loyal sceptic he was, at least in his origins, he believed that
our moral life could consist of the most extraordinarily varied and
idiosyncratic beliefs – anything which 'seems good' counts as good for a
presocial individual, who comes equipped with the same kind of elaborate
and contingently given moral language as an entire society might possess
(Hobbes being notoriously confident about the logical possibility of
private language). The central ethical problem is then intercultural conflict, and it is resolved by a retreat similar to that of Grotius towards the
minimal principles of self-preservation and no unjustifiable injury (the
latter in Hobbes' formulation being the injunction to 'seek peace' with
one's fellow men unless doing so endangers one). But even after the
negotiation has been completed, and a *modus vivendi* worked out, there is
potentially (on Hobbes' account) a great deal of moral variety: since the
Leviathan ought to police only those beliefs and practices relevant to our
physical survival, everything else (including much of our religion) will in
general be up to individuals to work out for themselves:[15]

There ought to be no Power over the Consciences of men, but of the Word it selfe,
working Faith in every one, not always according to the purpose of them that
Plant and Water, but of God himself, that giveth the Increase ... [and] it is
unreasonable in them, who teach there is such danger in every little Errour, to
require of a man endued with Reason of his own, to follow the Reason of any
other man, or of the most voices of many other men; Which is little better, then to
venture his Salvation at corsse and pile.

A similar case might be put forward even for Locke, whose rights
theory was again by no means the whole of his ethics, and who articulated
it in the particular context of a cultural clash about the government of
England and (once more) the settlement of North America.

---

[14] See in particular my *Hobbes* (Oxford: Oxford University Press, 1989); 'Grotius, Carneades and Hobbes' *Grotiana* NS4 (1983), pp. 43–62; and *Philosophy and Government
1572–1651* (Cambridge: Cambridge University Press, 1993).
[15] *Leviathan*, ed. Richard Tuck (Cambridge: Cambridge University Press, 1991) p. 480. See
for example Alan Ryan, 'A more tolerant Hobbes?' in *Justifying toleration*, ed. Susan
Mendus (Cambridge: Cambridge University Press, 1988) pp. 37–60).

II

How did the idea come about (which is by no means peculiar to Taylor) that these classical rights theorists were seen as reductivist in his sense, and that they believed that a moral life should be reduced to those elements which are derivable from the fundamental rights? I myself believe that this was largely a development of the eighteenth century, and that Taylor's assimilation of these seventeenth-century 'liberal' writers to their late eighteenth-century successors has obscured a vitally important difference between them. The obvious break is provided by Kant, who was openly contemptuous of the 'sorry comforters' and their hetero-geneous collection of ethical principles; Kant was a foundationalist of the first kind outlined above, who believed that all moral prepositions had to be tested for validity against a fundamental axiom. Utilitarianism, too, was reductivist in this sense, and again the first utilitarians were very hostile to Grotius and his successors – so hostile, of course, that they abandoned the use of rights theories completely.

Various movements earlier in the eighteenth century presaged this break; like Taylor, but for different reasons, I would single out deism as a key element in the story. Although the writers from Grotius to Locke were clear precursors of the deists, they were not actually prepared to abandon Christianity, and one reason for this was that they did not think that the necessary minimal theology was also *sufficient*. Even Hobbes, the closest to deism of all of them, believed that since religious utterances were simply culturally specific ways of honouring the Creator, there could (and may be should) be a wide variety of theologies in which each man sought salvation in his own fashion (though always of course within the hedges laid out by the Leviathan). What marked out the early eighteenth-century deists was the fact that they believed that we should thin down our actual religion to the universal core, and from there it was a short step to doing the same for our ethics.[16]

However, the important point for our purposes is that the late eighteenth-century ethical theorists who sought out a more profoundly foundationalist ethics than the seventeenth-century writers had provided were not straightforward rights theorists of the classical kind. One of the clear historical oddities of *Sources of the self* is the desire on Taylor's part to assimilate the rights theorists to the utilitarians and Kantians, regardless of the fact that both Bentham and Kant believed that they had

---

[16] It should be said that there are intimations of this approach in Grotius's *De veritate*, as part of this work involves defending the superiority of Christianity to Judaism and Islam on the grounds that its moral message is closer to the natural, minimal religion than the elaborate codes of the other creeds.

crossed some vital boundary separating them from Grotius and his successors. As we have now seen, this may not merely have been historically misleading: at least one strain of modern liberalism, that drawn in our time largely from Hobbes and Locke, but with its origins in Grotius, may retain enough of its ancestry to be immune to the criticisms Taylor has levelled at it.

11   The political theory of strong evaluation

Daniel M. Weinstock

Reading Charles Taylor's work, one is struck both by its breadth and by its remarkable consistency. An underlying intention of Taylor's writings as a whole has been to oppose the reductive impulse which has marked many of the human sciences since the seventeenth century, and which seeks to account for various aspects of human life in terms provided by explanatory theories derived from the natural sciences. Thus, he was an early critic of behaviourism in the philosophy of psychology, and has defended an 'expressivist' theory of meaning against the truth-conditional theories which have become something of an orthodoxy in the philosophy of language. In these fields and in many others, Taylor has sought to restore a dimension of meaning and significance which is too often ignored by philosophies of man of a more naturalistic bent. Taylor himself has characterised his work as that of a 'monomaniac', pursuing 'a single rather tightly related agenda'[1] through a number of seemingly unrelated areas of philosophy.[1] My intention in this paper is to take Taylor at his word, and to assess the consistency of his contributions to the areas of the philosophy of action and of political philosophy.

One of Taylor's principal philosophical achievements has been to discredit a view of human agency according to which action can be understood solely in terms of agents' preferences and of their efforts to satisfy these preferences, and to suggest the greater plausibility of a model emphasising agents' second-order reflection upon such preferences, and the evaluative frameworks which make such second-order reasoning possible. His work in this area has provided an important impetus for the gradual displacement of the belief–desire model as the dominant paradigm in the philosophy of action.[2]

I have benefited in writing this paper from the comments of Sam Black, Elizabeth Elbourne, Kai Nielsen, Michel Seymour and Brian Walker, and I wish to record my thanks to them here. I also wish to thank the Social Science and Humanities Research Council of Canada for post-doctoral funding which has made this essay possible.
[1] Charles Taylor, 'Introduction', *Philosophical papers*, p. 1.
[2] For an example of his influence on contemporary discussions, see J. David Velleman's important *Practical reflection* (Princeton: Princeton University Press, 1989).

Taylor has also been concerned in much of his work to argue against some of the principal claims of liberal political philosophers such as John Rawls and Ronald Dworkin, on behalf of a conception of political life more attuned to human beings' communal nature, and to the important goods which flow from practices of collective self-rule. According to Taylor, the emphasis placed by liberal political theorists upon governmental neutrality with respect to competing conceptions of the good life renders liberalism incapable of adequately giving expression to the fact that there are certain types of human goods which can only be secured by collectivities acting in concert. Taylor's political writings have thus placed him within the 'communitarian' camp in contemporary philosophical debates.[3]

Although these two strands of Taylor's work seem to be addressed to quite different agendas, it is clear that he sees them as proceeding from the same basic intuition: both the belief-desire model in the explanation of action and the doctrine of liberal neutrality are in his view manifestations of an approach to the study of human affairs that ignores the horizons of meaning and significance against the backdrop of which human beings lead their lives.

My aim in this paper is to suggest that these two strands of Taylor's thought are actually in tension with one another. Tersely stated, my claim will be that the social conditions required in order to foster the development of the 'strong evaluators' his philosophy of action advocates are better secured under liberal political institutions grounded upon procedural values of toleration and mutual respect than they are under communitarian arrangements in which citizens seek to attain an encompassing common good through the workings of their political institutions.

My argument will proceed as follows: first, I will point out an important ambiguity in Taylor's account of agency, having to do with whether that account is to be understood *normatively* or *descriptively*. I will argue that it is best understood as a normative thesis, describing the manner in which human beings deliberate practically *at their best*, when they are fully instantiating some potentiality latent within all humans. Understanding Taylor's arguments about 'strong evaluation' normatively has the important consequence of allowing for circumstances in which the development or the exercise of this capacity *can go wrong*, and conversely, of circumstances particularly appropriate for the development of the capacity.

Second, I will turn my attention to Taylor's critique of liberal political practice, in order to try to show that, at least as regards the issue of

---

[3] This is partly the result of other- as opposed to self-ascription. See Allen Buchanan, 'Assessing the communitarian critique of liberalism', *Ethics*, 99 (1989); and Stephen Mulhall and Adam Swift, *Liberals and communitarians* (Oxford: Basil Blackwell, 1992).

neutrality, it is mistaken both as regards the question of the *justification* of neutrality, and with respect to its implications for *political practice*.

Third, I will argue that any form of political organisation centred around a conception of the common good not ultimately reducible to the affirmation of the social conditions required for the pursuit of a diversity of less encompassing forms of good is going to be less likely to ensure the social conditions required for the development of strong evaluators than liberal political institutions.

I

Taylor's theory of human agency, spelled out in a number of earlier papers as well as in the first section of *Sources of the self*[4] revolves around the notion of 'strong evaluation'. A strong evaluator is an agent capable of second-order reflection upon her desires, whose practical deliberation is guided by 'a language of evaluative distinctions' identifying certain types of actions as base, noble, courageous, etc., rather than simply by calculations of the probable outcomes associated with the pursuit of given desires. A person whose deliberations were premissed solely on such cost/benefit considerations would according to Taylor be a 'simple weigher'.[5] The concepts in the terms of which we evaluate strongly are moreover not given to us through sheer individual fiat; rather, they stem from the traditions and latent understandings of our human communities (hence their necessary embeddedness in linguistic forms), and are perceived by us as 'articulations' of the intrinsic goodness of those things external to us toward which our desires and feelings implicitly direct us.[6] Such articulations can be more or less perspicuous, and an important part of human reflection according to Taylor consists in refining these articulations, so as to bring them closer to the goods they seek to express. This kind of reflection exerts an influence upon our desires, helping to shape and direct them, so that our articulations become at least partly constitutive of these affective states. The goods we recognise in this manner are plural, and yet Taylor argues that their pursuit is unified and rendered coherent by our acknowledgment of an architectonic 'hypergood', a source of ultimate value such as freedom, benevolence, obedience to God, and the like, which shapes and constrains our pursuit of less ultimate goods.[7]

---

[4] I take the most important to be 'What is human agency?', 'Self-interpreting animals' and 'The concept of a person', all in *Philosophical papers*, I; the relevant chapters (1–4) of *Sources of the self*.

[5] These distinctions are originally introduced in 'What is human agency?'

[6] For the notion of an articulation, see 'Self-interpreting animals', pp. 63ff.

[7] The notion of a 'hypergood' is introduced and discussed by Taylor in *Sources of the self*, pp. 62–75.

Taylor's account of 'strong evaluation', traced across the various writings mentioned above, provides us with a subtle and compelling phenomenology of agency.[8] One of the most striking claims Taylor makes about his account is that it partly defines our concept of human agency and of personhood, in that we would not recognise as fully human a being who did not engage in the kind of evaluation described above. A person for Taylor just *is* a being who cannot but deliberate practically within evaluative frameworks, and for whom such frameworks function, as Taylor puts it in *Sources of the self*, as 'transcendental conditions'.[9]

There is, however, an air of implausibility about this claim. Surely Taylor does not want to maintain that it is a necessary condition of one's being a person that one be self-consciously engaged in the process of searching for increasingly perspicuous articulations of the goods to which one's feelings and desires are a response. Is Taylor here offering an objective, minimal condition of personhood, analogous to Locke's characterisation of a person as 'a thinking intelligent being, that has reason and reflection, and can consider itself as itself, the same thing, in different times and places', determined 'only by identity of consciousness', or to Strawson's 'primitive' concept of a person as 'a type of entity such that *both* predicates ascribing states of consciousness *and* predicates ascribing corporeal characteristics ... are equally applicable to a single individual of that single type'?[10] This seems to raise the entry conditions for personhood to an impossibly high level, since it is not at all clear that people generally engage in the fairly sophisticated exercise in reflexive self-understanding and self-constitution which strong evaluation involves. Perhaps Taylor wants to say that it is a condition of *moral* agency that an individual be engaged in such a process?[11] Even here, though, I would suggest that this is a counterintuitively strong requirement for moral agency: we do not withhold our normal 'reactive attitudes' from others simply because they do not have an articulation of the background values which guide them in their actions; our notion of moral responsibility does not normally require that its ascription be conditional upon individuals being responsible not only for their actions, but also

---

[8] For a critique of this account, and particularly of its articulacy requirement, see Owen Flanagan, 'Identity and strong and weak evaluation', *Identity, character and morality: essays in moral psychology*, ed. Owen Flanagan and Amélie O. Rorty, (Cambridge, Mass.: MIT Press, 1990).

[9] *Sources of the self*, p. 32. The strong claim is made in various places including ibid., p. 27, and 'What is human agency?', p. 33.

[10] John Locke, *An essay concerning human understanding*, ed. P. H. Nidditch (Oxford: Clarendon Press, 1975), chapter 27; and P. F. Strawson, *Individuals: an essay in descriptive metaphysics* (London: Methuen, 1959), p. 102.

[11] 'Moral agency ... requires some kind of reflexive awareness of the standards one is living by (or failing to live by)'. See 'The concept of a person', p. 103.

for the moral frameworks which are somehow at the basis of their actions.[12] Even simple weighers, it seems, can be held responsible for their actions.

A more plausible position than this can be constructed on the basis of some of Taylor's perhaps more cautious statements on the centrality of strong evaluation to our conception of the person. In various places, Taylor claims that it is the *capacity* for strong evaluation which marks persons off from other types of living creatures.[13] Persons would on this view be characterised as having a latent potential for the type of reflection which strong evaluation involves, but one that can be more or less developed. Saying that it is a necessary condition for personhood that the being to whom it is ascribed evaluate strongly would therefore not be a flatly descriptive claim, as is the case with Locke's self-conscious intelligent being or Strawson's bearer of physical and of mental predicates, but rather a claim to the effect that the being in question has to a significant degree developed a certain potentiality which it has to the extent that it is human. This would mean that there could be *failure* to develop the traits characterised with strong evaluation while remaining in the sphere of the recognisably human in a manner which would not be possible with Locke's or Strawson's characterisations. And most importantly for my present purposes, we might also be able to specify conditions which would make it more or less likely that the traits associated with strong evaluation develop more or less fully.

Taylor's writings on human agency seem to allow for a number of ways in which human beings might fail to develop their capacity for strong evaluation. I want for the purposes of this paper to highlight two.

First, a person might fail to realise that the terms in which she deliberates practically situate her in a framework of qualitative contrasts. Though her actions would clearly seem to situate her within such a framework, she might lack the self-consciousness required to become aware of the fact that they refer back to a horizon of values, rather than simply being 'value-neutral' manifestations of her basic capacity for rational agency. Taylor takes the utilitarian and Kantian strains in the Western moral traditions as instances of theories – and of associated moral outlooks – which, in the attempt to *abstract* from the epistemologically unseemly business of articulations of goods, actually end up remaining uncritically in the grip of a particular value or set of values (the aspiration to human freedom in the case of the Kantian, the values

---

[12] I take the notion of a 'reactive attitude' from P. F. Strawson, 'Freedom and resentment', *Proceedings of the British Academy*, 68 (1962).

[13] 'What is human agency?', p. 28; and 'The concept of a person', p. 103.

associated with the 'affirmation of ordinary life' in the case of the utilitarian), which must be appealed to in order to make sense of the types of deliberative procedures they recommend. To put it tersely, strong evaluation for such persons is *an sich* and not yet *für sich*.[14] The problem for such unreflective agents is the following: since fully realised strong evaluation involved undertaking the articulation and refinement of a conception of the good, they will necessarily remain at a fairly primitive stage of development, since such an undertaking requires that they gain awareness of themselves as standing within a framework of values.

Second, a person might, unlike the wholly unreflective agent described in the previous paragraph, be alive to the importance of strong evaluation, and yet be carrying out her practical deliberation by means of a framework of values that does not constitute a perspicuous articulation of the goods toward which her feelings draw her. Taylor's view is that people in this situation can be brought round to more satisfactory accounts of the goods they recognise through a process of reasoning in transitions, which consists in a series of 'error-reducing' moves from one articulation to another.[15] Yet such reasoning might be unavailable to agents not because of any lack of awareness of the importance of strong evaluation, but rather because of an insufficient awareness of *alternative* conceptions of the good which might serve as more fully adequate articulations.

This analysis of the multi-tiered structure of Taylor's account of human agency permits us to appreciate that it is only the *capacity* for strong evaluation that can plausibly be taken to constitute a necessary condition of personhood. It must therefore also allow for an account of the conditions under which the full fruition of these capacities is more or less likely to occur.

My principal claim is that in the context of modern societies marked by a vast array of coexisting conceptions of the good and of quite different cultural forms, the political conditions required for the development of the capacities involved in strong evaluation are best secured under liberal institutions which prescind from promoting any particular conception of the good or cultural form. Now in his writings in political philosophy, Taylor has been critical of liberal political philosophy, particularly of its neutralist pretensions. My task in the following section will therefore be to defuse Taylor's principal objections to liberal political practice, before turning in the final section to a consideration of the grounds for my principal claim.

[14] This alleged systematic self-deception on the part of utilitarians and Kantians is explored by Taylor in *Sources of the self*, pp. 77–90.
[15] Taylor, 'Explanation and practical reason'; see also *Sources of the self*, p. 72.

II

Taylor's critique of liberal political philosophy can conveniently be divided into two general categories. First, in a series of influential essays, Taylor has questioned the self-understanding that liberal political philosophers have manifested regarding the central values of the liberal political edifice. Whereas they tend to view such notions as autonomy, freedom, equality and the like as somehow foundational, or as deliverances of pure reason, Taylor shows that the importance they have within liberal political philosophy can only be accounted for given a logically prior commitment to certain human capacities and to the social forms required to foster and sustain them. He adduces a number of transcendental arguments to show that it is only on the assumption that we positively value the development of certain human traits that we can explain the value we place upon providing the individual with moral and political rights, or with a fair share of certain economic goods. Thus liberal values such as rights and fairness are shown to have a derivative, as opposed to a foundational, status.[16]

Second, some of Taylor's writings target liberal practices. His objections at this level are directed principally at liberal political philosophy's claim that government ought to remain neutral among the coexisting cultural and moral forms of life within its midst. He fears that this construal of government's role cannot accommodate certain political claims which citizens concerned to advance a common good might legitimately want to make, and that it might actually end up being practically unviable, since citizens viewing one another solely as rights-bearers might end up being unable to generate the commonality of purpose required to sustain free institutions. In this section, I will principally be concerned with this range of arguments.

Taylor's arguments against liberalism are often difficult to assess because they tend to be addressed not at particular liberal thinkers but rather at liberalism as a general civilisation trend.[17] Thus, what might constitute a decisive argument, say, against the rights-foundationalism of a Robert Nozick will be importantly wide of the mark in assessing the more holistically based liberalism of John Rawls. And attacks on liberal contractualism will bear on the arguments of liberal thinkers such as

---

[16] This strategy is deployed by Taylor to account for the value of (respectively) autonomy, liberty and theories of distributive justice in 'Atomism', 'What's wrong with negative liberty?' and 'The nature and scope of distributive justice', all reprinted in *Philosophical papers*, II.

[17] The point has been made most recently by Mulhall and Swift, *Liberals and communitarians*, p. 101.

Locke, Kant or Rawls but will be irrelevant for the work of liberal philosophers like Ronald Dworkin and Bruce Ackerman, who explicitly disavow appeals to contractarian devices. Despite the broad manner in which Taylor has chosen to define his liberal target, however, my remarks in this section will take their cue from the writings of John Rawls. Although his writings are contested even within the liberal tradition, this choice seems justified in the present context by the fact that, as opposed to other liberal writers such as Raz, Galston and Macedo, he places considerable emphasis on that aspect of liberal practice which Taylor is most concerned to rebut, namely the requirement of liberal neutrality.[18]

It seems clear that the first range of criticisms addressed by Taylor to liberal theories is importantly wide of the mark as far as Rawlsian liberalism is concerned. Political principles for Rawls are justified by reference to an ideal of the person, which in turn is required to make sense of some of our strongest moral 'considered convictions', as well as of the main tenets of the political cultures of constitutional democracies.[19] Neither the principles of justice, nor the set up of the original position, nor again the 'primary goods' which are at the centre of the deliberations of the agents in the original position, have the kind of foundational status which would make them fall afoul of Taylor's strictures against 'liberal' modes of justification. In Rawls' work, whether 'early' or 'late', political principles are not to be understood independently of the commitment to the fostering of certain human capacities (a 'sense of justice' and a capacity to conceive, to revise, and to carry out one's own conception of the good life), the development of which is taken to be best ensured under political institutions governed by Rawls' famed two principles of justice. Taylor might want to argue with Rawls about the nature of the valued human capacities we find latent in our considered convictions and in our public political culture, but he cannot argue that Rawls justifies his preferred political principles without any awareness of the human goods which they subserve.

The second aspect of Taylor's critique of liberalism seems more damaging to Rawlsian liberalism. The core of his concerns about liberal practice have to do with the issue of neutrality, the claim made by a number of liberal political philosophers, including John Rawls, that government institutions ought to remain scrupulously neutral among the conceptions of the good and cultural forms of life in the midst of which they exist.

---

[18] I thank Brian Walker for having pressed me to provide justification for this limitation of my discussion.

[19] The centrality of ideals of the person for Rawls' conception of moral and political justification has been well highlighted in Samuel Scheffler, 'Moral scepticism and ideals of the person', *The Monist*, 62 (1979).

According to Taylor, political neutrality is a morally unattractive goal, because it prevents citizens from pursuing certain legitimate collective goods through their political institutions; and it might even render liberalism practically self-defeating, by placing moral obstacles in the path of a community's enacting measures to oppose practices and ways of life which strike at the very foundations of its traditions and institutions. Let me first in this connection consider a species of the moral argument put forward by Taylor in response to recent work by Will Kymlicka.

In an important recent book, Kymlicka has argued that the kind of mainstream liberal philosophy exemplified by the work of Ronald Dworkin and John Rawls is capable of accommodating the type of collective cultural rights claims on behalf of which a number of communitarian writers had attacked liberalism. In his view, individuals can only avail themselves of the capacities of choice and self-direction which liberal philosophers emphasise if they are members of viable cultures which provide them with a range of options upon which to exercise these capacities. Cultural membership is therefore, according to Kymlicka, a primary good just as vital as more traditional ones such as individual freedom and material well-being. Liberal political philosophy can thus accommodate certain types of collective rights claims, as long as these are justified with reference to the individual's need for a viable cultural environment within which to develop his individual capacities.[20]

Taylor's reply to this argument has been to claim that, while Kymlicka's argument might very well do for '*existing* people who find themselves trapped within a culture under pressure, and can flourish within it, or not at all', it does nothing to 'justify measures designed to ensure survival through indefinite future generations'.[21] His concern is that though this liberal derivation of collective rights might ensure the continued existence of a cultural structure of which individuals can, if they choose, avail themselves, it does not ensure the survival of a community which *will* choose to identify itself with the culture in question.

Now from the perspective of Rawls' theory of justice, the distinction between the interests of presently existing people and those of future generations is untenable. If, as Kymlicka has urged, cultural belonging is to be viewed as a 'primary good', its fair distribution according to Rawls is not restricted to already existing people. Rather, the principle according to which it is to be secured must be determined within the original position, that is, from a point of view where 'the parties do not know to

---

[20] Will Kymlicka, *Liberalism, community and culture* (Oxford: Clarendon Press, 1989), chapter 8.
[21] Taylor, 'The politics of recognition', Taylor et al., *Multiculturalism and 'the politics of recognition'*, pp. 40–1 fn. See also Taylor, 'Shared and divergent values', p. 61.

which generation they belong or, what comes to the same thing, the stage of civilisation of their society'; they cannot therefore settle on a principle which would handle the cultural claims of different generations un-equally. Although Rawls' consideration of the problem of intergeneratio-nal justice is mostly concerned with determining a just rate of social saving, it is clear he intends his reflections to have a more general scope, imposing upon each generation the responsibility to 'preserve the gains of culture and civilisation'. For Rawls, cultural 'primary goods' cannot be secured fairly by the basic institutions of society for 'already existing people' without provision being made for future persons to enjoy the same levels of security.[22]

But perhaps the core of Taylor's 'future generations' concern lies elsewhere. The justification for collective rights claims envisioned by liberal theory makes reference to the need individuals have for a stable cultural structure outside of which the exercise of the individual's capacity for choice would be inconceivable. But, as has been pointed out by Allen Buchanan, this justification cannot give solace to people con-cerned to ensure the survival of *this particular cultural community*. It requires that there be cultural structures at the disposal of individuals, but remains silent on the question of which cultures must thus be protected and promoted.[23] For all that liberal theory would seem to require, there is nothing wrong with the disappearance of minority cultures, so long as the culture of the surviving majority is capable of integrating the members of these minorities. It does not seem to matter to Rawlsian liberals which *particular* culture provides individuals with the cultural primary goods required for the meaningful exercise of their capacity for choice, so long as the cultural conditions for the exercise of that capacity are, in some way or other, provided for. This reformulation of Taylor's objection main-tains the essence of his concern that liberalism is unable to countenance the 'love of the particular' required to account for the true patriot's relation to her community, without invoking the dubious distinction between political measures designed to secure cultural protection for 'already existing people' and those aimed at future generations.

I believe that Rawlsian liberalism allows us to give expression to this kind of 'love of the particular'. Perhaps the most important primary good, Rawls tells us, is that of 'self-respect', which includes 'a person's sense of his own value, his secure conviction that his conception of his good, his plan of life, is worth carrying out'.[24] The social bases of such self-respect

22 John Rawls, *A theory of justice* (Cambridge, Mass.: Belknap Press, 1971), pp. 284–93.
23 Allen Buchanan, *Secession: the morality of political divorce from Fort Sumter to Lithuania and Québec* (Boulder, Col.: Westview Press, 1991), p. 55.
24 Rawls, *Theory of justice*, p. 440.

can, according to Rawls, only be secured when others recognise the value of our activities and goals, when there is some associative framework within which individuals can acquire a certain level of confidence in the worth of their pursuits.

Now in *A theory of justice*, Rawls implies that the political framework provided by the basic structure of society governed by his two principles of justice suffices to achieve this purpose. This is because in that work, Rawls conceived of individuals' conceptions of the good in an overly individualistic manner, without giving any weight to the important role which one's membership in a particular community might come to play in one's overall conception of what a good life would look like. That one views one's social relations to others through the prism of the principle of equal liberty and the difference principle provides individuals with as much social recognition as Rawls once believed they needed.

The major change in Rawls' work since the mid-1980s has been his greater appreciation of the importance of citizens' embeddedness in particular communities differing greatly from one another in their moral and cultural orientations.[25] The impact of these changes upon Rawls' work has been abundantly canvassed by others. One change that has not been adequately addressed, however, either by Rawls or by his commentators, is the modification which this new appreciation imposes upon the specification of the social basis of self-respect. Given that people's conceptions of their good are now seen by Rawls as inextricably intertwined with their identification with distinct communities, he must accept that the social basis of self-respect is violated in cases where the potential disappearance of one's cultural community is met with indifference by one's fellow citizens, or with the claim that there is nothing of moral importance that one can draw from one's own culture that cannot also be drawn from the cultures with a higher chance of survival.

It is important to note, however, that the kind of justification which Rawlsian liberalism is capable of providing for political measures aimed at protecting particular cultures cannot be used to protect a cultural community *at the expense* of other such communities. If self-respect is a primary good, then the social conditions which underpin it must be distributed fairly. A political community which affirmed the protection and promotion of one particular sub-community's culture as being of special importance would not be ensuring the social bases of self-respect for members of other cultures within the broader community, unless grounds of a particular kind could be adduced for this prioritisation,

[25] Rawls is most candid about this change in the conception of political community underlying his work in the introduction to his recent *Political liberalism* (New York: Columbia University Press, 1993), pp. xvi–xviii.

among which, as I have argued elsewhere, would figure the greater risk faced by that cultural community of disappearing, combined with a plausible claim to the effect that the granting of the social bases of self-respect to the members of other communities would increase these risks.[26]

Rawlsian liberalism can therefore go a very long way in accommodating one of Taylor's principal concerns with liberal neutralism. Not only can it recognise a stable cultural structure as a primary good for members of this and of all subsequent generations, it can also, in virtue of the central primary good of self-respect, accommodate citizens' 'love of the particular', which gets expressed in the claim that the goods which accrue to them through their membership in a cultural form of life should be derived from their participation in *this particular* cultural community rather than in the cultural form that has the best chance of survival. The only constraint is that this claim be given political weight regardless of the cultural community from which it emanates. In a culturally diverse society, this constraint will require that government not actively promote any one culture, but rather that it provide its citizens with the means with which to pursue their lives as communal beings, whatever the culture their community embodies happens to be. While Rawlsian liberalism need not be neutral about human beings' nature as cultural beings, it must in conditions of cultural plurality remain neutral between the various cultures which coexist in a given society, lest it undercut the capacity of some to fully exercise their capacities as cultural beings.

The second objection Taylor voices against liberal neutrality has to do with its viability. In 'Cross-purposes', he argues that a neutral regime is mired in a form of pragmatic self-contradiction, since it cannot without violating its own neutralist strictures enact political measures designed to resist individuals or groups whose ways of life constitute an assault upon the very foundations of the community's life. A viable polity must, according to Taylor, make room for 'patriotism', which involves 'a common allegiance to a particular historical community' and a 'socially endorsed common end' of 'sustaining this specific historical set of institutions and forms'.[27] If it is not to fall foul of the neutrality requirement, however, the proceduralist liberal regime must treat the conflict between 'patriots and antipatriots' in the same neutral manner as it would a struggle between, for example, 'people with homo- and heterosexual orientations'. And, according to Taylor, this sets up the conditions for the liberal state's court of law 'undermining the very regime it was established

[26] See my 'Libéralisme, nationalisme et pluralité culturelle', *Philosophiques*, 19 (1992), p. 141.
[27] Taylor, 'Cross-purposes: the liberal–communitarian debate', p. 176.

to interpret' by giving satisfaction to an anti-patriotic challenge (e.g. to having certain historical figures treated as heroes in the schools).[28]

Two interpretations of this concern are permitted by the language of Taylor's text. The first has to do with patriotism construed as an allegiance to a 'particular historical community' (e.g. the Americans, the Québécois, the French, etc.). With respect to this first interpretation, it is certainly true that liberal neutrality *can* countenance attacks upon an historical community's self-conception embedded in a particular understanding of its own history and traditions. But this, I would argue, is a good thing, both from the point of view of political morality and from the point of view of the health of the polity. For the questioning of a political community's own self-conception is a normal component of the community's development, and can only be labelled 'unpatriotic' from the standpoint of a group which has an interest in artificially 'freezing' one particular moment of a community's evolving self-conception. A community's imagination of its own history and its understanding of its supposedly immutable traditions is in fact both fluid and constrained by contemporary concerns.[29] Furthermore, different sub-groups within the broader *political* community frequently possess different historical understandings, often expressive of profound conflicts between themselves and the larger community, of the very nature of the political community's identity and self-conception. Collective memory is always thoroughly embedded in the present; it is highly fluid and thoroughly political. To claim that a particular community's historical conception of itself stands beyond politics, and should therefore be immune from contestation, is to employ political means to enshrine a specific self-conception, and to render it immune from the normal process of challenge and redefinition. It would be invidious for the state to enshrine particular mythologised self-understandings in the context of on-going political contestation and the evolution of values which characterise the healthy society. Rather the state should defend standards of evidence and free enquiry so that the members of different sub-groups can participate in a spirit of openness and mutual toleration in the on-going process of defining and redefining the community's identity. Far from being unpatriotic, the challenges which are currently being made to the status of certain historical figures in North American history constitute contributions to the on-going *moral* debate as to what is to count for us as patriotism.[30]

[28] Ibid., pp. 176–7.
[29] Eric Hobsbawm, 'Introduction: inventing traditions', ed. Terence Ranger and Eric Hobsbawm, *The invention of tradition* (Cambridge: Cambridge University Press, 1983), pp. 1–14.
[30] On social criticism internal to the traditions of a community, see Michael Walzer, *Interpretation and social criticism* (Cambridge, Mass.: Harvard University Press, 1987).

Another interpretation of the 'patriotism' concern is perhaps permitted by Taylor's text, especially by his equation of patriotism with an allegiance to 'this specific historical set of institutions'. One might read him as implying that liberal regimes are paradoxically constrained on their own first principles to be neutral about themselves, that is, to lack the moral resources to legislate against conceptions of the good within their midsts which strike at the very foundations of liberal *institutions*. In other words, Taylor might be taken to be reformulating Robert Frost's oft-quoted quip that the liberal is the person who cannot take his own side in an argument.

This objection is premised upon what I take to be a mistaken view of the justification of liberal neutrality. Briefly stated, I would argue that it takes the fact that neutrality at the level of political *practice* requires of governments that they not privilege certain conceptions of the good to the detriment of others as sufficient warrant to assume that its *justification* is similarly premised upon this type of principled avoidance with respect to issues of the good life. This, I would argue, is not the case: the most convincing justifications of political neutrality are based not upon the claim that neutrality is valuable in itself, nor upon any kind of scepticism with regard to the good, but rather upon the conviction that, especially in contexts of moral, cultural and political diversity, individuals will best be able to pursue their own conceptions of the good when government abstains from the explicit endorsement of any one such conception. This practice of abstinence is premised upon the idea that in contexts of diversity, the good life is best abetted by government when it provides people with 'all-purpose means' (such as Rawlsian primary goods) to pursue their particular conceptions of the good, whatever those conceptions happen to be, rather than on the idea that liberal institutions are both practically and epistemologically geared against questions of the good.

An appreciation of this line of justification of liberal neutrality leads to the recognition that practices of liberal neutrality have bounds. The justification of neutrality is, broadly, consequentialist: it is good that government abstain from doing anything more than providing its citizens with all-purpose primary goods, because this will allow individuals to pursue their own conceptions in a climate of toleration and mutual respect. There are therefore also consequentialist grounds for the *limits* of liberal neutrality: a liberal régime need not (and I would suggest more strongly, must not) countenance conceptions of the good which recommend actions the intent of which is to destroy the institutions within the context of which alone the pursuit of diverse conceptions of the good is possible. If the justification of political institutions derives in part from the desirability of the states of affairs they give rise to, then these institutions cannot be justified in acting (or refraining from acting), when such action or inaction detracts from the pursuit of the aimed-at goods. This is especially the case when this involves attacks upon the integrity of the framework of institutions within which the untrammelled pursuit by individuals and groups of the good life is made possible. Although I cannot do the exegetical spadework required to substantiate this claim here, I believe that Rawlsian liberalism fits this model, both at the level of justification and at that of practice. Briefly, Rawls believes neutrality to be justified by reference to the capacity it affords individuals and groups to pursue their conceptions of the good, and it is restricted to what he calls 'permissible comprehensive conceptions of the good', that is, conceptions of the good which are compatible with liberal-democratic institutions.[31]

I have argued in this section that some of Taylor's main attacks upon liberal political philosophy fail, either because the concerns they voice can be incorporated into the body of liberal theory, at least as it is represented in the work of John Rawls, or because they are not worth pursuing, especially in the context of a heterogeneous society comprising a plethora of cultural forms and moral and political conceptions. This has not been an exhaustive survey of Taylor's arguments; in particular, I have had to set aside a discussion of his arguments against liberalism on behalf of a republican conception of participatory self-rule, conceived of as a necessary bulwark against the atomisation and excessive litigiousness of liberal citizens who think of themselves exclusively as rights-bearers. I believe that here again, Taylor's arguments do not have the desired force. First, the functioning of institutions allowing a radically diverse ensemble of groups to pursue their conceptions of the good in an atmosphere of toleration and trust can come to be perceived by citizens of a liberal régime as a good in itself. This may come about even when the working of these institutions is not the primary focus of citizens' political activities, and when they are more actively involved in the associations of civil society where activities may be more in tune with the various aspects of their complex identities than the state could ever be.[32] Second, it seems clear that individual rights are not incompatible with community virtues; rights can remain uninvoked in the context of well-functioning associations, but become crucially important when such associations begin imposing unacceptable sacrifices and injustices upon some.[33]

---

[31] On the limits to conceptions of the good within a neutralist framework, see John Rawls, 'The basic liberties and their priority', *The Tanner Lectures on human values*, III, ed. S. M. McMurrin (Salt Lake City, University of Utah Press, 1982).

[32] I take this to be the governing idea behind Rawls' idea of a 'social union of social unions'. See *Theory of justice*, especially p. 527.

[33] The point is made by John Tomasi, 'Individual rights and community virtues', *Ethics*, 101 (1991).

I want now to return to the theme of the first section, to show that especially in such social circumstances, the social conditions required for the full development of the capacities involved in strong evaluation are best secured under liberal institutions.

III

In the first section of this paper, I identified two ways in which a person could fail to develop the deliberative capacities which Taylor identifies with strong evaluation. I now want to suggest that a Rawlsian liberal polity would be *better* suited to providing the social conditions required for the fostering of these capacities than would a communitarian polity organised around the pursuit of a more particularistic common good.

Let me consider the first potential source of failure to develop one's capacities for strong evaluation. It arises when an individual is insufficiently self-aware to realise that he stands within a moral framework, that her practical judgements always presuppose a range of evaluative distinctions identifying the worthy from the unworthy, the noble from the base. She uses the vocabulary at hand unreflectively, and is as such debarred from realising her capacity for strong evaluation.

My claim is that individuals are less likely to remain in this unself-conscious and therefore unself-critical state when they live among people whose judgements and feelings are the manifestations of quite different conceptions of the good. We are more likely to fail to realise that the terms and concepts which we employ in our practical lives are manifestations of a particular overall conception of the good life if we are surrounded exclusively by like-minded people; in these conditions, it is easier not to reflect upon the particular moral framework within which we lead our practical lives, and to think that 'the way we do things 'round here' is simply *the* way things are done. It is when we are confronted with quite radically different forms of life that we are moved to reflect upon the underlying sets ,of concerns which account for our judgements, actions and beliefs. This is partly for the Hegelian reason that full self-consciousness requires recognition by others, that I can only become an object of concern for myself once I have become one for others;[34] and partly for the Foucaldian reason that contact with radical otherness has the effect of problematising our own practices, revealing their dependence upon contingent moral frameworks which, far from being inscribed in the very order of things, come to be seen as fallible, limited, allowing of further

[34] G. W. F. Hegel, *The phenomenology of Spirit*, trans. A. V. Miller (Oxford: Oxford University Press, 1977), p. 111 (par. 178).

refinement. Both the questioning gaze which others will cast upon me and the appreciation I gain of the difference of others will have the effect of heightening my own self-consciousness, my awareness and problematisation of those understandings and moral presuppositions which lie at the basis of my judgements and actions.

Thus, I have argued, the self-consciousness which is a necessary first step on the road toward the full development of strong evaluation is most likely to occur in conditions of moral and cultural plurality. This does not in and of itself entail any political conclusions. Only a short step, however, is required to generate such conclusions. Indeed, the effects upon my own self-consciousness of contact with others will only occur if I respect them, if I view them as equals. I will not be shocked out of the complacency which consists in not realising that my own judgements are the expression of a quite contingent and limited set of moral assumptions if I view my neighbour's actions and behaviour with disdain and contempt, or if I am made to think that there is a good reason for my way of life to be granted priority. The tragic irony of the master's situation, as poignantly brought out by Hegel, is that the recognition he secures from the vanquished slave cannot be the occasion for his coming to full self-awareness, because this recognition is not that of an 'independent consciousness', but rather that of a being conceived as inferior.[35]

My claim is that a society which does not through its institutions of government privilege a particular form of life, but rather recognises the equal importance of all permissible 'conceptions of the good' and promotes its citizens' capacity to pursue them, is most likely to avoid the master's sorry situation, and to secure for its citizenry the social bases of full moral self-consciousness. In a society in which our institutions and principles of justice manifest respect for the capacity of individuals to pursue conceptions of the good, but do not place a premium on one conception to the detriment of others, we will be more likely to develop the reflexivity with respect to our own background moral frameworks which is required to begin down the path of strong evaluation than we would be in a community which affirmed a substantive common good.

Now Rawls' theory of justice is structured so as to achieve precisely this aim: the hypothetical situation of choice which generates its principles of justice mirrors a political ideal of the citizen he finds latent in the political cultura of Western democracies. It centres on an idea of the citizen defined in part by her teleological orientation toward seeing her particular activities and pursuits within the overarching logic of a conception of the good or 'plan of life', and in part by her willingness to carry out her plan

---

[35] Hegel, *Phenomenology of Spirit*, pp. 116–17 (par. 192).

of life within a fair structure that does not privilege or denigrate any other particular conceptions. It thus seeks to give rise to a society in which citizens identify strongly with a conception of the good, but also have a full moral appreciation of the equal status of other such conceptions. Such a society would, I claim, be best suited to instilling in moral agents the kind of moral self-awareness which would be required for strong evaluation.

The second manner in which an agent might fail fully to actualise her capacity for strong evaluation is by being locked into an articulation which is only an imperfect approximation of her good, of the overall conception of the good toward which her more specific pursuits seem to point. A strong evaluator is someone who is constantly engaging in the dialectical process of refinement of her conception of the good as a function of her increasingly perspicuous understanding of her reactions and feelings, and whose reactions and feelings alter as a result of the modifications made at the level of her articulations. The question arises, how do such refinements and alterations come about?

In a recent paper,[36] Taylor suggests a model of practical deliberation which he believes provides the best account of the transitions which might take us from one articulation of the good to another. According to this *ad hominem* model, modifications in one's moral framework are effected by error-reducing moves whereby, taking one's bearings within one's present moral position, one comes to see another position as necessitated given a premiss one already accepts, as giving rise to the dissipation of confusions and contradictions within one's present position, or as affording a more satisfying characterisation of a predicament one is facing. The model is contrasted to the foundational, 'apodeictic' view of reasoning inherited from the Enlightenment epistemological tradition, according to which argument must proceed from the ground up, as a function of ultimate, indubitable criteria. Justifying one's moral position thus consists, on this view, in showing how it flows from these criteria, the criteria themselves being independent of the position being defended; showing an opponent's position to be wrong similarly means showing its incompatibility with these independent criteria. The central contrast is between a conception of reasoning in terms of absolute criteria, and a conception which eschews any thought of such independent criteria, but which still maintains that the transition from one conception to another can be rationally warranted.

How may certain types of social arrangements be more likely than others to foster our capacity to engage in this type of deliberation? In

---

[36] Taylor, 'Explanation and practical reason'; see also *Sources of the self*, p. 72.

general, I would say that, at a minimum, a society committed to the promotion of this aspect of strong evaluation would have to abstain as much as possible from imposing psychological or material costs upon citizens for modifying their conceptions of the good, as well as the activities and forms of life which are associated with them, when deliberation seems to indicate that such a modification is required. It should be the force of the better argument, rather than extrinsic social or psychological factors, which determines whether such a transformation is decided upon by an individual. More positively, a society devoted to strong evaluation on the part of its citizens would provide them with both material and institutional means to exercise their ability to revise and re-articulate their conceptions of the good.

Political communities organised around the pursuit of a substantive common good run the risk of falling short of the minimal, negative requirement set out above. Governments that set out to privilege a particular culture, or religion, or ensemble of career paths through the workings of their institutions do so by attaching psychic or material costs, or by imposing legal obstacles, upon those whose deliberations have led them away from the particular common good in question, when they do not simply make use of their monopoly of force. One might plausibly argue that these disincentives make it unlikely that many people will choose to engage in the – potentially quite costly – exercise of revision and re-evaluation which is one of the marks of strong evaluation.

A liberal régime which shows its commitment to strong evaluation through the provision of the means – material and institutional – with which to foster its citizens' potential as teleologically oriented beings fares much better both with respect to the minimal to the more positive social conditions listed above. As far as the negative conditions are concerned, its abstention from the promotion of any particular permissible conception of the good means that it is likely that there will at any given time be within the society a plurality of such conceptions sharing a public space. Now Taylor makes it clear that the type of practical deliberation which will give rise to our being able to come up with better overall accounts of our good is paradigmatically dialogical. A society in which a variety of conceptions of the good existed, and in which people viewed each other, despite their differences, with respect, would be one in which the type of exchanges required to fuel our capacity for re-evaluation and re-articulation of the good would be much more likely to occur than in a society in which the workings of political institutions themselves privilege a particular conception of the good.

As regards the positive condition, that society provide people with the social bases for the exercise of this capacity, I believe that Rawlsian liberalism once again has much to offer. Remember that in *A theory of justice*, the hypothetical situation of choice from which principles of justice emanate is designed so as to reflect the two human powers which, according to Rawls, we deem most importantly relevant for a theory of justice. These are 'the capacity for an effective sense of justice' and 'the capacity to form, to revise, and rationally to pursue a conception of the good'.[37] Generally speaking, one might say that the constraints imposed upon the participants through the 'veil of ignorance' are meant to represent the former capacity, while the specification of the 'primary goods' is intended to reflect the latter.

Primary goods are conceived by Rawls as 'all-purpose means' with which individuals can pursue whatever specific conception of the good they choose, without prejudging the nature of the good that will be pursued. Rawls does impose some constraints upon what is to *count* as a conception of the good from the standpoint of the justification of principles of justice; more specifically, he proposes a specification of the nature of the practical deliberation which is to give rise to a rational conception of the good, and seeks to tailor his account of primary goods to fit this view of practical deliberation. The constraints upon deliberation are epistemic, so that ideally, a rational life-plan for a person would be 'the plan that would be decided upon as the outcome of careful reflection in which the agent reviewed, in the light of all the relevant facts, what it would be like to carry out these plans and thereby ascertained the course of action that would best realize his most fundamental desires'.[38] Given this epistemic constraint, it is important that we adopt a fallibilist attitude toward our conceptions of the good, that we view them as *revisable*.[39] Now political arrangements can contribute to the likelihood that we will adopt such an attitude toward our conceptions of the good by providing us with goods and resources which, while they encourage us to live our lives in function of *a* conception of the good, do not contribute to tying us down to one particular such conception, and set up conditions in which it is likely that we will reflect upon our conceptions critically and with our minds open to what other conceptions might have to offer. As Buchanan has shown, Rawlsian primary goods can be seen as fulfilling these conditions, since they include goods such as freedom of person and freedom from arbitrary arrest, which are '*conditions of the pursuit of ends in*

---

[37] The importance of a conception of the moral person for the specification of the original position is clearest in John Rawls, 'Kantian constructivism in moral theory', *The Journal of Philosophy*, 77 (1980), pp. 520, 525; see also *Theory of justice*, p. 505.

[38] Rawls, *Theory of justice*, p. 417.

[39] This point owes much to an important article by Allen Buchanan, 'Revisability and rational choice', *Canadian Journal of Philosophy*, 5 (1975).

general', wealth, educational opportunities, etc., which are 'best thought of as *maximally flexible assets*', and freedom of speech, thought, assembly and the like which are '*required for rationally formulating, criticizing, and revising one's life plan or conception of the good.*'[40] To this list we might want to add the social condition that there be available an adequate range of options upon which individuals can meaningfully exercise their capacity for choice (a condition which finds one expression in Kymlicka's argument for the importance of a stable cultural structure for the exercise of individual capacities).[41] In sum, to the extent that we want the principles which govern the workings of our political institutions to reflect the conception we have of ourselves as teleologically oriented beings, capable of forming, revising and rationally pursuing a conception of the good, and to the extent that we view the capacity to revise this conception (for example so that it coheres to a greater degree with our most fundamental desires) as central to the deliberative processes which give rise to these conceptions, a thin theory of the good such as that represented by Rawls' list of primary goods, and the principles he specifies to distribute these goods fairly, seem best qualified to serve as the social basis for the development of the requisite deliberative capacities. They have the twin virtues of not imposing psychic or material costs upon individuals for engaging in the revision of their conceptions of the good when rational considerations warrant such a revision (since the recognition by governmental institutions of primary goods as centrally important to individual well-being is not biased toward any specific conception), and of recognising that citizens none the less place great importance on their nature as teleologically oriented beings, beings who cannot but live in function of an overarching life-plan, by tailoring primary goods as a reflection of this central moral power.

The upshot of the foregoing discussion of Rawlsian primary goods for Taylor's views on strong evaluation is this: the capacity to refine one's moral framework, one's conception of the good, in the direction of increasingly perspicuous articulations of the goods toward which one's actions and reactions point is best promoted under social arrangements in which individuals are provided with a fair share of social means with which *to* pursue a conception of the good, but not with means which are particularly geared toward any *one* such conception. Again, therefore, a capacity which is central to the full development of strong evaluation would appear to be much better secured under liberal institutions which

[40] Ibid., pp. 402–3.
[41] For the importance of an adequate range of options as a condition of individual autonomy, see Joseph Raz, *The morality of freedom* (Oxford: Clarendon Press, 1986), pp. 373–7.

attempt to establish a fair framework within which individuals can pursue conceptions of the good than under communitarian institutions oriented toward the realisation of a common good.

An assumption of the foregoing discussion has been that Rawls and Taylor mean roughly the same thing when they speak, respectively, of 'conceptions of the good' or 'life-plans', and of 'moral frameworks'. On the face of it, this might seem a problematic assumption, since Taylor's notion seems to refer to a network of values whereas Rawls' would appear to pick out a range of activities. Although I can only assert this baldly here, I would claim that these are in fact complementary notions, in that we cannot really make sense of a framework of values without thinking of it alongside activities and practices involved in the pursuit of these values, nor can we think of an overarching life-plan which would be independent of any reflection on the question of what gives life worth, of the goods of which the life-plan seeks the attainment. Given this complementarity, conclusions applying to the social conditions required for the revision of Rawlsian life-plans are directly relevant to those which underpin the capacity for the refinement and re-articulation of Taylorian moral frameworks.

IV

I have argued in this essay that if we value the capacity which, according to Charles Taylor, marks us off as human, and if we accept, as I think we must, that basic social and political arrangements figure prominently among the various forces either promoting or inhibiting the various traits which make up the ideal strong evaluator, then we ought, especially in contexts of moral and cultural diversity, to support liberal political institutions which strive for neutrality among different conceptions of the good life. My argument has involved unpacking Taylor's notion of strong evaluation to show the various ways in which it might fail to develop strong evaluators, and to suggest that the social conditions required to ensure this development are best secured in the context of a Rawlsian liberal regime, rather than under the more communitarian or republican arrangements recommended by Taylor in his writings on political philosophy. Along the way, I have attempted to defuse a number of independent objections made by Taylor against liberal political philosophy, especially against its understanding and support of a requirement of political neutrality. In particular, I have wanted to indicate that liberal political need not be as averse to talk of the 'good life' as its Aristotelian and communitarian critics have claimed, and that in contexts of moral and political plurality, it might even be *more* suitable than their views to the development of a fully flourishing, teleologically oriented person. Unlike many of the other targets at which he has taken aim over the course of his philosophical career, liberal political philosophy need not be viewed as part of the general civilisational drift away from meaning and significance about which Charles Taylor has so justly warned us.

12 Philosophy and political judgement in a multinational federation

Guy Laforest

Charles Taylor has spent a good part of his adult life in a struggle to avoid the breakup of the Canadian federation. Much of his philosophical work can also be regarded as an attempt to understand and to interpret the sources of our malaise for others, in Canada and elsewhere. As a human being and as a philosopher, Taylor has himself benefited greatly from this effort. To borrow from his own appropriation of Hegelian concepts, his involvement – to be more specific, the numerous defeats that he has suffered – has worked like a series of enabling transitions leading to higher, more lucid stages of self-consciousness. From a state of better knowledge in Canadian affairs, Taylor has been able to move to a more refined understanding of our modern Western civilization. And vice versa.

Over the past thirty years, Charles Taylor has written at length on Canadian and Québec politics. This segment of his work, in itself, deserves an interpretive essay that would provide readers with the appropriate historical background.[1] As an introduction to this project, I shall sketch out here a critical analysis of the position adopted by Taylor in the latest chapter of our seemingly endless constitutional saga, from the demise of the Meech Lake Accord in 1990 to the referendum held on 26 October 1992, when Canadians were asked whether or not they were in favour of the unanimous agreement concerning constitutional reform reached by political leaders two months earlier in Charlottetown, the cradle of the Canadian federation. The referendum project, supported by Taylor, was defeated by a substantial majority of Canadians, and suffered the same fate at the hands of both Québec's citizens and the native peoples of the country.[2]

---

[1] Taylor's collected essays on Canadian politics are now available in English as *Reconciling the solitudes: essays on Canadian federalism and nationalism*. I believe they will become essential to those who will attempt a systematic analysis of his philosophical work.

[2] In Canada, the results were 54.4 per cent – 44.6 per cent in favour of the 'No'. In Québec, the 'No' won with a majority of 55.4 per cent – 42.4 per cent. The native population rejected a package that would have recognised their inherent right to self-government by voting 62 per cent against.

My hypothesis is that the variations and nuances in Taylor's political beliefs, in the last two years of our 'national unity' crisis, can best be understood when we take into account the 'therapeutical wisdom' best exemplified by the structure of Aristotle's *Politics*. Aristotle does not ignore Plato's fundamental question: what is the ideal state? Indeed, he devotes book VII of the *Politics* to a discussion of political ideals and educational principles. It seems to me, however, that the thrust of the *Politics* is elsewhere, in questions such as the following: what sort of constitution is desirable for what sort of civic body? (book IV), and how can we preserve the stability of imperfect regimes such as democracies and oligarchies? (book VI). Aristotle and Taylor never forget that philosophical and political deliberation are always constrained by the circumstances at hand in any particular society. For both of them, the words of Benjamin Barber ring quite true: politics is the world of the uncertain, the evanescent and the malleable.[3] In a recent essay, Taylor reiterated such a view:

Governing a contemporary society is continually recreating a balance between requirements that tend to undercut each other, constantly finding creative new solutions as the old equilibria become stultifying. There can never be in the nature of the case a definitive solution.[4]

Charles Taylor's philosophical project clearly amounts to more than simply a reformulation of Aristotelian prudence. As a keen reader of both Hegel and Herder, Taylor knows a great deal about the role of nationalism in the modern identity, and about the drive towards recognition which animates it. For the philosopher who is proud of his origins in Montréal, Québec, and who cherishes his citizenship in a moderately successful Canadian federation as well, the insights of German philosophy concerning the nature of nationalism clash with the realistic principles of Aristotelian therapeutics. Such is the tension that I wish to illustrate in this paper. To make my case, I must lift the curtain a little on some events in recent Canadian history.

I

In the early 1980s, Canadian political leaders made the most far-reaching structural changes to a federal system that had evolved gradually from the Burkean and imperial connotations of the British North America Act, becoming over time a moderately decentralised and smooth-working

---

[3] Benjamin Barber, *The conquest of politics* (Princeton: Princeton University Press, 1988), p. 208.
[4] Taylor, *The malaise of modernity*, p. 111.

regime. In the post-1945 period, our federal state had been facing two major challenges: the demands for more powers and symbolic recognition made by successive Québec governments on behalf of a rising nationalist movement in the province, and the increasing assertiveness of the four westernmost provinces, as they asked for a greater voice in central institutions and for enhanced regional control over natural resources. The constitutional reform of 1982 was the brain-child of Pierre Elliott Trudeau, prime minister of Canada almost without interruption from 1968 to 1984. Through this reform, Trudeau realised two of his dearest dreams: the repatriation in Canada of the control of the amending formula for our fundamental law, which had since 1867 remained in the hands of Westminster parliamentarians for lack of an agreement between the federal and provincial governments of our country; and, perhaps more importantly, the entrenchment in our constitution of a Charter of Rights and Freedoms which did much more than secure the legal and political rights of individual citizens. For Trudeau nurtured yet another dream: by granting a schedule of linguistic rights in a symmetrical fashion to English- and French-speaking individuals, no matter where they hailed from or where they lived in Canada, by recognising the nature of the country as a multicultural mosaic and by appealing to the non-territorial identities of citizens and groups alike, he sought to foster a greater and unmediated allegiance to Canada as a political community, over and above provincial and regional commitments.[5] Extremely influenced by the deep-seated anti-nationalism of Cold War liberal thinkers such as Elie Kedourie, Trudeau attempted in 1982 to crush once and for all the hydra of Québec nationalism that he had despised since the days of his youth. (It is interesting to note that Charles Taylor and Pierre Trudeau shared a bilingual and bicultural background in Montréal, at a time when rigid Catholicism and an authoritarian brand of politics characterised Québec.)

The constitutional reform of 1982 was promulgated after having been accepted by Trudeau, by federal parliamentarians as well as by the leaders of all provinces, with one exception. The Québec governments of sover-eignist premier René Lévesque, and its federalist successors, have to this day refused to give their stamp of approval to Trudeau's reform project. Is the 1982 constitution legitimate in Québec? Trudeau maintains that it is, since it was approved in the federal Parliament by 71 of the 75 Québec representatives in the House of Commons, most of whom were members of his own party. Many of his critics, myself included, argue that it is not,

---

[5] Alan Cairns, *Disruptions: constitutional struggles, from the Charter to Meech Lake* (Toronto: McCelland and Stewart, 1991), p. 117.

on the theoretical ground that sovereignty is shared in a federal regime, and because this principle was violated when the legislative powers of Québec were reduced without the consent of either the people, the government or the legislative assembly of the province.[6]

The lingering doubts concerning the legitimacy of the 1982 constitution were fed by the politicians, in both Canada and Québec, who replaced the warriors of the early 1980s. The Conservative leader Brian Mulroney became prime minister of Canada in September 1984, with a promise that he would strive to obtain Québec's adherence to the new fundamental law of Canada in a spirit of honour and enthusiasm. The efforts of Mulroney and of his counterpart in Québec, Liberal leader Robert Bourassa, were rewarded three years later when provincial premiers unanimously agreed to sign the Meech Lake Accord. In the main provision of this agreement, the principle of Québec's existence as a distinct society was affirmed and elevated as a rule of interpretation for the whole Charter of Rights and Freedoms. Charles Taylor applauded the new initiative, seeing in it the first formal acceptance by Canadian institutions of Québec's self-definition. Three years later, in the absence of the required unanimous ratification by provincial legislatures, the Meech Lake Accord became a missed opportunity. Fuelled by a coalition of opinion leaders and groups opposed either to the political process leading to Meech Lake – steeped in the spirit of executive federalism – to its decentralising thrust, or to its oblique acknowledgement of the legitimacy of Québec nationalism, the forces of the opposition, led by former prime minister Trudeau, had carried the day. Canada's constitutional impasse was total. The Québec government set up an extraordinary parliamentary commission to reflect upon the future course of the province. I shall now examine the role played by Charles Taylor in this process of collective deliberation.

II

Taylor was one of the first experts to appear in front of the members of Québec's constitutional commission in the autumn of 1990. His presence there was certainly justified in virtue of his international reputation as a philosopher. However, this was not, in the eyes of a broader public, the main reason for his involvement in the commission's work. In his home

---

[6] For a Lockean interpretation of this chapter in Canadian history, see my book *Trudeau et la fin d'un rêve canadien* (Sillery: Les Èditions du Septentrion, 1992). Interestingly, the native peoples of Canada had their ancestral rights enshrined in the new constitution, albeit in a broad and vague fashion, but their consent was not deemed to be required. Ten years later, in the referendum of October 1992, their consent was required, and the Charlottetown Agreement, if it had been accepted by the people, would have transformed the requirement of this consent into a legal necessity.

province, at least until very recently, Taylor was mostly seen as the preeminent federalist intellectual of Montréal's English-speaking community, and as the *éminence grise* of Canada's social-democratic political organisation, the New Democratic Party. If they were old enough, or sufficiently knowledgeable, his fellow Quebeckers could recall that he had returned from his studies in England in the early 1960s to take part in Québec's Quiet Revolution and to help the New Democratic party take roots in the majority French-speaking province. Between 1966 and 1971, Taylor even served as national vice-president of the NDP. In his attempt, in earnest hermeneutical fashion, to find a synthesis that would 'fuse the horizons' of English-speaking Canadians of various cultural origins – and their anxieties concerning unity – with those of French-speaking Canadians and Quebeckers – afraid of losing their identity in America – Taylor met a formidable political foe in Trudeau. He was personally defeated by Trudeau in the federal elections of 1965 and, in the end, all his attempts to gain a seat in the House of Commons proved unsuccessful. Taylor wanted to integrate the modernising and communitarian aspirations of Québec's neonationalists in a more decentralised Canadian federation. Trudeau's solution, which prevailed at the time, was substantially different, resting squarely on individualistic premises. In his view, no concessions should be made to Québec nationalists, for nothing short of independence would satisfy them. Rather, Canada should become a fully bilingual country to make the liberal principle of equality of opportunity available to all, including French-speaking citizens.[7] For Trudeau, the constitutional reform of 1982 and the entrenched Charter of Rights and freedoms were the greatest accomplishment in his persistent struggle. For Taylor, the demise of the Meech Lake Accord in 1990 meant that nothing had been solved, that the bonds and character of the political community had to be reconceived. This was the thrust of his address to Québec's parliamentary commission in December 1990.

In his brief as well as in his oral presentation, the philosopher from

---

[7] Taylor's writings on Canadian politics in the two decades following Trudeau's access to power in 1968 are characterised by a number of criticisms, at times directly and on other occasions more obliquely, addressed to the Liberal prime minister's approach to political theory and practice. In 1970, Taylor thought Trudeau had gone too far by invoking the War Measures Act and suspending civil liberties in his struggle against organised terrorism in Québec. Ten years later, when the nationalist premier of Québec, René Lévesque, presented in a referendum a project to restructure the relationship of his province with Canada along the lines of sovereignty-association, Taylor relinquished the Chichele Chair in Social and Political Theory at Oxford to fight side by side with Trudeau against the fragmentation of the Canadian federation. He made it completely clear, however, that his rejection of the perceived extremism in Lévesque's project should not be seen as an endorsement of Trudeau's view reducing Québec nationalism to a form of parochialism or tribalism. On this point, see Charles Taylor, 'Why do nations have to become states?'

McGill argued that Quebeckers now had a unique opportunity to redefine their political identity and allegiances. At least as a starting point, he invited them to see their society as liberated from any previous engagement. His analysis and his conclusions were quite radical for a federalist, particularly for one seen as an intellectual leader of the English-speaking minority. Taylor argued that the death of Meech Lake had dispelled the ambiguities in the beliefs held by federalists in Québec. The hesitations concerning whether or not the Canadian regime should be just reformed or rebuilt from scratch had vanished. The perceived refusal to recognise Québec as a distinct society after such an acknowledgement had been given by governmental leaders, meant that the Canadian constitution of 1867 was thereafter morally dead in Québec.[8] Citizens of the other provinces and their representatives should be warned that no cosmetic replastering of existing institutions would be deemed sufficient. Symbolically, Taylor opined that all interested parties should go back to Charlottetown, where the federal adventure was first conceived in 1864.

After such a dramatic statement, Taylor turned his attention to the sceptics who were wondering about the need to pursue the dialogue with Canadians from the rest of the country. Why would they be inclined to engage in radical constitution making with Québec after having rejected the Meech Lake Accord? Taylor replied to the doubters that, in a way, it would be easier to start anew rather than to engage in a mere reform. Once Québec made it clear that it wanted to move beyond the regime started in 1867, a number of misunderstandings would simply dissolve. There would be no further attempts to contain Québec within the parameters of a system defined as a multicultural mosaic, where all provinces are equal and where there is only one nation, namely, the Canadian one.

Beyond the bitterness surrounding the Meech Lake affair, Taylor identified the factors that his fellow citizens should ponder in their deliberations: the nature of Québec as a distinct society, as well as the political expression and main homeland of a nation; the need to build an open economy in an era of globalisation; the goal of staving off all forms of external political hegemony. An asymmetrical and decentralised federal alliance with Canada remained Taylor's favoured option. It would create a greater space for the French language on the continent, and enable Canadians and Quebeckers to better protect their form of mixed economy as well as their intertwined network of social programmes, while keeping all the options open with regards to the development of the North. He also argued that a federal dialogue would offer the

---

[8] Taylor, 'Les enjeux de la réforme constitutionelle', reprinted in *Rapprocher les solitudes*, p. 66.

best opportunity for a comprehensive and just resolution of the demands of the native peoples.

Taylor returned to the National Assembly a year and a half later, in the spring of 1992, at a further stage in the unfolding of our constitutional saga. In the meantime, the Québec government had decided to hold a referendum either on sovereignty or on a renewed form of partnership with Canada, no later than the end of October 1992. As the resentment associated with the failure of Meech Lake had started to fade in public opinion, the liberal government of Robert Bourassa was sending signals suggesting that it would clearly prefer a new federal partnership. It was desperately waiting for such an offer. When Charles Taylor came to address the committee set up to study these offers, a group of federal parliamentarians had just published a major report launching a new round of negotiations. Taylor did not embark upon a detailed analysis of this report. Rather, he chose to go to what he perceived as the heart of the matter. From Québec's perspective, he argued, there were three dimensions to the constitutional debate: a new division of powers between governments, precautions to be taken in order to avoid the dangers linked to a minority status in Canada, and the matter of recognition. He considered the third dimension as the key to the resolution of the crisis. What counted first and foremost was the recognition of Québec's distinctiveness, the consensus around the idea that the promotion of this distinct society should be a fundamental objective of the federation.

It is often said that recognition is of little importance, that it is 'only' a matter of symbols ... As if symbols were without importance. As if societies, and particularly democratic ones, did not nourish themselves on symbols, on concise and sharp expressions of their common agreement.[9]

Taylor insisted that Québec's thirst for recognition was crucial for two reasons. First, he had no doubt that it was a profound aspiration of a great majority of citizens in the province. Moreover, he prophesied that the absence of a common understanding on the status of Québec as a distinct society would be the source of recurrent misunderstandings. Therefore, Québec's fundamental goal should be to secure an appropriate recognition of itself as a distinct society within Canada. On this point, Taylor pronounced himself satisfied with the relevant provisions in the federal report under study. Taylor was as forceful on the consequence that should flow from the recognition of Québec's distinctiveness. Our political partners should clearly accept the principle of asymmetrical federalism. They already accepted it in the daily business of the régime.

[9] Taylor, 'Les grandes lignes d'une solution constitutionnelle', p. 10 (my translation).

This agreement should now be elevated to the status of a formal, legal principle. Taylor even went on to say that the recognition of the principle of asymmetry – according to which Québec should have unique powers in view of its nature and situation in America – was more important than the positive recuperation of any one of these responsibilities, on matters such as communications, manpower and training, etc.

Five months after Taylor's second appearance in Québec's National Assembly, the political leaders of the federal and provincial governments, along with the delegates of the native peoples and of the Northern Territories – finally admitted into the inner sanctum of executive federalism – concluded two years of discussions by giving their agreement to the Charlottetown Agreement. Shortly thereafter, the referendum machinery was activated for 26 October, 1992. Canadians and Quebeckers, were about to be asked whether or not they agreed to the renewal of the Canadian federation on the basis of this agreement. During the campaign, Charles Taylor debated the project at McGill and approved of it. Considering what he had said earlier in Québec City, I want to claim that it would have been quite rational and consistent for him to reject the Charlottetown Agreement. However, when I make room for his considerable sympathy towards Aristotelian therapeutics, his position in late 1992 continues to make sense. By going more deeply into the matter, I hope to nail down a couple of tensions in his articulation of theory and practice with regard to the management of national and ethical pluralism in a federal regime. This could provide him with an opportunity to shed greater light on the assumptions and premisses constitutive of his outlook on Canadian politics. To do this in an adequate fashion, I need to consider yet another of Taylor's pronouncements between the failure of Meech Lake and the short-lived euphoria of the Charlottetown Agreement.

In the winter of 1990–1, Taylor undertook to write a background paper comparing the values espoused by Quebeckers and Canadians from other provinces. Entitled 'Shared and divergent values' the paper, prepared as part of a comprehensive project for the Business Council on National Issues, was widely discussed in English-speaking Canada.[10] In Québec's National Assembly, Taylor had provided his fellow citizens with a list of reasons for preferring the federal option, once the distinctiveness of their society had been sufficiently recognised. When he delivered his paper on values in January 1991 to a select group formed by the executives of blue chip corporations, and, indirectly, to a wider audience in English-

[10] See Taylor, 'Shared and divergent values', pp. 53–76.

speaking Canada, he used a different strategy while continuing to oppose fragmentation. He outlined two models of liberalism. The first model respected the parameters defined by such thinkers as Dworkin and Rawls; it was strictly procedural, demanding that the state should be neutral, disengaged from any substantive vision of the good life. I shall let Taylor himself specify the contours of the second model, relevant according to him for Québec:

Quebeckers, therefore, and those who give similar importance to this kind of collective goal, tend to opt for a rather different model of a liberal society. On this view, a society can be organised around a definition of the good life, without this being seen as a depreciation of those who do not personally share this definition. Where the nature of the good requires that it be sought in common, this is the reason for its being an object of public policy.[11]

When a society follows the second model, it is imperative that it treat fairly the minorities who do not share its collective goals, and it is equally necessary that it uphold what Taylor considers the core of liberal rights: life, liberty, due process, free speech, free practice of religion. He then interpreted the Meech Lake saga as a clash between the two forms of liberalism, explaining English-speaking Canada's refusal to recognise Québec as a distinct society – and the consequences that would flow from it on the Charter of Rights and on the division of powers – as a sign of the progress made by proceduralism. The next quote will sound quite prophetic:

COQ (Canada Outside Québec) saw that the 'distinct society' clause legitimated collective goals. And Québec saw that the move to give the Charter precedence imposed a form of liberal society that is alien, and to which Québec could never accommodate itself without surrendering its identity.[12]

Taylor persists in believing that the two models of liberalism and the various self-definitions of Canada's national communities can and should be reconciled within the institutions of a single political regime. Indeed, he considers genuine respect and pride *vis-à-vis* these forms of what he calls 'deep diversity' as a fundamental characteristic of Canada's political covenant. Quebeckers and the native peoples should not be asked to give an unmediated allegiance to the country as a whole. Beyond Trudeau's dream of uniform citizenship for everyone, Taylor implored Canadians to accept the principle of a 'plurality of ways of belonging' to the federation.[13] He proposed his notion of deep diversity, capable of integrating

---

[11] Ibid., p. 70.   [12] Ibid., p. 71.
[13] Ibid., p. 75. For Taylor, it is possible to be a Quebecker first and foremost while remaining loyal to Canada. I should add that recent studies on the intellectual history of Québec tend to support Taylor on this point. See Raymond Hudon and Réjean Pelletier,

procedural as well as communitarian models of liberalism, open to multiple conceptions of citizenship, as an example that Canada could provide for the complex societies of Europe and of the world in the late twentieth century.

Pondering Taylor's paper and his address of January 1991 to Canadian business leaders, there are four points that must be made. First, it is interesting to note that as Canada's preeminent political philosopher, he situated our predicament right in the middle of one of the most important debates in contemporary Anglo-American thinking, between the apostles of procedural liberalism and their communitarian adversaries. There is indeed a peculiarly theoretical quality to the Canadian debate, which is largely about the meaning of liberal justice in a federal society. Beyond Taylor, this quality can be seen for instance in the work of Will Kymlicka, who attempts to broaden Rawlsian liberalism by making room in its framework for cultural membership as a primary good, and in the reflections of Ronald Beiner on citizenship and on the relationship between theory and practice.[14] Second, Taylor makes it plain that reflections about the Canadian dilemma are fraught with meaning for the world in our era of resurgent nationalism. I shall return to this point in the conclusion of this chapter. Third, I would claim that, although other people have made significant theoretical contributions to the debate, Taylor's voice is about the only one to reach the pinnacles of intellectual influence in both French-speaking Québec and English-speaking Canada.[15] This renders his role both quite unique and extremely frustrating. He knows as well if not better than anyone else the complexities in the intellectual and political histories of both societies. He has devoted a considerable amount of his energies as a pedagogue to creating greater understanding between Canada's cultural and national communities. Throughout the years, he has used his vast knowledge to put forward a number of measured and prudent compromises, most of which were rejected because, as he put it in 1979, 'The extreme positions always seem to win out here'.[16] One could say that although the ship of state is being governed imprudently in both Canada and Québec, Taylor, like a beacon,

ed., *L'engagement intellectuel: mélanges en l'honneur de Léon Dion* (Sainte-Foy: Les Presses de l'Universitié Laval, 1991).

[14] Will Kymlicka, *Liberalism, community and culture*, (Oxford: Clarendon Press, 1989), and Ronald Beiner, *What's the matter with liberalism?* (Berkeley: University of California Press, 1992).

[15] Pierre Trudeau wields the same kind of transcultural influence, but it stems more from his identity as a politician. There are other voices that can be heard in the two official languages of Canada (those of Christian Dufour, Pierre Fournier, Daniel Latouche and Philip Resnick), but their work has not yet received the critical acclaim accorded to Taylor's.

[16] Taylor, 'Why do nations have to become states?', p. 32.

persists in sending signals in order to prevent the defenders of the extreme positions from sending the federation into oblivion.

My fourth point will be a controversial one. In his presentation on shared and divergent values in Toronto, Taylor argued that the locomotives on a collision course were two models of liberalism, one dominant in Québec while the other reigned supreme in the rest of Canada. This argument is highly debatable. While the Supreme Court of Canada has been rather sympathetic to the procedural creed in the jurisprudence of the first ten years in the history of our Charter of Rights, while such values as state neutrality and symmetrical equality in the relationships between individuals have established themselves more and more in the minds of the citizenry, and notwithstanding the polemical pronouncements of some intellectual figures who would boot Québec out of Canada to secure the triumph of liberal proceduralism, I would claim that the 1982 Charter of Rights and Freedoms, as well as the political culture of English-speaking Canada, make ample room for Taylor's two models of liberalism.[17] The Charter defines and protects the ancestral rights of the native peoples, it grants provincial communities a number of economic and legal privileges that are clearly collective in their nature. In a sense this issue is an empirical one that could be resolved by an independent study. For my purposes here, I just wish to claim that the Canadian federal government's own understanding of the issue, in the documents it published in the preliminary stages leading to the Charlottetown Agreement favoured my interpretation in a way that helps reveal some of the tensions in Taylor's position. I shall illustrate this first with an excerpt of the proposals submitted by the federal government to the people of Canada in September 1991:

In the Canadian experience, it has not been enough to protect only universal individual rights. Here, the Constitution and ordinary laws also protect other rights accorded to individuals as members of certain communities. This accommodation of both types of rights makes our Constitution unique and reflects the Canadian value of equality that accommodates differences. The fact that community rights exist alongside individual rights in our Constitution goes to the very heart of what Canada is all about.[18]

In theory at least, the preliminary document put forward by the federal government suggested that legal and moral claims were legitimate beyond the realm of individual rights in Canada. In one of the most important

---

[17] This thesis is supported by David Elkins, 'Facing our destiny: rights and Canadian distinctiveness', *Canadian Journal of Political Science*, 22, 41 (1989), p. 709. The argument about the need to reject Québec in order to rescue liberal proceduralism in Canada is made by David Bercuson and Barry Cooper, *Deconfederation: Canada without Quebec* (Toronto: Key Porter Books, 1991), p. 16.

[18] *Shaping Canada's future together*, constitutional proposals of the Government of Canada (Ottawa: Supply and Services Canada, 1991), p. 3.

sections of the August 1992 Charlottetown Agreement known as the 'Canada clause' because it purported to identify the fundamental characteristics of the political community as a whole, it was formally affirmed that 'Canadians are committed to a respect for individual and collective human rights and freedoms of all people.'[19] If my interpretation is correct, and if these documents do indeed suggest that the conflict between Canada and Québec is not about two models of liberalism, where else should we look for an explanation of our current troubles?

I think Taylor was on the right track in his paper on shared and divergent values when he surmised that, in the aftermath of the failure of Meech Lake, 'Quebeckers will no longer live in a structure that does not fully recognise their national goals.'[20] After having been thwarted in their quest, Quebeckers have in a sense become keener in their thirst for recognition, and the scope of their desire has been enlarged. It seems to me that in the 1990s, the goal is to achieve the recognition of Québec as a distinct society either within a Canadian federation that accepts its multinational nature, or outside of it. A new political covenant must make room for the national aspirations of the various peoples constitutive of Canada. The Charlottetown Agreement failed to meet this first requirement; moreover, it did not pass the test of the criteria proposed by Charles Taylor in his presentations to Québec's parliamentary commissions in 1990 and 1992.

The Charlottetown Agreement and the preliminary documents leading to its formulation work with the premise that there is such a thing as one nation in Canada and a national government in Ottawa, in short, a single all-encompassing 'Canadian identity'. Rather than belabouring the point unduly here, I will quote an excerpt which establishes clearly that the framers of the document were literally obsessed by their desire to affirm the national identity of Canada and the national nature of its central government. The relevant passage is taken from a section which gives exclusive jurisdiction to the provinces in the fields of labour market development and training:

There should be a constitutional provision for an ongoing federal role in the establishment of national policy objectives for the national aspects of labour market development: factors to be considered in the establishment of national policy objectives could include items such as national economic conditions, national labour market requirements, international labour market trends and changes in international economic conditions.[21]

---

[19] *Consensus report on the constitution*, Charlottetown, 28 August 1992, p. 1.
[20] Taylor, 'Shared and divergent values', p. 65.
[21] *Consensus report on the constitution*, Section 28, p. 11.

Charles Taylor has claimed all along that there is no consensus on the issue of national identity in Canada. By persisting in postulating the existence of an unproblematic Canadian sense of nationhood, the Charlottetown Agreement remained a prisoner of what Taylor calls 'our great historic misunderstanding'.[22] This lacuna casts a shadow over Taylor's own position on such matters as identity and recognition in the Canada–Québec debate. Addressing Québec's parliamentary commission in March 1992, Taylor had expressed his satisfaction with the formulation of the clause recognising Québec as a distinct society within Canada. In the light of his previous positions, I believe Taylor should have been alerted by the fact that whereas the Meech Lake Accord had maintained a prudent silence over matters of national identity, the 1992 proposals reframed the recognition of Québec as a distinct society within the parameters of Canadian nationalism. There was a second dimension in Taylor's remarks concerning Québec as a distinct society. He recommended that the negotiators for the French-speaking province make the acceptance of the asymmetry principle, with regard to the division of powers between levels of government, one of their fundamental demands. Considered from this angle, the Charlottetown Agreement should have been very disappointing for him, since Québec did not make any real gains on this point. The agreement included some asymmetrical elements, such as the establishment of a process for administrative arrangements, but there was no consensus on the formal and symbolic aspects of asymmetry. In sum, the 1992 constitutional proposals regarded Québec as a distinct society, but also as a province just like all the others in the Canadian nation. In order to further explain Taylor's position, I now turn my attention to Aristotelian politics.

III

Charles Taylor has integrated a number of Aristotelian insights in his understanding of ethics and politics. With the Stagyrite, and against Plato, he does not think class struggles can be eliminated from human affairs. Realistically, our aim should be to tame the tensions and conflicts of interest that will nevertheless remain with us.[23] Since human beings are self-interpreting animals, Taylor also believes that moral thinking cannot aspire to the precision of a theoretical science. Like Aristotle, he argues that ethical knowledge is a matter of perspicuous articulations that have

---

[22] Taylor, 'Alternative futures: legitimacy, identity and alienation in late twentieth century Canada', p. 217.
[23] Taylor, *Philosophical papers*, II, p. 65.

to be frequently re-evaluated.[24] The following passage will lead us to the Canada–Québec predicament:

If this all means that there may be no such thing as *the* coherent set of principles of distributive justice for a modern society, we should not be distressed. The same plurality emerges in Aristotle's discussion of justice in *Politics* III and IV ... This need not reduce us to silence, but it means that there are no mathematical proofs about distributive justice. Rather the judgement of what is just in a particular society involves combining mutually irreducible principles in a weighting that is appropriate for the particular society, given its history, economy, degree of integration.[25]

In the reflections about models of liberalism and notions of citizenship that I outlined earlier, Taylor made it plain he did not believe that a single solution could be imposed on all modern democracies. Observing the cities of his time, Aristotle noted that his view concerning the ideal constitution was 'beyond the reach of most states', thus forcing him to study the sort of régime 'which it is possible for most states to enjoy'.[26] In the discussion which follows, he established the merits of mixed régimes dominated by the moderating influence of the middle classes. He is forced also to admit the historical infrequency of régimes in which the middle classes can exercise their role. This brings him to examine the relationship between the various kinds of constitution and the forms of civic body. As the analysis progresses, Aristotle has to make more and more room for the complexities and nuances of real life. I sense the same kind of evolution in Taylor's political philosophy as he is drawn closer and closer to the current dilemmas of his country. What corresponds for Taylor to Aristotle's preference for the mixed régime – the polity – is precisely the vision of a multinational federation that can accommodate at least two models of liberalism and a plurality of ways of belonging to the political community as a whole. This would be the right form of constitution for a civic body characterised by deep diversity. But what should a philosopher (or a political scientist) do when the citizenry decides to adopt a constitution different from the one he deems adequate for this particular civic body? A retreat to the world of contemplation would certainly be a dignified choice for the philosopher. Aristotle opts for a different path. This is the moment where his therapeutic instinct really triumphs:

We have also to consider the particular way in which each constitution is likely to degenerate – i.e. to explain from what a constitution is most likely to change to what. In addition we have to suggest the policies likely to ensure the stability of

---

[24] Ibid., p. 137.   [25] Ibid., pp. 312–13.
[26] Aristotle, *The politics*, edited and translated by Ernest Barker (Oxford: Oxford University Press, 1958), book IV, chapter 11, p. 180.

constitutions, collectively and individually, and to indicate the means which may best be employed to secure each particular constitution.[27]

In Aristotle's own imperfect world, most constitutions were democracies or oligarchies rather than aristocracies or polities. In these circumstances, a thinker also had to identify the means whereby the imperfect régimes would be able to domesticate 'the passion for equality which is thus at the root of sedition', thereby reaching a temporary state of stability. In Charles Taylor's own imperfect country, the constitution at hand is not the one which accepts the multinational nature of Canada and the multiple forms of citizenship that come along with this fact. Rather, it is still the old British North America Act – the same one Taylor proclaimed morally dead in Québec – accompanied by the reforms Pierre Trudeau initiated in 1982. Taylor endorsed the Charlottetown Agreement in our recent referendum not because it corresponded exactly to his vision of federalism, but rather because he came to see in it a formula capable of restoring some stability to the 1867–1982 constitutional order. He had to see some progress in the inclusion of community rights alongside individual rights in the 'Canada clause', as well as in the recognition of the native peoples' inherent right to self-government. In the end, this modest but real progress prevailed in his mind over what he had said earlier concerning Québec's requirements with regards to recognition and asymmetry.

I would surmise that there were three additional reasons explaining Taylor's position during our referendum. First, he had indicated that the causes of diversity and pluralism would be better served by a political union between Canada and Québec, rather than by having each society follow its own independent path. I take it that he also includes in his balancing act the signals that the failure of the Canadian experiment could send to the international community. Finally, one also senses that even if all the right arguments were in favour of the sovereignist option for Québec, Charles Taylor would move in such a direction with an extreme reluctance, if at all. I was struck by an interview he gave in the weeks following the October 1992 referendum, in which he said that 'Maybe if we can cool things for a while, we can avoid fragmentation and carry out some of the compromise by administrative order.'[28] The thrust of Taylor's work until now has been precisely to show that the thorn in the Canadian side belonged to the symbolic order, not the administrative one. In moments such as this, Taylor demonstrates practically what he has

---

[27] Ibid., book V, chapter 1, p. 203.
[28] Karen J. Winkler, 'A scholar seeks the multicultural middle ground', *The Chronicle of Higher Education*, 9 December 1992, p. A-8.

lucidly explained in his philosophical anthropology, namely the place of pre-articulate elements in our moral experiences. In his nuanced advocacy for Canadian federalism, philosophical reason is not the only weapon.

In politics and ethics, a form of epistemological modesty has characterised the itinerary of Charles Taylor. Much of this can probably be attributed to the sinuous contours of political judgement in a multi-national federation such as the one he has experienced in Canada. As I write, the symbolic thorn – fed by the drive towards recognition that animates both Québec and the native peoples – is still endangering the Canadian body politic. Taylor must know that it could be his own *moira* to play an important role in the exercise of the kind of radical therapeutics required to remove this thorn once and for all.

Part VI

Reply and re-articulation

Charles Taylor replies

Introduction

Isaiah Berlin

I was very moved by the kind words of Isaiah Berlin, who has been an inspiring teacher and friend for many decades. In the high-powered but rather arid and parochial philosophical world of Oxford after the war, he opened new windows on the world and history, made us aware of possibilities undreamt of in the standard curriculum. His tremendously wide sympathies, and unparalleled capacities of expression made these come alive for us, even across wide gaps of culture and history. I am greatly in his debt, as are a great many others of my generation, as well as those older and younger than myself.

As he points out, though we share a great deal, we don't see eye to eye. He gives a sketch of some of the differences in a few paragraphs. I'm not sure the gap is as wide as it seems in his description. Or rather, I would say, the differences run very deep metaphysically and theologically; but they narrow somewhat in the practical judgements about our situation in society and history.

Berlin has tirelessly pointed out the irreconcilable conflict that we frequently face between different goods which we cannot help subscribing to. The modern vogue of ethical thinking, which tends to try to derive all our obligations from some single principle, has tended to hide and muffle these conflicts. His reminders have been salutary and important, but too little heeded.

I very much agree with him on this: human beings are always in a situation of conflict between moral demands, which seem to them to be irrecusable, but at the same time uncombinable. If this conflict is not felt, it is because our sympathies or horizons are too narrow, or we have been too easily satisfied with pseudo-solutions. To take a prominent contemporary example, today we are aware of the increased liberty, respect for human rights, control over our environment, acceptance of diversity which has come with modernity; but we also know that we have paid a price in the increased fragility of some human bonds, and in our relation to nature. We are torn two ways; and everywhere we turn, this conflict surfaces in concrete dilemmas: when weighing the costs of 'development', or in our relations to other, not yet fully 'modernised' cultures. We don't have any formula to render these two demands harmonious. We can only make difficult judgements in which these demands are balanced against each other, at some sacrifice to one or both.

This is, I believe, our actual situation, and in this regard I would say that Berlin's thinking has been a surer guide than mainstream moral philosophy. I suppose that where I disagree is that I am reluctant to take this as the last word. I still believe that we can and should struggle for a 'transvaluation' (to borrow Nietzsche's term *Umwertung*) which could open the way to a mode of life, individual and social, in which these demands could be reconciled.

I don't think this is totally chimerical. We have made some such advances in history. For a long time, our ancestors couldn't conceive how to reconcile popular rule and public order. Now the most law-abiding societies are democratic. That this may have been achieved at the cost of other values has to be allowed, but the original dilemma was not insurmountable. Of course, the whole history of the twentieth century shows how dangerous this kind of aspiration can be. The too quick belief in a specious solution can wreak terrible destruction, as the sad story of Bolshevism shows beyond question. The distinct nature of the demands, in their full richness and power, have to be kept before our eyes, lest we trick ourselves that we have met them with cheap substitutes, like Leninist 'democracy'. In this regard, Berlin's immensely eloquent and penetrating work is and will remain indispensable reading for a long time to come.

I   Foundations

Susan James

I am grateful to Susan James for forcing me by her careful analysis of Descartes to try to be less fuzzy about a transition which plays a crucial role in my picture of the modern identity. James opens her piece with a description of this transition: 'from a belief in an external guarantor of moral values to a confident reliance on the internal guarantee of reason – to what?' (p. 7)

Now this is not quite the transition I had in mind. Or rather, since there is more than one transition involved here, this is not the transition that I think Descartes to have been a hinge figure in – which presumably is what is at stake between us. What is at issue for me isn't 'guarantees', and the direct upshot of the change isn't moral relativism.

I want to come back to this later. It might help first if I tried to say what I think the transition is. Obviously, I was operating in *Sources of the self* with something like 'ideal types' in Weber's sense, while at the same time I was commenting on historical figures, who never quite fit the types. This has led to some confusion, not all of which is in the minds of readers. I think it casts light on the development of the last four centuries to see it as moving from an epoch in which people could find it plausible to see in the order of the cosmos a moral source, to one in which a very common view presents us a universe which is neutral, and finds the moral sources in human capacities. Obviously, neither of these views is unanimously held in its time. But each in its time is widely held, and seems to everyone a position to be taken seriously, whereas the other seems strange and far out.

I took Plato as my representative figure of the first position. The cosmos, ordered by the good, sets standards of goodness for human beings, and is properly the object of moral awe and admiration, inspiring us to act rightly. If we think of this as a representative starting point, then we can identify a common end point in a view which sees us human beings as set in a neutral universe, in which we pursue the goals of survival, prospering and knowledge (this latter either as instrumental to the first two or as pursued in its own right). What inspires moral admiration now is our capacities, for reason, for intelligent control of nature, and transformation of our condition with foresight and determination. These capacities set the standards we should live up to.

Now it is clear that the transition doesn't mean that the cosmos becomes simply *irrelevant* to what we do. Obviously, it still in a way determines our action. If our goals are knowledge and control, then we can only achieve these by taking account of the world we live in. But the kind of taking account is very different. It is no longer that this world offers, as it were, patterns of goodness, but rather that paying close attention to it, and adapting to it, are essential to achieve *our* favoured goals, which now command our moral awe and admiration.

Now, as James points out, my claim about Descartes was not that he completed this transition, but rather that he pushed us a good way along it (p. 18–19). But I wouldn't take as evidence of his being still in an early stage that virtuous 'qualities depend quite explicitly on an understanding of things outside ourselves' (p. 16); because this is still a feature of the most radically human-centred end point. I think there are some cross-purposes between James and me here. We are not talking about the same transition.

What *is* a reflection of incompleteness – and here I agree with James – is

Descartes' invocation of Providence, which is still so close to the Stoic mode. (There were of course later references to Providence in the eighteenth century which were fully compatible with the modern human-centred construal.)

But this notwithstanding, it seems to me that Descartes took giant steps in negating the Platonic view and towards the human-centred outlook. The very invocation of *générosité*, seeing in it the key to the virtues, is a sign of this. Generosity in its seventeenth-century sense, rather different from its contemporary meaning, was that lively sense of one's own honour which kept one from doing the base things which might compromise it, and inspired one to the noble deeds which suited it. To make this the key, replacing what wisdom had been for the Socratic tradition, is a giant step towards that concentration on the sources within, foreshadowing Kant's articulation of the 'dignity' of the rational agent as a crucial moral notion. To be inspired to some action by 'generosity' is to be moved by the sense that I owe it to myself and my high status (in this case, as a being capable of rational control). The focus of moral awe and admiration is turning inward.

Another telling detail where I want to take issue with James: I characterised Descartes as having made an important shift in the Augustinian tradition. Undoubtedly, he stands within it, because he sees a road to God within; and more particularly, because he takes up that mode of argument for the existence of God which starts off from my having a sense of perfection which is far above my own imperfect being. This is, indeed, a crucial Augustinian theme. But the atmosphere has subtly and decisively altered. In Augustine, the move towards the discovery of God within, even when carried out by reasoning, is inseparable from a path of devotion. Only the rightly loving soul can come to see God. With Descartes, the reasoning process which nets us God as a crucial stage in our foundational argument is separated off from this spiritual background. There is indeed, an analogous preparation, in the ability to grasp the real distinction between soul and body which the First meditation in particular is meant to inculcate in us. Failing to make this distinction is a kind of analogue (or for some of his Port Royal followers, a fruit) of original sin. But a crucial accent has been displaced. The acute religious sensibility of a Pascal could not fail to pick up on this. We shouldn't either.

I don't mean to imply for a minute that Descartes himself was not genuinely devout. Many anachronistic readings turn on the inability to recognise his real religious convictions. Just that a crucial disintrication is taking place here, which had important consequences.

While I'm at it, I will take the occasion of James' exacting critique to try to clarify some other distinctions which I tried to use to explain the transition. The first is substantive versus procedural. These are terms applied to rationality or reasoning, and represent different conceptions of it. We have a substantive conception of rationality when getting it right is a necessary condition of being rational. Perhaps we might better put it: where getting it right is a definitional condition of being rational.

A procedural view, on the other hand, turns from the result of our thinking to the process, and identifies a proper procedure the following of which amounts to being rational. There are many rival accounts of this, of course. In some contexts, the procedure is deductive reasoning, and there have been battles over just which contexts these are. Then there is the famous historical controversy between the Cartesian variant, stressing clear and distinct inferences, and the empiricist counterposition, which focuses on rules of evidence, the methodologies of induction. All these have in common a focus on procedure.

But just as the main transition to inward moral sources doesn't involve just *ignoring* the external world, so the move to procedural reason doesn't shed all concern for substantive correctness. The procedure is after all an alethetically oriented one. So some assurance is sought that it will generally hit the mark. This is given us, for instance, in Descartes' argument to the existence of a veracious God, which closes off the worrying possibility that we are being systematically misguided by a malicious demon. In the other camp, over the course of the centuries, there has been much worrying about the justification of induction. These arguments made sense, indeed were unavoidable, precisely because the procedure was *not* definitionally tied to getting it right.

So after the shift, getting it right is still playing a role, but it's a different role. It is now indirect, at a distance, as it were, not definitional. Does this mean that the shift is unimportant? I think not, because it goes along with the inward turn and the aspiration to foundationalism. With a procedural conception of theoretic reason, we turn towards our own thinking processes. We turn to reflexive self-examination. This is a key element in the whole epistemological shift of modern philosophy, and the accompanying ambition of founding our knowledge claims. Together with the resolutive-compositive method, it produces the typical structures of modern epistemology.

This brings me to a second distinction of mine which James criticises, that between the found and the constructed. Here there has been misunderstanding, and I apologise for not being clearer in *Sources of the self*. What is constructed is our picture of the world, if we follow the Cartesian method of breaking down our putative representations into simple components and then assembling them only in rigorous obedience to our canonical procedure. The procedure itself follows standards, but I wasn't claiming that these were constructed. James quotes me in my reference to 'the rational thing to do, where this term is now defined by the standards imposed on the orders we construct in order to live by them' (p. 17). The relative clause '[that] we construct' here attaches to 'orders', not 'standards'. Rationality is defined by the standards applied in construction, i.e. by the canonical procedure.

There is also an analogous move, I believe, from the substantive to the procedural in the domain of practical reason, which is complexly related to the one I've been describing in the theoretical domain, and also to the main transition I have been discussing here. In the practical domain, it is Bentham and Kant who have offered the most influential rival procedures.

I'd like in concluding to return briefly to the point I adverted to in the beginning. If there have been some cross-purposes between James and me, it is perhaps because we are not talking about the same transition. First, it should be clear why relativism is not the direct upshot of the one I'm focusing on. Rather this transition has generated a strong human-centred ethic, with a strong view of human dignity. I recognise that this has in various indirect ways helped a slide into relativist modes of thought, but that is another matter.

My problem with the upshot of this transition is thus different from James'. I have no difficulty with what this ethic affirms, at least in some variants. I bridle at its denial of all sources outside. And here the only issue is not the theological one: should we recognise God? Indeed, this in a sense is not the principal issue involved in *this* transition, because the destruction of the meaningful cosmos was so much the work of orthodox Christians, from Occam through Descartes and beyond. The big issue repressed by *this* kind of human-centredness is, to put it very broadly and loosely, what is our moral relation to the universe which surrounds us?

Now here I think we are not in such an impasse as James seems to suggest. I believe that ways out are already being explored. I'm referring not only to certain spiritual outlooks which have fed the ecological movement, but also to the place of epiphanic art, and the development of 'subtler languages', which, while built in a sense on personal resonance, take us beyond the subject and open us to moral sources outside. (This connects to my reply to Mette Hjort.)

I think this shows that James and I are focusing on different issues. She speaks of my proposing a return to 'a God who is an external arbiter of right and wrong' (p. 8). But my concern in *Sources of the self* was not arbitration, but precisely *sources*. To look first for an arbiter is to reverse the proper order. No one can find an arbiter in God who has not first found a source therein. Or where people do, you can be sure that something rather sick and oppressive is going on.

Richard Rorty

I am glad to continue the exchange with Richard Rorty, which, as he remarks, goes back now over a number of years, and from which I have learned a great deal. I am happy to hear that he feels the same about it. Perhaps one day, this exchange will bring a final clarification; if not substantive agreement, at least an agreed formulation of the differences. But I think we have still some way to go before we get to this point. It seems so hard to get a final, clear fix on just what is at stake between us. There are passages where I find myself nodding in agreement, but then suddenly the text veers off on to a terrain where I can't follow. At moments 'realism' seems to be a mere scarecrow, something that needs to be exorcised rather than refuted. But then it appears rather that in refuting it, we are preventing ourselves from saying something we still have to say.

I suppose one place to get at the difference relates to the scheme/ content distinction. Whereas Rorty, following Davidson, seems to think this is something we should put behind us, it seems to me evident that we cannot do without it. We are using it all the time. Once again, I think Rorty has focused on a caricature of what he's attacking. He asks: 'can we distinguish the role of our describing activity, our use of words, and the role of the rest of the universe, in accounting for the truth of our beliefs?' (p. 23). A rhetorical question, to which the answer is plainly 'no'. The inference is, that we must drop 'the third dogma of empiricism', the scheme/content distinction.

The assumption which underlies this inference is that the only way to make sense of the distinction would be to disaggregate and isolate somehow a component of pure precategorised reality, which could then somehow be compared or related to language. But this is a chimaera, of the same family as 'nature's own language', which Rorty has agreed to take out of the play, for the moment.

This assumption is very shaky. Compare: you can't make sense of a form/colour distinction, unless you can somehow separate off a pure colourless form and a pure formless colour. You can't? So drop the distinction. To which the answer would quite legitimately be: we don't need this feat of metaphysical disaggregation. We've identified two ways in which inseparable form/colour combinations can vary, and that allows us to distinguish them.

Trivially: yesterday there were twelve chairs in this room; today there are only ten. The language of classification is the same, what has changed is the reality described. Less trivially: Aristotle: the sun is a planet; us: the sun is not a planet. What brings about this change is not reality, but our adopting a different scheme.

Now this gets untrivial, because once we can identify schemes as alternative ways of describing the same reality, we can sometimes rank them. Our description is better, because it is part of a scheme which allows us to describe reality better. There are very important matters about how things work in our galaxy which you can't get a handle on unless you can distinguish stars from the planets (in our sense) which orbit around them. A way of talking which puts the sun and Mars in the same category is going to be incapable of dealing with these. So it has to be replaced.

Now I don't quite understand where we part company, because I haven't appealed to anything in this example that Rorty doesn't also accept. There are things which are causally independent of us (here stars and planets, particularly those of our own system). These things are causally related in various ways. Further, these things can be classified in different ways. Some alternative classifications are rivals because they purport to allow us to come to grips with the same questions: here issues about the motions and causes of motions of the earth and the heavenly bodies. Between these, we can sometimes show that one is superior to the other, because it allows us to make plain important features of motion and the causes of motion which the other fudges, misrepresents or makes unstatable.

Now, coming to see this at no point involves somehow grasping the world independently of any description. And it is also true that there are other modes of classification of heavenly bodies, e.g. in terms of their colours or aesthetic properties, which can in no way be ranked alongside Aristotle's or Kepler's, because they are not related to the same question. So a scheme can't be compared to reality unframed by any scheme. And not all schemes can be ranked, because some raise quite different questions. Indeed, questions only arise because there are schemes. But when all this is said, some schemes can be ranked; and ranked because they permit us to grasp, or prevent us from grasping features of reality, including causal features, which we recognise as being independent of us.

This is the nub of what I want to call realism. It involves ranking (some) schemes, and ranking them in terms of their ability to cope with, allow us to know, describe, come to understand reality. I can't see what's wrong with saying this. More, I can't see how one could invalidate any one of these formulations without substituting another with the equivalent sense. On pain of failing to make distinctions between schemes; or schemes which are rivals versus schemes which are not; or schemes which are better and those which are worse; or on pain of being unable to articulate why some are better and others worse.

There is, of course, another very important area in which we want to distinguish something like scheme and content, and that is where we are dealing with the different 'takes' of very different cultures on nature and the human condition. Here I think the Davidsonian rejection of the distinction runs us into incoherence or worse. The standard danger here is ethnocentrism, misunderstanding the other because he/she is interpreted as operating with the same classifications as we are. The differences in behaviour are then often simply coded as bad versus good. For the more unsophisticated *conquistadores*, the Aztecs had to be seen as worshipping the devil. It's simple, *compadres*, you either worship God or the devil. Ripping out hearts, is that worshipping God?? It follows ...

What is needed is not the Davidsonian 'principle of charity', which means: make the best sense of them in what we understand as sense; but rather: coming to understand that there is a very different way of understanding human life, the cosmos, the holy, etc. Somewhere along the line, you need some place in your ontology for something like 'the Aztec way of seeing things', in contrast to 'our way of seeing things'; in short, something like the scheme/content distinction. To fail to make this can be, literally, lethal. This allows us to give a perfectly good sense to my phrase about the world waiting for Kepler. The shift to Kepler's description, unlike that about the chairs above, was a shift to a new scheme, which allowed a superior description, in virtue of what we now recognise to be features of the universe which are continuing. This can come out in our being able to put these descriptions also in the past tense, as Rorty agrees.

The contrast I want to make is with the kinds of changes in self-understanding which change us. Here we get something which fits neither of the categories mentioned so far. When I come to see myself as having resented your attitude all these years, or as being in love with someone, there can be a change which is not just the recognition of a continuing reality. It may be phrased that way, but the feelings also change in being so acknowledged. But nor is it simply a matter of changing realities justifying changing descriptions, as with the chairs. There is a change of description which also alters what is being described. And yet, we can also sometimes rank the descriptions as being more or less self-clairvoyant, or more or less self-deluding. There is a complexity of relations here, which is not captured simply by saying that I make some predicate true of myself by taking on the description, as Rorty seems to be saying (p. 25–6). It is trivially true that I make the predicate 'self-confessed coward' true of myself for the first time by acknowledging that I am a coward. So do I make the predicate 'self-described Montrealer' true of myself when I answer your question where I come from. But the whole dynamic between description, reality and truth, noted in the previous paragraph will normally be absent in this second case.

This is the interesting dynamic to explore. But how can one do this without saying something about the different ways in which sentences can be true? Or perhaps, otherwise put, made true by whatever makes them true? It might be tempting to follow Rorty in just abandoning a host of troubling expressions. But not if one becomes incapable of saying important things, or is forced to banalise important distinctions.

II   Interpreting modernity

Quentin Skinner

I am glad of the chance to continue the debate with Quentin Skinner that we started in the exchange in *Inquiry*. He directed some powerful criticisms at the portrait of the modern identity that I drew in *Sources of the self*. That portrait can be challenged in a host of places, because I claim to be describing features of the outlook of people in the modern West which are very widespread. I often used the pronoun 'we' to describe us contemporary denizens of North Atlantic societies. Skinner objects that I have frequently presented an outlook which is very far from universal in our societies. I have to plead guilty to this, although I don't think it necessarily invalidates the enterprise, for reasons I will go into in a minute.

However, let me say first that I am still very much in disagreement with Skinner about the examples he brings up. One of the features I think is widespread is our valuation of autonomy, which is often prized among other reasons because it permits each person to develop their own mode of being, or find fulfilment in their own way. I invoked Mill as one of the articulators of this value. Skinner wants to take issue with this, and he instances the present attack on pornography by radical feminists (p. 40–1).

I cannot see in what way this represents a counterexample. I can think of few cases in which a political position is more squarely situated within the Millian structure of argument. Mill's principle in one of its famous formulations is 'that the only purpose for which power can be rightly exercised over any member of a civilized community, against his will, is to prevent harm to others. His own good, either physical or moral, is not a sufficient warrant.'[1] The radical feminist attack on pornography attacks it precisely as a vicious form of harm to others. There is no challenge

---

[1] John Stuart Mill, *Three essays* (Oxford: Oxford University Press, 1975), p. 15.

whatever to the principle that people should be left free to develop in their own way, as long as they don't trespass on others. Skinner somehow thinks that I have been ignoring the ferocity of attacks on 'liberal complacencies'. But this quite misplaces the issue. The central emphasis on autonomy is precisely what is shared by both liberals and radicals in our culture. They are fiercely opposed to each other in their interpretations of what harm amounts to, but they share much of the modern belief in freedom, and in this they see things rather differently from our premodern forebears.

And also from some of our contemporaries. My claim here *is* vulnerable. Yet Skinner seems to have perversely chosen the most inappropriate examples. Think of the strange (some think unnatural) alliance against pornography of radical feminists on one hand and those defending traditional codes of decency on the other. These latter really do think that people ought to be protected in this regard from their lower instincts. They are really not part of the Millian consensus.

So is Skinner right to protest, even though he may have got the wrong examples? Perhaps. I still think there is a point to the kind of portrait I am drawing. My claim is that the general understanding of the human subject in individualist-expressive terms has seeped into our culture, and in a sense saturated it. Those who resist some of its manifestations, as for instance those elements on the right who are keen on censorship, also feel its pull in other ways. A sensitive study, like that by Steven Tipton,[2] shows how the assumptions of expressive individuality can infiltrate the culture of revivalist 'born-again' Christianity in the United States. I know that this claim is hard to pin down in exact terms. But it may nevertheless be an insightful way of regarding our contemporary society.

I am also unmoved by a second example Skinner brings up. He objects that many people no longer consider marriage and the family as important for their identity. Very true. As I tried to explain during our *Inquiry* exchange, I see the focus on the value of ordinary life as having taken a wide range of forms. Relationships are still a central concern of people's lives, even when they take forms which are widely different from the traditional family. I think this is a significant continuity, even though there is rupture, and sometimes rebellion involved. I confess to being not quite clear here on what the basis of Skinner's objection is. He seems to think that my remarks about the thinness and shallowness of ties, and about the eclipse of solidarities, which include those of birth and family, must make me a foe of any kind of relationship which differs from the traditional family. He further seems to think that in embracing the family one embraces all its injustices.

---

[2] *Getting saved from the sixties* (Berkeley: University of California Press, 1982).

In the world in which I live, I see people who are struggling with multiple demands and goals, which include aspirations to intimate ties which will not turn out shallow, and which include the desire to keep or recover closeness with siblings, parents and other relations. They have a lot of trouble sometimes putting this together with the demands of autonomy, fulfilment and their own integrity. But in this complicated world that's what they're struggling with. Such people are found both within traditional-style marriages, and in other kinds of relationships, and sometimes in none at all. In short, lots of people are struggling to put together self-fulfilment and intimate and deep and lasting relationships. I claim no credit for pointing this out. I hoped only that some of the account in *Sources of the self* might cast some light on the background to our commitment to both these ends. One can see that there is a struggle here, without necessarily being committed to everything which is wrong with the patriarchal family.

Skinner and I seem to be talking past each other in these passages. He sums up his critique here by saying that 'the institutions he [Taylor] invokes to save us from meaninglessness are just those which, according to many of "us", are most likely to betray our interests and threaten our liberties' (p.42). Now I wasn't aware of invoking anything to 'save us from meaninglessness'; that wasn't one of my purposes in writing the book. Rather, what I was saying was something like: the relationships which we enter into partly because we feel that they are essential to a full human life frequently pose threats to our interests and restrict our liberties. Out of the dilemmas that thus arise, there is no easy way.

Cross-purposes also seem to dog the discussion about whether modernity represents some kind of moral gain. It is not an objection to the proposition that some important goods have been given their due for the first time, to point out that some have also been lost. The principle of the universality of rights, for instance, that we live in a civilisation which does not tolerate slavery, I consider a gain. Of course, we still have to make an overall judgement, whether the gains are more important than the losses. But what moral realism requires is that one be able to identify certain changes as gains or losses. I think we can, and also that there have been significant gains.

I also think there have been losses. But here again, I find some of Skinner's examples unconvincing. He cites the figures of citizen and monk as among those which have been rendered unavailable to us (p. 43). Here I am bound to say that I find the account of modern European history hard to recognise. I realise the presumption involved in a philosopher challenging an historian on this, but I can't help raising objections to the global explanation. His basic claim is that 'the evolution was partly engineered by powerful ruling groups' (p. 44). This is meant to be a rival to an account which can explain the evolution partly in terms of the inherent force of certain ideas.

Now the language in Skinner's text does seem to remind us of the English Reformation under Henry. Certainly, the monks were suppressed, and the break from Rome carried through, by a revolution from above. But we're looking here at the longer-term evolution of a civilisation. Can the whole impact of English Protestantism on politics and culture be laid at the door of the Tudor régime? Why do some changes imposed from on top take on a life of their own, and others signally fail to do so (as, for instance, Lenin's seems to have failed in Russia)? Far from engineering the continued evolution of Protestantism, 'powerful ruling groups' in England were severely incommoded by it in the following century.

More radically, in what sense is it true that the citizen is no longer with us? Yes, there is a tension here too between the political culture which tends to treat us as essentially 'consumers of government', and the political culture of democracy. But the latter is very much alive, and has been vehicled in the last two centuries in large part through the image of the citizen drawn from the same ancient sources as the Renaissance ideal. Of course, there are differences, which have to do with a host of things, not least the scale and complexity of modern societies. But it would be too simple to say that the citizen has been elbowed aside. Some analogous points could be made about the monk. Monastic spirituality is alive and well in the twentieth century.

I want lastly and very briefly to touch on Skinner's discussion of theism and Christianity. It is hard to come to grips with this, because our background assumptions are so different. I don't mean here that I am a believer and he is not. This wouldn't prevent some kind of understanding about the nature of the phenomenon we're discussing. But it is here that we are poles apart.

Skinner argues that we cannot be confident that 'we have no reason to fear the Christian faith' (p. 47). He probably thinks he is arguing against me here. But I think it is very evident that we have reason to fear the Christian faith. I think that we have reason to fear any belief which holds out hope of major transformation in human life, including several atheistic views, some of which have caused quite a bit of havoc in our century. I also think that this is not necessarily the only consideration. Perhaps if we determined only to put our faith in something which gave absolutely no cause for fear, we might end up also without hope for human beings.

'The death of God', says Skinner, 'leaves us with an opportunity, perhaps even a duty, to affirm the value of our humanity more fully than ever before' (p. 47). Great. The issue is: what kind of affirmation can one make? I don't want to prejudge this. I have a hunch that there is a scale of affirmation of humanity by God which cannot be matched by humans rejecting God. But I am far from having proof. Let's try to see.

In my view, this is the question: how much *can* you affirm? Just talking of 'opportunity' or 'duty' is beside the point. As though you could just turn it on. And as though once you had, the resulting commitment would be no cause for fear. This is perhaps the ultimate 'liberal complacency'.

Michael L. Morgan

I am grateful to Michael Morgan, first for having reformulated much of what I said in *Sources of the self* so clearly; and second, for the interesting discussion of Buber and the important analogies between epiphanic art and certain modern understandings of revelation. I can see connections now which I barely sensed before.

What I'd like to do here, is try to respond to the challenge of the third part of Morgan's paper, where he raises all the difficulties of understanding religious faith, and living it, in the context of modernity and a genuine pluralism. Now I think some of the difficulties are more apparent, others are very real. Let me take one of the first kind first.

My account does give a kind of primacy to our moral and spiritual experience. Someone will believe in the God of Abraham because God figures in his/her best account. I believe in God, because I sense something which I want to describe as God's love and affirmation of the world, and human beings. I see this refracted in the lives of exceptional people, whom I'll call for short saints, as well as hearing faint echoes in my own prayer life. Of course, the last few sentences are an extremely oversimplified and schematic account of the confused searching, alternation of doubt and confidence, hope and despair, which actually constitute what one might call my spiritual life. But it may suffice to bring out certain typical features of religious faith.

What I believe in is what figures in my best account of the world, history, and my experience as a moral and spiritual being, but what figure in this account are experience-transcendent things. The God who figures in my account is not a function of my experience, although of course my *belief* in him, access to him, is. In a parallel fashion, I believe in trees, rocks, cars, because they figure in the 'best account' of my experience. This sounds strained, only because there is no rival hypothesis even remotely as plausible. But the trees, rocks, cars, are anything but functions of my experience, and I won't survive long if I entertain this delusion.

Again, I speak of 'my' best account, but this may just as easily be 'our' account. No one thinks totally alone; the Cartesian ideal is unrealisable integrally. I think with, sometimes also against, but largely at least in the terms offered by my community. There is in particular a lot of trust in anyone's spiritual life, unbelieving or believing. For instance, we are moved by the lives of what we see as exceptional people, and we find ourselves drawn to accept, in order to deepen and explore further, what they offer as *their* best accounts. Or we have a more diffuse sense that there is some wisdom, some deeper understanding of human life, in the ways of a given community, ours or some other. We join this, or remain in it, in the hope and trust that we can become more deeply rooted in this understanding. So when I speak of 'my' best account, I don't mean one that I would identify as totally self-generated. I just mean the one which in fact makes most sense to me.

My community, my history, exceptional models, and my own reflection, have all combined to offer me a language in which I make sense of all this. I will almost certainly become aware, in our world, that there are other languages in which very closely analogous experiences and happenings are encoded by other people. For instance, exceptional individuals, showing very similar spiritual strengths, will account for their lives very differently in other spiritual traditions. Thus, in the above short account of myself, I used the term 'love'. I was giving a Christian 'spin' to the things which seemed to point to God, e.g. extraordinarily saintly people, or my own experience of prayer. But I know that people and meditation experiences not totally unlike the ones I focus on are given a quite different account among Buddhists, for instance, in whose discourse, 'love', 'God', and also 'saint', for that matter, don't figure.

I have given a Buddhist-Christian example here, but the point is more general. It also holds between believers and unbelievers. An atheist friend of mine and I may both admire, say, Martin Luther King, but have a quite different account of the sources of his moral and spiritual leadership.

Now the account I am giving of religious belief is quintessentially modern. It is modern in my last point, in facing up to the puzzlement of the plurality of religious and other outlooks. But it is also modern in giving the epistemological foreground to our moral and spiritual experience. As I mentioned above, we could also say that our empirical beliefs about the world follow our 'best account', but there seems to be no question of rival views between which we have to adjudicate, when it comes to trees, rocks and cars. It is appropriate to speak of the 'best account', because we are self-confessedly in a domain where we only see muddily and uncertainly, and with lots of hesitation, whatever we think we see. That's how *we* tend to see our predicament when it comes to

spiritual outlooks. But at an earlier phase in our civilisation, the epistemological status of God, while never being the same as that of trees and
rocks, was considerably less problematic than it is today.

Thus it is clear that my account doesn't leave much place for the five
ways of proving the existence of God propounded by Aquinas, *provided*
(which is by no means unproblematically given) that they are meant to
convince us quite independently of our moral and spiritual experience,
that one can take them as an unbeliever would, as showing the
inescapable rational cogency of certain conclusions, regardless of their
spiritual meaning to the thinker.

Nevertheless, however modern this account of belief is epistemologically, it doesn't actually exclude any premodern objects of faith. Morgan
is right to point out the tendency among moderns (Kant is a prominent
example he cites) to move away from a conception of the divine–human
relation as one of command, towards views more respectful of human
autonomy. Still, this is in principle quite independent of the account I'm
offering in terms of the epistemic primacy of experience. People can arrive
at what to them is a best account which very much figures an angry,
jealous, commanding God. Indeed, some of our fundamentalist contemporaries seem to have done just that. One mustn't confuse the epistemological level with the substantive one.

Now it might be objected that fundamentalists would probably not
accept very readily my epistemology. They might be happier with a
discourse of absolute proof, self-authenticating revelation, or the like.
That is quite likely, but it is no objection to my thesis. It would just show
that they too were confusing the two levels. My thesis claims to be about
what actually makes one's spiritual outlook plausible to one. We can be
deluded about this. I think believers in the five ways (taken in the
'disengaged' spirit mentioned above) are so deluded. They would never
find them remotely convincing, if they weren't already moved to do so by
their feel for what makes sense of their moral and spiritual experience.
Indeed, I don't think anyone was ever so convinced by a 'disengaged'
proof of this kind. Only in an era in which very few people had an
alternative account of moral experience, and few even understood well
what it would look like, would this weakness of the five proofs remain
unnoticed.

So I don't think that my account of religious faith rules out any
substantive view, up to the most 'transcendent' and non-human-centred.
Indeed, I don't think my view is all that human-centred, although it is
hardly fundamentalist. But I wasn't trying in offering this picture to
delegitimate, say, fundamentalism, as polemical lay epistemologies have
tried to delegitimate religious belief. Let the best account win, but we can

only say *a posteriori* that their account is not best. Hence, one seeming difficulty with my account, that it allegedly can't allow for full-blooded religious traditions as objects of legitimate belief, disappears on closer examination.

There is another problem which can't be explained away. And that lies in the ecumenical dimension. I made the point above: we are aware today that there are other accounts of and ways of animating what we all have to recognise as authentic spiritual lives of the most arresting quality. This is an empirical statement. It does not cover all existing modes of belief. Certain positions seem shallow, others bogus, others frankly evil. One sees this as one looks across the range of cults available in our society today – we don't have to go farther afield, to movements like the Nazis for instance, though here is clearly a case of the latter type. But the number of spiritualities which command our profound respect is plural; of that there is little doubt.

No one has a good account of this. Many people suppose that we all relate to some ultimate reality which we each see partially – the story of the blind men and elephant is meant to illustrate this. Something like this probably holds, but it is of no immediate help. No one can yet stand, even dream of what it would be to stand, at the point where these perspectives join. It may even be in principle beyond human power. To think that we can already make the synthesis is just to propound some weakly beneficent generalities, in which all the particularities of the living traditions are washed out. But it is through the particularities that they animate our lives. Even if we suppose that the ultimate reality is neither God's love as I understand it, nor Nirvana as understood by a Buddhist, I cannot relate to it as a *je ne sais quoi* which is neither. The route of Nathan the Wise is the road to post-Enlightenment banalities, which lose their transforming power very quickly.

What does this call for? Everybody has to put it in their own language, so I'll frame it in mine. I have to recognise that there is another relationship to God (my term), which I don't fully understand, but which I have to respect. And part of respecting it is coming as best as I can to understand it. But that means precisely not trying to reduce it to some common denominator, not trying to fudge the differences with Christianity, because very often the power of this other faith resides in what differentiates it from mine. We have to come to be able to understand – and therefore also admire – spiritualities which are nevertheless not ours.

We will, of course, learn from each other, and borrow considerably. A number of twentieth-century spiritual figures have already done so: for instance, Gandhi, Thomas Merton, John Main, not to mention Buber whom Morgan discusses. But we shouldn't delude ourselves that all the distance can be closed by such borrowing. We need a radical break with the exclusivity claims of the past, the claims to have got it simply right against all others, while recognising that this doesn't put us in a new superior, synthesising position, which in its own way would be simply right against all others. Needless to say, this 'we' here includes the unbelievers among us as well.

Jean Bethke Elshtain

I am grateful to Jean Bethke Elshtain for tracing so well in her work, and now putting together here again, one of the roots of the modern ideal of self-determining freedom. I mean the ideal of freedom as self-control, an ideal whose highest expression would come in a self-making. I tried to describe the growth of this out of the stance of disengagement in *Sources of the self*, but it also has a more specific basis in the evolution of modern political philosophy, and she has brought this to light. The ideal of self-control, or more radically, self-making, is one facet of the modern self, one way to give a sense to the appeal to be ultimately self-responsible, to be free agent as against a victim, or a being shaped by others; it is one way of understanding the demand to be oneself, or 'authentic'.

Elshtain has a challenge for me. The ideal of control can make monsters of us. It can lead us to shut out a lot of reality: the realities of our dependence on others, on the world in which we live, on the 'ontological givenness' involved in being human. Otherwise put, it can make us define any such dependence as a limit, something to be reduced to the minimum; something to be combated. It loses the ability to distinguish between those givens which we should be struggling to acknowledge and those which we rightly want to alter, or even bring under control. It leads us into a metaphysical snowstorm, in which all contour is lost, and everything around us is seen as an obstacle to be combated. So there are ideals of self-making, such as that of the late Foucault, which seem to leave no metaphysical room for the acknowledgement that our identity is also a gift from others, that disciplines can also free us, that some things in the shape of the natural world and of human life command our respect. And these ideals are surprisingly popular among educated people in our society.

Elshtain's challenge for me, if I understand it, can be simply put: am I not being too unambiguously upbeat about the modern identity? Can one be unambiguously upbeat about it when it also generates ideals like this? To the latter question, the answer seems to me to be clearly, no. But is the thrust of my work sliding towards a 'yes'? It could be, but I hope not.

I have been trying to read phenomena like those ideals of self-making which are blind to dependence ('I'll call them 'blind' for short) as *aberrations*. What do I mean by an 'aberration'? Well, first of all, something terribly wrong. I won't try to argue this here; I concur with Elshtain on our judgement on these ideals. But by 'aberration', I mean something more than this; I mean that it is the twisted form of something good. My thesis is that these blind ideals are dependent on spiritual aspirations which are good. They are dependent in that the ideals wouldn't have arisen historically without the underlying aspirations; they piggy-back them, in a sense; and they still depend on these aspirations to make sense. They are in an important way parasitic.

Roughly, I believe that there has been, *inter alia*, a move in modern Western culture towards our taking charge of our natural environment and social relations, taking responsibility for them; there has also been a growing ideal of authenticity, that one be true to one's own peculiar potential as a human being. These are two strands among others, but they are enough to make the point. I consider both of these to have opened important new dimensions of human flourishing. This is not to say, of course, that they have not been difficult to combine with other valuable things in human life; that there has not been and will not continue to be lots of tension and conflict around them. But to me they are human gains.

I consider the blind ideals of self-making to be (at least partly) aberrations in relation to the aspiration to take responsibility, because these ideals arise from an occlusion of the context which gives the aspiration its sense. Taking responsibility can be seen to be a good given what human beings are, their powers, their potentials, their way of being. Taking responsibility specifically for our environment is a good in the context of the natural world, of its place in our lives, and in those of our descendants, and of the respect we owe it. To exult in the fact of control outside of both these contexts, human and natural, is to take joy in power for itself, a kind of joy which can easily tip over into a love of violence, because nothing manifests raw power so completely and convincingly as violence.

The blind ideal of self-making denies the context which makes it believable as a human ideal. It trades on a confusion. It draws some of its force from the modern aspiration to take responsibility, but it suppresses what gives this aspiration its sense and its force. Seen this way, it is what I call an aberration, where something good becomes bad through the non-recognition of the context which gives it sense.

I want to argue that modernity is full of these; classical utilitarianism is a good example. I mean the original theory as we find it in, say Bentham, which was both a psychology and an ethic. Its moral psychology can't recognise the understanding of good which implicitly powers it.

It might be argued that this perspective only makes visible a part of the story. It makes it sound too much as though the blind ideal of self-making were just the aspiration to responsibility which had lost awareness of its essential context. But what if someone wants to break with this aspiration altogether? What if they quite consciously want to exult in power, and even violence? This has not been absent from the modern world. Fascism and Nazism are just the most spectacular cases. In addition today there is a fashion for theories which proudly declare themselves 'anti-humanist', and which often draw on sources which explore and express the fascination for violence (e.g. Bataille and Artaud, as sources of Derrida and Foucault). There are profound moral options in play here, and not simply unconsciousness or inadvertence.

I think we need both perspectives to understand these ideals: that is, both that which sees these forms of blind self-affirmation as a simple falling off from what is good in modern emancipation, a losing from view of the essential context; and that which brings out the polarity between an ethic in continuity with the Platonic-Christian affirmation of the goodness of being, and those views which want to reject this root and branch. So there is certainly something misleading in talking just in the first perspective of these ideals as aberrations. This I have tended to do perhaps too much, and Elshtain's challenge here is also a valid criticism.

Notwithstanding, I think it would be equally wrong just to revert to the other perspective. (I'm not in any way implying that Elshtain is just carrying on the argument into the next issue which must arise.) In fact, the vogue for 'anti-humanist' theories shows a great deal of confusion. Many people adopt Foucault and/or Derrida as a modality of critique of power relations, of domination and inequality, from a basically egalitarian perspective.[3] These writers themselves have often spoken as supporters of a more conventional Left. Plenty of people swear by Foucault or Derrida who are plainly operating in their moral or political lives out of a sense that all human beings are equally worthy of respect, who are vegetarians and attracted by non-violence, who are in an utterly different spiritual universe from Bataille. They are responding to the suggestion that relations of domination and inequality are more subtle and pervasive than we thought, and need a more radical exposure and critique. But their goals are indistinguishable from the many generations who preceded them in the 'humanist' Left. A lot of confusion reigns.[4]

---

[3] See Richard Bernstein's discussion in 'Serious play: the ethical-political horizon of Derrida', Bernstein, *The new constellation* (Cambridge: Polity Press, 1991).

[4] This point was made some years ago by Vincent Descombes; see his review of David Hoy's collection, *Foucault: a critical reader, London Review of Books*, 4 March, 1987. Descombes showed how this somewhat bowdlerized 'Left' reception of Foucault tended to dominate

Motives, also, are very mixed, no doubt. Many people who would never consciously and expressly break with a humanist politics are excited by the more radical critique of all hitherto existing religion and metaphysics which they sense in these neo-Nietzschean theories. Some feminists are drawn by the separatist consequences which seem to be strengthened by the sense that relations of mutuality can always be decoded as modes of domination. And so on. A single grid will never do justice to the phenomenon.

This is all the more so when we take it at its fullest stretch. In the last paragraphs, I've fallen into talking of certain fashionable 'postmodern' theories. But the range of blind ideals of self-control and self-making go way beyond this. There are protagonists of unchained technological control, say over human genetics, who have never heard of postmodernism and probably never will.

Elshtain has a point. I have tended to stress perhaps too much the 'aberration' perspective. But in making the necessary correction, it is important not to lose it from sight. That is because there is too much simplistic thinking which just collapses the two, which sees the aspirations of modernity itself as partaking of blindness. It is a thinking which moves from the undeniable fact that the aspiration to take responsibility involved the displacement of *some* limits, to the conclusion that this aspiration inherently amounts to a rejection of *all* limits. In other words, it confounds the original aspiration and its aberrant form. This is a bad mistake, indeed, a potentially catastrophic one for us who cannot but share the modern identity.

III   Natural and human sciences

Clifford Geertz

I found Clifford Geertz's paper immensely interesting and instructive. He has explored areas which I have all too little visited, and should have seen more of.

I also take to heart his criticism, and welcome the correction. It would be crazy to think of 'natural science' as a single unitary procedure, arching down from the seventeenth century to today. That image was a creation of positivism, cherished for instance by the 'unity of science' movement. It was an invention of philosophers, which, in a way which I have never fully understood, managed to impose itself on some practising

in America, while the somewhat darker, more problematical, anti-humanist side was better understood in France.

scientists, though much less in the non-human than in the human sciences. One of the uses of this myth was to erect a canonical model for the human sciences. It is this model which I have been trying to combat, and in this Geertz is in agreement with me. I hope I haven't myself fallen victim to the image, and come to believe that it is true of some home territory, running uninterrupted from particle physics through geography to biology and much else besides, even if inappropriate for, say, sociology and linguistics.

Certainly I have been no friend to the notion of a neat divide between sciences of mind on one side and nature on the other. The really difficult, and to me really interesting, and as yet unsolved problems have precisely to do with 'putting the mind back into nature', in the words of Gerald Edelman, which Geertz quotes (p. 90–1). One of my earliest, and continuing, philosophical enthusiasms was for the work of Merleau-Ponty, who strove for something which could perhaps be captured in Edelman's phrase.

There is, however, a place where I still feel like resisting the thrust of Geertz's argument. That is where he agreed with Rorty in wanting to bury all versions of the Diltheyan distinction between *Natur-* and *Geisteswissenschaften*. I think some form of this distinction – albeit profoundly reformulated in the spirit of Gadamer – is still very useful. This is not because I want to mark off two big, internally homogeneous domains, sharply demarcated from each other. As I have just indicated, I have no sympathy for either aspect of this idea. What I rather retain from the Diltheyan enterprise is the attempt to get clear on what makes a science really successful, what makes accounts insightful and illuminating. Exploring this may seem at times circular: one identifies successful examples of a given kind of study, then tries to formulate just what makes them so, and then turns back in the light of this perhaps to challenge some of one's original set of examples. In fact, there is no other way to proceed, unless one is in possession of some foundationalist key.

What remains Diltheyan is the conviction that different domains of study yield different answers to this question. There don't have to be just two. But there is a set of features of human beings which makes it so, that being illuminating and insightful about them involves something rather different than being illuminating and insightful about, say, stars and even amoebas. Now what is important in the Diltheyan project is not simply staking out this terrain – although that still has its uses in a culture where reductive explanations still flourish (let's not forget that a Nobel Prize has recently been awarded to a protagonist of an extremely reductive, homogenising mode of explanation in the social sciences). What is interesting and important is the attempt to define what the difference consists in. And here is where I would prefer to speak of a 'neo-Diltheyan' study, because one can be engaged in this project while wanting to set aside, or at least substantially modify, most of what Dilthey himself wrote about forms of life, explanation versus understanding, and the like.

I think this work is extremely important and absolutely indispensable to an enterprise like that of Edelman, for example. He is trying to define a new kind of physiological understanding of our embodied mental life. To some degree, he has to proceed by defining this in contrast to the regnant ways of construing this life. And so it is not surprising to see Edelman square us against and criticise models of function based on the digital computer, for instance. But carrying through this criticism involves getting clear how a model of this kind distorts, what it 'leaves out', fails to capture, or forces into an alien mould. We cannot but be engaged in the Diltheyan (or 'neo-Diltheyan') project of defining the difference. Here we are in the domain where resources drawn from the philosophical tradition, together with those of the specific domain, can be fruitfully combined, in the best Merleau-Pontyan fashion.

I'm not sure I've understood the difficult arguments that Edelman puts forward. But part of his criticism of the computer model seems to focus on what is normally considered one of its strengths, viz. that a computer operates with uninterpreted calculi. The calculus may be interpreted somewhere for some agents, and the computer may be hooked up to the external world in a fashion which is mapped by this interpretation, but the actual working of its programs can be accounted for without reference to this hook up. If I have come even close to the general thrust of Edelman's argument, he seems to be saying that we living embodied minds don't function in this manner. Cortical integration can't be understood unless we take into account the real world environment, not just as the distal cause of changes which could have a sufficient description in intracortical terms. Put in terms of the philosophical tradition, units of cortical integration can only be adequately defined by taking into account what they relate to 'out there'; paralleling the Brentano–Husserl thesis of intentionality for mental contents, that we can only define them in terms of what they are 'of'.

This piece of self-explanation doesn't come to grips with the valuable points that Geertz makes in his paper. If I can put it in the form of self-criticism, I have certainly been too focused on the polemic in the social sciences, and this has narrowed my focus. And perhaps he is right, that the continued attack on the image of unified science, while serving to expel it from the human sciences, has helped to accredit it as an image of 'natural science'. I hope that I am mellowing with age. One of the advantages of growing old is that one sees these various fads for reductive explanation outrun their own credibility and self-destruct, as their 'degenerating' nature as research programmes becomes more and more evident. I have seen behaviourism disappear over the horizon; the strong AI model is following in its train; and with a few more years of life I shall see rational choice go the same way.

Not that I regret attacking these various targets, because one can always learn something neo-Diltheyan along the way. My first book was a vicious attack on, a stab to the heart of, behaviourist psychology. Because it was my thesis (which I lingered over a bit too much), and also because of publishing delays, the victim was dead before the knife entered its vitals. But I never considered the time wasted. I learned a lot. It is just that this lesson, as it has sunk in over the years, has cured me of the belief that it depends on us, humanist St Georges, to slay the dragons.

As I become less focused on the polemic, I am more capable of appreciating the importance of the new frontiers of scientific thinking which I have paid too little attention to, some of which Geertz mentions here: such as the historical understandings of scientific theorising, and the impending revolutions which may sweep away even our contemporary maps, not to speak of the outmoded ones we have been cherishing. I am grateful to Geertz for opening some more windows in the overheated room of my theorising.

Vincent Descombes

I found Vincent Descombes' paper very exciting, because I think he is getting a hold on some of the deep assumptions which have bedevilled discussion of the whole issue of 'objective spirit', and in this way helping us to get beyond certain confusions which have kept us from finding the right categories to talk of social life.

The first imprisoning assumption was the picture of the 'subject' as the sole possible locus of meaning. This meant that any attempt to come to terms with the existence of meanings which go beyond those created or entertained by individual agents would come to be seen as the postulation of some mysterious collective super-subject. Then the manifest oddness, not to say repulsive unbelievability of such postulations would be invoked to discredit any attempt to clarify the supra-individual element in society. Thinking returned to the sterile grooves of 'methodological individualism'. Another result of all this was that even those who were unimpressed by the strictures of methodological individualism had to struggle to liberate themselves from distorting modes of thinking, and only slowly and confusedly are becoming capable of formulating an adequate social ontology. We have all been very confused, as Descombes shows. Thinking in terms of texts, languages, structures, helped to get out of the straightjacket of atomism, but these new terms were (and still are) also frequently misunderstood, or used in several incompatible ways, or misapplied. Descombes points out some of the confusions in my use of the notion of interpretation for instance.

I think that what emerges from Descombes' study is that we have to think of two ways in which sociology (this term used here in the generic sense of any study of society) requires us to think supra-individually. The first is the one he invokes with the term 'dyad' at the end of his paper. We have to allow for what I want to call common actions as well as for individual acts. The difference I'm trying to mark between an individual and a common action lies in the agents' understanding of who is acting. I understand my individual acts as mine, but in common action, there is a common understanding that we are operating together. This is different from the case where a lot of individual actions dovetail, even if each one of us understands that and why they dovetail. As we are all caught together, cursing and fuming in the five o'clock traffic, we all understand well enough how this commonality comes about, but we do not understand ourselves to be acting together.

Some common actions consist of many of us performing identically out of a sense of common purpose (in this latter respect, unlike the traffic jam case); as we stand in the central square shouting 'down with the government'. These 'mob' actions have received a certain amount of attention from social theorists (including both Durkheim and Mead), but they are far from being the paradigm or central cases of common action.

Much more important and pervasive are actions where different roles are distributed among the participants. The conversation is perhaps the paradigm of these, as Descombes' example makes plain. One speaks and the other listens, then the roles reverse, but unlike singing in unison or chanting slogans in the square, there is always a difference of role at any one moment. And yet this is a paradigm common action. Because it is essential to the individual utterances' being interventions in a conversing together, that they are together attending to this issue, or enjoying their mutual repartee, or whatever the focus may be. Conversations make their foci matters for *us*.

As Descombes points out, speaking in a conversation is very different from saying the same words alone in one's room in an attempt to practise one's accent or one's elocutionary style. What makes the difference is that in the first case, and not in the second, the individual action of making this remark has to be understood as part of a common action of sustaining the conversation. 'Behind the question "who is speaking?" there must therefore be the question "who is speaking with whom?", a question which requires as an answer a dyad or a polyad rather than a monad' (p. 117).

This is one distinction between individual and supra-individual which one has to have in one's social ontology; since otherwise one is incapable of accounting for the distinction between, say, solitary linguistic practice and conversational speech. And this would be a pretty crippling disability for any social theory. Beyond this, there is a second locus of the supra-individual, which is the one which Descombes sets out to circumscribe under the term 'objective spirit'. In order for there to be both common and individual action, there has to be a socially understood repertory, from which these actions are drawn. In order for there to be different speech acts both in conversation and solitude, there has to be a language. Language provides the most obvious, and in some ways perhaps the most essentially human form of this relationship, and we are drawn to make it the paradigm or model. So that we see getting married or divorced, entering or breaking a relationship, becoming a leader of the group or stepping out of leadership, as related to the understood repertoire which makes them possible in a way analogous to the relation between speech acts and the common language they are couched in.

Language is supra-individual in a different way than common action. A way which seems more difficult for us to understand and define. Talking in terms of atomism or supra-individuality seems to press us to ask the question: where does language reside anyway? And this seems very difficult to answer.

There is an atomist answer to this question. A language resides in the minds (or brains) of the individuals who speak it. This is very questionable as a sociological answer. It is not just that each of us is inducted into a language as something which preexists us. Nor is it just that any one of us, however erudite, never manages to master a whole language. Each one of us understands ourselves as using a language which we don't fully command. Even as we use certain words, we gesture beyond our own grasp of them to a proper sense which perhaps only some specialists really master. Our implicit speech intentions, if we were to spell them out, would have to be formulated in terms of a language which no single person fully possesses.

Could we think of the language as a capacity distributed between all the individual speakers? This would be to have too restricted a notion of language. In effect, if we want to situate language, we would have to place it at two levels, identified by the Saussurean terms *langue* and *parole*. It is not just an interiorised capacity possessed by a set of speakers at a given moment. This capacity only maintains itself by its continuous exercise. The phenomenon language can only be understood at these two levels. Without *langue*, no *parole*, because the individual's acts of speech are only possible against the background of the repertory, the code. But without *parole*, no *langue*, since this latter is not only sustained but continually redefined in the former.

It is not just a question of trying to place the capacity (the *langue* component). The whole of language also embraces *parole*, and this takes the form primarily of common actions. An individual reduction is out of the question. Apart from the final demise of atomism (when will this victory of reason and good sense finally occur?), what comes out here is the strange and paradoxical ontological status of language – a status which is strange and paradoxical only against the background of our regnant distorting assumptions. It can't simply be placed in the realm of action, because it provides the background or framework within which actions of a certain kind become possible at all. But at the same time, it cannot be clearly relegated to some other domain – e.g. 'structure', or some realisation of structure in the brain – because this background is only continuously there through and in the form of its realisation in action.

Once we see this paradoxical status, we can see how atomism can be laid aside without landing us in some positing of a super-subject. Languages – and other repertories with the same structure – have to be taken as irreducibly social realities. They are not agents, but nor can they be reduced to facets or features of agents – even collective ones. We also have to see that they cannot be well understood by some other images as well, which we have tried to grasp them with: such as texts, for instance, or 'structures', understood simply as systematic causal agencies, and not as backgrounds of meaning. This is convincingly argued by Descombes.

As I indicated earlier, I am not entirely happy with some of my uses of the image of interpretation. Descombes shows what is inept in looking on the ordinary application of a repertory in a society as an interpretation (p. 111–13). In fourth-century Alexandria, one who went off to be a hermit couldn't be said to be 'interpreting himself' as a hermit, in the way that we might say this of someone who chose to live a life on the margins of a modern city. The Alexandrian didn't 'interpret himself' as this; he *was* a hermit.

And yet, there is an important point which I was struggling to make with this perhaps inept image, and which we have to find a way of getting at. As we come in the situation of intercultural comparison to understand better the differences in outlook and understanding between different civilisations, we can come to see the different languages and repertories which are at home in these cultures as offering different takes on a common human condition, which can be gestured at by referring to certain inescapable nodal points; as Peter Winch does in 'Understanding a primitive society' by borrowing the phrase from Eliot about 'birth, copulation and death'.[5] We are born, we die, sexual relations and some form or other of family relations are essential in our lives; we strive for one or other form of love, companionship. It matters less that we cannot define this common lot in a way which every culture could subscribe to, than that we all sense that these nodal points offer the sites of really illuminating comparisons between human societies.

In some sense, then, we could say that different languages encode different ways of understanding our common condition. It was this which I was trying to gesture at with the word 'interpretation', but it is probably a mistake to use this already overloaded term once more in this context. We're still struggling to find the language in this domain, but Descombes in this and other of his writings has helped considerably to dispel confusion and increase our clarity.

IV   Philosophy in practice

Mette Hjort

I read Mette Hjort's paper with great interest. I sensed, of course, that what I had written in *Sources of the self* must have some relation to contemporary controversies in literary theory, but didn't fully understand what the relation was. I have to confess that I still don't have an adequate grasp of this, but Hjort's paper has perhaps put me on the track of some useful questions.

Hjort tries in a sense to place me on their map. But I don't yet recognise myself. Thus, she states five theses that jointly define a position called 'aesthetic autonomy' (p. 129). She suggests that I am committed to three of these. But I can't find a non-strained reading of any of them that I would subscribe to. The first states that the artist is a genius. What do I think of this? Well, in the sense we use the term these days, some artists are, and lots of others aren't. But the same could be said for scientists, political leaders, performers, philosophers, etc. Is the gift of these exceptional people natural or social? How could it be all one or the other? Maybe the idea here is that what distinguishes an exceptional person from others is not their upbringing but their natural endowment. This seems plausible, but just as much for Einstein and Kant as for Mozart.

The third thesis says that 'art is untouched by means–ends calculations'. I'm not sure what this means, but I can imagine giving it content with the understanding that there are features or qualities which make for

[5] Peter Winch, 'Understanding a primitive society', *Understanding and social inquiry*, ed. Fred R. Dallmyr and Thomas A. McCarthy (Notre Dame: University of Notre Dame Press, 1977), pp. 159–89.

excellence of a work of art (not at all necessarily the same for all of them), and others which are irrelevant. Means–ends calculations aimed at the irrelevant features don't contribute to the excellence, and may in certain cases even detract from it. When, under threat from Zhdanov, Soviet writers modified their texts, it was often to their detriment. The thesis would then be a normative statement: art ought to be untouched by such calculations – although of course it often is.

Read this way, the third thesis would seem to require some version of the fifth, which Hjort also ascribes to me: the world of art is autonomous and governed exclusively by a set of specifically aesthetic norms and conventions. Now if this means just that there are some considerations which are external to aesthetic excellence, in the sense of the previous paragraph, then I do agree with it, and with the associated reading of thesis three. But this fifth claim is often taken in a much stronger form: that the aesthetic is a domain quite unrelated to any other, and in particular, the moral or spiritual. This I emphatically do not believe, as is evident from the later chapters of *Sources of the self*. This is not to say that the relationship is simple, and easy to state. It's evident that aesthetic excellence doesn't just amount to spiritual or moral depth, for instance. But the two cannot be neatly dissociated either, in my view.

So I do subscribe to versions of three and five, but in a weak form which I can't imagine anyone denying. To do so, we would have to hold that *no* consideration at all could be external to art, and no purposes could be detrimental. There is certainly, in distinction from this, a strong form of aesthetic autonomy, but with this I strongly disagree.

Hjort sets out three features of defining 'legitimate' over against 'popular' taste today: that one privileges form over function, that one is 'disinterested' in utility, function or even truth/falsehood, that one favours the conceptual, abstract, formal (p. 134). I am, needless to say, completely out of sympathy with this position. To put it very simply, I think (at least some) art has to do with the truth, and that is why I was concerned with the 'epiphanic'. Indeed, I find that the polarisation set up here between 'legitimate' and 'popular' leaves out a lot. If we could only join one or other of the camps described here, we would be in a parlous condition indeed.

In short, I can't find my way into the disputes as defined here. But perhaps I can say something about a central point that Hjort seems to be making, in her invocation of Bourdieu. I am a great admirer of one aspect of Bourdieu's work, his fine definitions of the role of theory and models in social science, and his understanding of the crucial place of practice. But I think his theory of cultural capital is pushed to a point where it becomes preposterous, and lands him in a form of ethnocentrism even worse than the one he has so painstakingly escaped with his theory of practice.

Theories of this global kind auto-destruct, because they make it impossible to answer crucial and inescapable questions about human life and history. This can be seen most clearly with utter vulgar Marxism. Following this we might want to explain, for instance, the Reformation in terms of the underlying economic interests of various social groups, because we firmly believe that this is all that really actuates people in history. But if this is true, then we cannot explain why people ever came to believe themselves to be responding to religious doctrines and stances. All right, for some actors the religious is just a pretext, a covering, a strategically presented justification. But it couldn't be this for *all* agents, or the pretext would lose its point. If there were no such thing as religious motivation, there would be no one to impress with a parading of piety, and no strategic advantage to presenting oneself as pious. At a certain point of uncompromising completeness, the reductive account auto-destructs. What vulgar Marxism needs and doesn't have is some account of why people are religious *überhaupt*.

Bourdieu's theory of social distinction through taste seems to me to be in the same pass. As soon as one renders total the explanation for people's taste in terms of their struggle for distinction and symbolic capital, the account leaves us incapable of understanding why taste can ever serve to distinguish. Unless art has some independent power for humans, in some way interpellates us and commands our admiration, then we couldn't possibly use it to enhance our position by defining our taste.

Defining taste hierarchies for purposes of social enhancement is very obviously an important social game in our civilisation. But it has in an important sense to be parasitic. Unless art has some 'aura', to use Benjamin's term in a broader sense, unless it commanded our attention or awe independently of the games of distinction, these would be powerless actually to advance anyone's symbolic capital. But if art has this independent power, then it follows that not all rankings can be artefacts of games of distinction. By universalising his account, Bourdieu renders it useless. Once it covers everything, it self-destructs.

All this means that there must be a question, parallel to the one about religion above (p. 226–30): what is it about art that commands our engagement with it, even love, admiration and awe? It would be surprising if there were a single, one-line answer to this question. It rather opens up a field of interrogation, but one of great importance if we want to understand ourselves. I believe that this point parallels one of the crucial arguments which Hjort develops in her path-breaking new work,[6] if I've understood her rightly.

[6] *The strategy of letters* (Cambridge, Mass.: Harvard University Press, forthcoming).

What I was doing in late chapters of *Sources of the self* involved suggesting a very partial and tentative answer in relation to some modernist works, which by no means excludes a host of other answers not only in respect of other works, but even regarding the ones I mention, which are after all complex and many faceted. Hjort understands this field incomparably better than I do, but I don't think that in offering such an answer I am necessarily denying the strategic dimension of art. Of course, I do want to say that strategic considerations related to purposes unconnected to the excellence of a work of art must be parasitic. They could never give us the whole explanation, for reasons I have just outlined.

This does obviously commit me to some thesis in this domain, *viz.* that there are some considerations external to a work of art, that is, for any given work there are some goals strategic pursuit of which is irrelevant and can be damaging to the value of that work. Toadying to Stalin or Mao or other such gruesome dictators offers an example in relation to certain works of literature. These considerations don't need to be the same for all kinds of art – although it is hard to think of a genre where obeying the directions of a Zhdanov would enhance value.

I don't see how a thesis of this kind could be plausibly denied, as a matter of fact. But leaving this aside, I don't believe that it amounts to denying the place of strategic considerations in the life and work of artists. All it is incompatible with is the thesis *either* that there are no external considerations, *or* that the strategic pursuit of external considerations offer the entire explanation for such discriminations as people make. In any other, more believable sense, the strategic dimension is not denied.

Similarly, I hope that my discussion of certain nineteenth- and twentieth-century works didn't involve a depreciation of today's popular art. There is a dynamic in some art of the last two centuries which pits an *avant-garde* against a supposedly uncomprehending 'philistine' public. I didn't mean to be taking sides for or against this in reporting it. In fact, my feelings about this are complex and many sided, and I haven't got room to go into them here.

I then wanted to note, for instance in the passage quoted by Hjort, that this dynamic gets caught up in today's media and art market in a certain bad faith where *avant-garde* posturing is in collusion with a market sustained by the very 'philistine' audience one is supposedly defining oneself against (p. 134). It seems to me that there is a kind of corruption involved here, and I do judge it negatively. But I don't understand the phenomenon judged here as 'popular art', and certainly not in the sense of the distinction Hjort makes (p. 135). On the contrary, it is partly constitutive of what she describes as 'legitimate' taste. The 'meat dress' that she cites, displayed recently in the National Gallery in Ottawa, is an excellent case in point. But popular art in some more genuine sense I in no way want to condemn.

I am still struggling to find myself in the unfamiliar world of literary theory. I hope, perhaps against the immediate evidence, that trying to come to grips with Hjort's paper has advanced me a little. In any case, I am grateful to her for giving me the chance to attempt it.

Patricia Benner

I have learned enormously from Patricia Benner's work, and from her personal example. She has helped to transform our understanding of health care by articulating facets of it which had fallen into a kind of limbo in the generalised accounts of it which tended to circulate in our civilisation; the accounts which tend to surface in public discussion and bureaucratic assessment. These facets were still very much alive to many care-givers, and particularly to nurses, on whom the role of giving day-by-day, minute-by-minute care tends to devolve. But they had lost some of their legitimacy, their importance was underrecognised, and they became easier to shunt aside in the face of other, more seemingly important facets.

We can see a good example of this in Benner's discussion of 'following the body's lead'. There is often a penchant to give priority to the use of what seems the most effective technology; negatively put, the priority is on reducing to a minimum the risk of failure through not having used the best technology available. This can be intrusive, alienating, even inhuman and therapeutically self-defeating. Sensitive judgements have to be made by someone who is attuned to the patient and can override this imperative on occasion. Now in a technological and bureaucratic civilisation, which values 'heroic medicine', and multiplies rules to avoid risk, the voice of sensitive judgement is often silenced. It can be made to appear pretechnological and arbitrary. Even those whose spontaneous response is to scale back the intrusive technology can be made to feel that their standpoint is somehow inferior, less skilled or 'scientific'.

Benner has helped to give this kind of standpoint a hearing. She has brought it to articulation. And she has done so principally by opening a space in which those who have this standpoint – principally nurses – can articulate it. The effect has been not only to give the public new perspectives and new terms. Important as this is, it is perhaps less important than the empowerment of the articulators themselves which has frequently followed. In telling their stories, in finding how much is shared by others, care-givers can come to a clearer sense of their perspective, and a firmer conviction of its importance and legitimacy.

The kind of standpoint illustrated by 'following the body's lead' was not only under a disadvantage through being at odds with our techno-logical-bureaucratic culture. It also fit badly into the canons of acceptable articulation, which tended – above all in the academic and bureaucratic worlds – to favour 'theoretical' statements in general terms, preferably 'experience-far' ones, purged of the heat of intense personal feeling. But to do something like following the body's lead, you have to be attuned to the patient's self-feeling and self-description, you have to be 'experience-near' to the utmost. Moreover, the kind of judgement you are making is one which cannot be rendered anything like adequately in general rules. This is a paradigm area where Aristotle's model of judgement by phronê-sis is at home. As Benner's story shows, sometimes the best medicine is 'anecdotal' (p. 140).

So this kind of articulation also requires a different medium. Under-standing, as in so much that is really important in human life, comes through narrative. Benner's work centrally features stories. The stories are those of practitioners, who often clarified and empowered themselves in telling them. Then they are retold, commented on and the comments lead us to other such stories. The comments allow us to see the relevance of the stories outside of situations immediately similar to the one being related. They permit us to see the more general structures and modes of thought which are blocking us here, like the ones I gestured at in talking of technological and bureaucratic civilisation, articulating itself in theory. But the comments would be much less incisive and penetrating without the stories. They help to give the stories a wider application, but the stories remain central to the enterprise.

The way of proceeding brings us close to how we really understand ourselves in our ethical lives. We are incapable, lacking insight, or in the grip of a dangerous obsession, when we try to proceed without such stories in moral thinking. This means that Benner's work has tremendous relevance not only for understanding health care but for the whole newly burgeoning domain of medical ethics.

It is in fact tremendously hard for us to think well systematically in a domain of this kind. By using the qualifier, I mean to acknowledge that many practitioners make wise and shrewd judgements in difficult situ-ations. But when we try to erect a systematic discipline of such matters, we tend to do rather poorly. Besides all the obstacles I mentioned above to clear general thinking in this domain, there is an additional difficulty. And that is, that the kinds of expertise that one needs to think well at this level are hard to combine.

I can perhaps make this point most simply by adverting to the two elements in Benner's texts which I mentioned above. The stories can only be generated by people who are actually working in care, with experience and sensitivity which comes with much practice. The general comments require familiarity with the broader context of society and the tradition of thought. And this you acquire by another painstaking apprenticeship, generally in the academy. It's very hard in the nature of things, in the time you need to become proficient in these different domains, as well as in the career structures of the different professions, to combine these two kinds of capacity. And yet effective general thinking about these matters, as much about the nature of health care, as about medical ethics, requires both of them.

To some extent one can overcome the difficulty through collaboration between people with the different capacities and backgrounds. But this itself doesn't work unless there are at least some people who have enough familiarity with the two to guide this collaborative effort. There have to be 'bicultural' people (to borrow an expression from my somewhat obsessive concern for Canadian politics) in order to get effective bicultural collaboration between lots of people with only one of these cultures.

Here is where Benner's special contribution has been so vitally important. Uniting experience in the field with philosophical reflection, she has been able to bring together in a fruitful way those who are only on one side or the other. She has made them able to speak usefully to each other. As one who has felt keenly the need to participate in this collaborative enterprise, without having the full means of doing so, I am very much in her debt for having given me a way in.

I hope that the collaboration will extend, over a wider and wider range of people and expertise, so that we can eventually become capable of dealing with some of the most intractable problems which lie on this ground between theory and practice.

V   Ethics, politics and pluralism

Richard Tuck

I found Richard Tuck's paper characteristically interesting and illuminating. I certainly hadn't grasped the theories of the early rights theorists in the framework which he offers. I'm sure it makes a difference, but I'm still struggling to see exactly what it is.

First, a quick note in clarification. The target, in 'Atomism', of my argument that the claim to rights can't stand alone without some understanding of human good, was Nozick and other contemporaries who think like him, not the classical founders of rights theory.

That doesn't mean that I think the classical thinkers' formulations are problem free. Tuck makes a crucial distinction between 'foundationalist' thinkers who seem to hold that all of ethics can be derived from a single principle – utilitarians and Kantians are prime examples – and definers of certain core demands which are universal. The core demands are not felt to be at the origin of all our ethical commitments. But they are – or clearly should be – part of everyone's ethical outlook. Only they allow alongside them other demands – e.g. conceptions of the good life, virtue, etc. – which are precisely what vary so greatly between different civilisations. Whatever we do about this variety – and that can include the greatest openness and willingness to learn from others – we can at least accept the universally binding nature of the core.

So described, the agenda of Grotius, Hobbes and Locke – the great founders – sounds tremendously relevant today. We too, are struggling to combine an acceptance of moral diversity with a convergence on agreed standards of human rights. We see developing today a more insistent demand that nations abide by certain such minimum standards than that they align their régimes with some norm. The impact of Amnesty International, for instance, is as great as it is just because it concentrates on core rights, as against more contentious issues.

But, how to justify these attempts to define a core? Now I think that the wrong way to try is through some epistemological distinction: the core would be in some way more obvious, less contentious and open to dispute, than understandings of the good life. This kind of distinction is made, of course, by certain modern Western theories, notably Kantian ones: the rule of right can be distinguished from people's conceptions of happiness (Kant), or of the good life (Habermas), and given a different, more secure foundation (in reason itself, or the commitments involved in discourse, or whatever). But this distinction is internal to *one* historical view. One couldn't ask an Aristotelian or a Thomist, let alone people from other cultures altogether, to buy this radical distinction between the right and the good, or between definitions of rights and those of human flourishing.

So a foundation of the universal core on a rights/goods distinction could only be a parochial foundation, and would have no title to win the assent of even all Westerners, let alone those outside. What does that leave us with? Another image that Tuck uses seems very good here: cultures are Venn diagrams which overlap at this core (p. 165). That is, they either do in fact now; or you could persuade each to converge on this overlap using resources internal to each. So you wouldn't try to make an Aristotelian culture buy into Kantianism as a prelude to signing the Universal Declaration; but you would concentrate on showing how from the Aristotelian outlook itself, certain fundamental immunities (life, liberty, bodily integrity, etc.) ought to be respected, certain discrimina-tions could no longer be defended, etc. (Of course, I mean 'Aristotelian' in the sense of the basic ontology; not a defence of every one of Aris-totle's doctrines, including those indefensible in the light of knowledge and experience gained today.)

So there are two possible discourses of the universal core. One is that of what Rawls calls the 'overlapping consensus', where one says roughly: we all seem to share an intuition that these human immunities are of unique importance, although we articulate this in very different terms, and draw the boundaries of these immunities differently. Let's see if we can come to some agreement on these boundaries, each from within our own horizons.

The other is the discourse of philosophical authority: see here, we have demonstrated (from out of our outlook, of course) that there is a funda-mental difference between (say) the rule of right and conceptions of the good life, religion, etc.; we have further shown that the first is more important and ought to trump the second. So kindly take your various religious, metaphysical and ethical conceptions and keep them out of the way of the Declaration of Rights which we hereby ground.

I'm not clear which of these discourses Tuck is attributing to the great founders. Conceivably they had some of each. They didn't live in our situation, and face the (politico-philosophical) need to distinguish them as we do. But (and this might be my prejudices) their discourse often sounds to me like that of philosophical authority. Does Hobbes leave any room at all for Aristotle's conception of the good life? Can Locke allow for a *polis* ethic? And when Grotius argues the justice of seizing aborigi-nal land, it sounds very much like a unilateral attempt to define the boundaries from out of a single authoritative discourse, trumping all others. We have a lot to learn from the founders, but a lot to unlearn as well.

When one really gets in an authoritative mode, it doesn't matter so much that one is not strictly 'foundationalist' in Tuck's sense; that is, that one does not claim to derive all the detail of ethics from the core. If the core is uniquely important; if it always trumps all the rest; then it is suffi-cient that one has grounded *all that matters* from a single source. This is, after all, what Kant, and foundationalist thinkers after him, e.g. Haber-mas, claim to do. There are other issues, which discourse ethics can't decide, e.g. what I and my culture consider a fulfilling life. But the deliverances of a discourse ethic must take precedence over these.

In other words, we don't ground everything, but we ground what trumps. If the great founders spoke the language of philosophical auth-ority, then they were such 'trump foundationalists'. I found Tuck's account of these founders extremely illuminating, but I am not yet convinced that he has cleared them of this charge (which is, after all only one in the eyes of our age).

Daniel M. Weinstock

I read Daniel Weinstock's carefully argued paper with great interest. It convinced me that I am still somewhat muddled, but I don't think the muddle is exactly where he places it. Nevertheless, a lot of things still need to be made clearer.

First, a quick word about 'strong evaluation'. I think this is something like a human universal, present in all but what we would clearly judge as very damaged human beings. But that is because I don't define it in quite the way that Weinstock suggests. I don't consider it a condition of acting out of a strong evaluation that one has articulated and critically reflected on one's framework. Clearly this would be to set too narrow entry conditions. I mean simply that one is operating with a sense that some desires, goals, aspirations are qualitatively higher than others. A true 'simple weigher' in all contexts in life would be a severely pathological case, incapable even of what we would call an identity, incapable of shame and much else.

Even if we take the caricature of the portrait we moderns make of the Homeric Age Greek warrior, or some of the unfortunate interlocutors of Socrates, where the level of reflection was at its lowest, we plainly have people who consider some modes of life higher than others. Some are 'honourable' and others 'shameful'. It's not simply the case that value flows from what you *de facto* want. The fact that it never occurred to them to challenge these frameworks is neither here nor there.

My mistake was in using the word 'evaluation', with its overtones of reflection and deliberate opting for one alternative rather than another. I should really find another term. But I won't go into that here, because the substance of Weinstock's criticism can still stand even after this terminological revision. It's true that I do value post-Homeric reflection about one's frameworks, and so if this should lead me to adopt a mode of liberalism which I have been criticising, then I'm in trouble, however you formulate it.

But am I? I'm not entirely convinced. I think Weinstock gives a very clear and fair account of much of what I've said on this issue. His instinct is right, even though he doesn't quite attribute this to me: the attack in 'Atomism' on modes of rights theory which try to deny their reliance on underlying notions of the human good was, as I indicated above in discussing Tuck's paper, written mainly with Nozick in mind. I don't think of this as applying to the theories of Rawls and Dworkin.

This brings me to the heart of my uneasiness with their kind of theory. Let me say one thing as a way of framing the debate. For me, it is not a matter of branding neutrality between various life conceptions as something wrong in principle. Quite the contrary, it is clearly an important good, even indispensable, in certain contexts of the modern liberal state. For instance, these states are neutral between different religious confessions, and it is extremely important that they be so. They should aim to provide the maximum freedom for their citizens to search out and practise various models of the good life.

So much is agreed. Where I disagree is in the absolute pretensions of this kind of theory; the claim to have found *the* principle of liberal society; or the principle which ought to trump all others wherever they come into conflict. I find this whole mode of thinking unreal. Here I think Aristotle did have an insight which has tended to get lost in modern philosophy. We don't and couldn't live our lives this way. Neither our individual lives, nor the lives of our societies. There are always a plurality of goods, vying for our allegiance, and one of the most difficult issues is how to combine them, how to adjudicate at the places where they come into conflict, or mutually restrict each other. I have no difficulty with the idea that offering the greatest scope for different modes of life and conceptions of the good is *an* important goal. I cavil at the idea that it can be *the* goal; that is, that it doesn't have at certain points to compose with other ends, which will require its limitation.

In short, the entire style of moral thinking which Bentham and Kant have in common, whatever their differences, i.e. that it makes sense to look for the single principle of morality, from which everything can be deduced, strikes me as utterly misguided in its very essence. And the analogous way of reasoning which these schools, in their mutually absorbed conflict with each other, have introduced into political thinking is equally unfortunate.

That's (one of the many reasons) why I'm unhappy with the term 'communitarianism'. It sounds as though the critics of this liberalism wanted to substitute some other all-embracing principle, which would in some equal and opposite way exalt the life of the community over everything. Really the aim (as far as I'm concerned) is more modest: I just want to say that single-principle neutral liberalism can't suffice. That it has to allow for other goods with which it will have to compose, and put some water in its wine, on pain of our forgoing other very important things. Or perhaps the case might be put more strongly; perhaps the integral realisation only of this principle verges on the impossible.

Let me try to indicate why I think this with three examples.

First, the case of cultural continuity, as in the situation of Québec today. Here I am not really satisfied with Weinstock's justification of this, just as I wasn't with Kymlicka's. The goal of some Québec legislation is to ensure survival and flourishing of the linguistic community. The attempt is to create a situation in which the probability is maximised that the children and grandchildren of existing Quebeckers, both home-grown and immigrant, will have French as their principal language. I tried to show how Kymlicka's reframing of the Rawls–Dworkin variety of liberalism can't encompass this. It argues from the needs of existing people, whereas this is concerned with future people. Nor does it help to point out that Rawls' original position can include the members of future generations, because the point is not that their interests are being considered as they might formulate them themselves, prior to any cultural identity; rather *we* are determining now what their cultural identity will be.

It doesn't seem to me that invoking the condition of respect helps either. I don't need to have any disrespect for French culture, to consider it inferior to English, if I decide that it isn't worth spending resources so that Franco-Ontarians can go on educating their children in French. Any more than the analogous American movements mean any disrespect when they turn their face against fostering minority Hispanic education. Many liberals of impeccable credentials are in this camp (including, I believe Rawls). Someone like myself who is sympathetic to cultural survival in these cases might judge that these people lack sensitivity and understanding, and that in this sense their respect is worth less. But they can't be taxed with sinning against this Rawlsian principle.

Survivance is just another matter. It is another good. I agree with Weinstock that it shouldn't be privileged at the expense of analogous survival needs of others, or of others' fundamental rights. But this concerns the judgements we would make of how to combine the goods. I don't think any useful goal is served trying to pretend that we aren't dealing with two independent goods which have to be combined.

The question which comes to my mind is: why go on trying to squeeze blood from a stone, trying to torture everything we hold dear out of the single canonical principle? It is very reminiscent of utilitarians trying to find ways of proving that the felicific calculus would never justify torture or gladiatorial combat on late-night TV. Why don't they just relax and admit that goods are plural, and save themselves all these strained arguments?

Second, the republican argument. As well as liberal, neutral societies, which offer freedom in the sense appropriate to these, we also live in democracies and value what Tocqueville called political freedom. Now our commitment to this is a commitment to a certain kind of good. Unless we value democracy purely instrumentally, as a bulwark for negative liberty, or as a condition of economic productivity, we will see intrinsic value in people being in charge of their own lives through institutions of self-government. We will be striving to make these more effective, to stave off citizen alienation, creeping bureaucratisation, the various forms of 'soft despotism', and the like.

There seems no sense to me in pretending that this is not another good we are seeking. And it also seems to me evident that this makes it difficult to be neutral all the way around. Of course, I agree with Weinstock about the dangers of canonising some versions of natural history. But consider another issue. We can somehow seek to inculcate in school this ethic of participation. This certainly goes against other world-views, which consider this kind of activity irrelevant, or even in some cases the service of anti-Christ. But should we be given pause by the thought that the convictions of some groups would be discriminated against here?

Of course, the liberal principle already allows from some discrimination, as Weinstock shows. It couldn't on pain of incoherence give equal value to views which denied liberalism itself. People who propose to apply Khomeini's *fatwa* against Salman Rushdie must be restrained by the law. There is no other way in a liberal society. But in the above example, I'm talking about a non-neutrality motivated not by the commitment to the principle of neutral liberalism, but by another good, that of participatory, citizen self-rule. We seem to be operating here out of a sense that there is another good at stake here, which justifies derogation from strict neutrality.

The third example. I believe that our present structures of work and career are terribly hard on people who want both to work and have children. Our society is operating on a model which grew up when women were generally confined to the home, when in fact today many women want to have and are in careers. Various measures are proposed to deal with this. One of them is more day-care. This is certainly important. The question is whether it goes far enough. How about people who want to take care personally of their children for more hours and over a longer period than a combination of day-care and maternity leave will allow? Such people abound today, and they are forced to make difficult, even agonising choices.

Well, we could go on and try a larger-scale revolution, changing our very concept of the continuing job or the career, to allow for someone maintaining a job or career, through fairly extended parental leaves, and also periods of part-time, flexible work, back to eventual full-time integration, with refresher courses built in where appropriate. This would require much greater re-organisation, and changing of hallowed patterns or work and career competition, than would, say, continuing the present pattern and building more and more day-care.

How do we decide which direction to go in? Of course, the fact that many people want to take care of their children longer, if I'm right about this, is a relevant consideration. But I cannot believe that our thoughts about what is a good pattern of life, both for the fulfilment of parents, and for the well-being of children is not going to enter our decision making here. Indeed, I cannot see how one could decide if one tried to factor it out. We can't give people everything they want when it comes to social spending. We have to make judgements about the relative weight and worth of different demands. And yet we are here in the midst of one of those controversial issues about modes of family life which has been put on the agenda of our society.

Neutral liberalism as a total principle seems to me here a formula for paralysis; or else for hypocrisy, if one tried to occlude the real reasons. It is at this point that it begins to appear more than costly; in truth, inapplicable.

Guy Laforest

I am grateful to Guy Laforest for his very fair-minded assessment of my contributions to the unending Canadian constitutional debate. The more so, in that we were on different sides in the last wrenching referendum confrontation. As he suggests, I was more than able to understand the objections of many Quebeckers to the Charlottetown Accord. It was indeed, a very imperfect document, which attempted to give recognition to Québec's distinctness in language which could nevertheless carry the assent of many people in the rest of the country who are rather suspicious of the whole idea, and are not always happy with Québec's difference. In the end, we should not be surprised that the Accord ended up being rejected in both halves of the country. For Quebeckers, the recognition was not clear and unambiguous enough, and, after the rejection of the earlier Meech Lake amendments, they were looking for something much more frank and unmistakable; they were no longer satisfied with a wink and a nod (as unsuspecting Albertans were recruited behind formulae which said less or more depending on the spin you gave them). But in the rest of the country, the distrust for existing leaders was such that the game of polysemic formulae backfired: people tended to project into them the most unacceptable interpretations, instead of resting assured that the best gloss was the one intended.

It seems clear to me that the Québec/Canada constitutional imbroglio will never be at a happy end (an unhappy ending is all to conceivable, and threatens again in the upcoming Québec election) until it becomes possible – if ever it does – to accept openly an asymmetrical form of federalism, instead or trying to operate in a framework in which, in spite of all adjustments, Québec is still placed as one among ten uniform provinces. I voted for the Charlottetown Accord not because I thought it was this happy end, but because I saw it as opening the road to such an eventual understanding. Very often in politics a half-understanding is better than no understanding, because if people live with it for a number of years, one can sometimes use this experience to allay their fears or their repulsion in face of the full, unambiguous arrangement which is at present beyond your reach. So I thought it might be with asymmetry after a number of years of the Charlottetown constitutional amendments.

I was also swayed by my fears about the possible consequences of rejection. One might well ask, after all these years, why go on struggling against the break up of Canada? On one reading, it might appear that more and more people on both sides are coming around to accept it. Why not just give in? My reasons for going on are partly a gut emotional identification with Canada, but this is continuously fed by a belief that the country has the potential to bring off a remarkable experiment in what I called 'deep diversity'.[7] I am also apprehensive about the climate in the successor states. I recognise the principled commitment of the *indépendentiste* leadership in Québec to building an open, tolerant, pluralistic society, with place for minority cultures. But I sense in the dynamic of the independence movement itself, in the passions it feels required to mobilise, the harbingers of a rather narrower and more exclusionist society. And very much the same can be said, *mutatis mutandis*, for the movements in English Canada which would be glad to see Québec go.

Separation would mean not only the failure of the Canadian experiment in deep diversity, but also the birth of two new states in a climate in some ways even less amenable to diversity than our present ambiguous condition. A society can succeed in accommodating real differences to the extent that its members can live with complex, many-poled identities. From this point of view, the ability of many Quebeckers to feel both Québécois and Canadian is not a regrettable in capacity to liberate themselves from a history of domination, but a potential growth point for citizen maturity and openness. I cannot see how the attempts of the separatist Parti Québécois to shatter this identity and pulverise one of its terms can lead to more *openness*, whatever else it might accomplish. An analogous point can be made about the simplified Canadian identity propounded by those separatists in English Canada who want to 'let Québec go'.

Both separatist movements are strengthened, and the attempts at

---

[7] See 'Shared and divergent values', reprinted in *Reconciling the solitudes*, pp. 155–86.

mutual understanding considerably hampered, by very strongly anchored misapprehensions about the possible bases of unity of a modern state (at least, I consider them misapprehensions). We are always being led to search for likenesses, points of convergence, common goals or values. Proposing in English Canada a model of the country as recognising diversity very often provokes the anxious question: but what will unite us?

This is indeed a very pertinent question. It is just that the answers recognised as legitimate are sometimes unnecessarily narrowed. Friendship is obviously very different from the political bond, but as Aristotle pointed out, there are analogies. Now friendship is often grounded partially on similarities, but it also can arise out of differences, which are felt by each party as enriching. And in particular, a long history together can make the interchange with some partner, precisely in his/her difference, internal to one's own identity.

There are political relations which bear some resemblance to this. And we can see them in Canada. For an indeterminate but large number of Canadians of both language groups, the history of their association with people of the other language has become part of their sense of their own national identity. The bond is precisely not based here on likeness, or (simply) on unity of purpose, but the sense of a partnership formed over the decades by a common history. Or to put it another way, one common purpose for these people is maintaining this association – one might say, conversation[8] – with people whom they recognise as different. For these people, this will be one strand of a many-stranded sense of Canadian unity. But it is an essential one. If this were to fray to the point of rupture – as it certainly has for many Canadians – none of the others would suffice to keep the country together.

The insistent demand for common traits, goals or purposes – not in itself, because plainly these have their importance, but as the only basis for Canadian unity – has the effect of delegitimating, and hence further weakening what is in fact an essential element of this unity. The ideas that Canadian unity must imperatively repose on a single, uniformly applied interpretation of the Charter, or that it requires a hyperactive and controlling central government, reflect this misapprehension.

There is no doubt that this is strong, and even perhaps growing stronger in our society. There are many reasons for this. But one surely is that this premium on unity as unanimity is very profoundly inscribed in

---

[8] This point had been eloquently made in a very insightful new book by Jeremy Webber, *Reimagining Canada: language, culture, community and the Canadian constitution* (Montréal: McGill-Queens University Press, 1994).

the models of democratic, popular government which we have developed over the last two centuries. This is obvious in one of the most famous and influential theories which has been taken up by some as the paradigm statement of the democratic ideal; I mean Jean-Jacques Rousseau's conception of *la volonté générale*. But it is widespread even among many who would repudiate the Genevan and all his works.

It is indeed true that popular government, construing as it does all the members of the political community as members of the same unit of *decision*, requires that they have a stronger sense of their unity than was required of the subjects of more authoritarian modes of rule. The old Austrian Empire governed the most diverse and mutually unrelated groups of people. Polish Galician peasants never saw Viennese bourgeoisie or Hungarian gentry; such people may even have been outside their horizons. This did nothing to undermine the stability of this empire – on the contrary – until the age when legitimate government came more and more to be conceived as popular. For the members of a modern electorate can't be that mutually ignorant and unconcerned. Or rather, when they are, it creates a profound tension, because it is understood to mean that some people are being left out, that they are not full members who count in the unit of decision to which supposedly everyone belongs, and which is usually spoken of as a 'people'.

This importance of the 'people' as an agent of decision has generally come to be construed as requiring *uniformity* of some or other kind as its only available ground. This presumption has only been strengthened by the considerable role that nationalism has played in the forming and identities of such peoples. So now we can easily come to believe that unity requires uniformity. Of course, we also believe in diversity; but now we all too easily tend to think that national unity has to be maintained *over against* the necessary diversity by some strong common traits. It requires some quasi-unanimity underlying the differences. This is not totally wrong; it is just radically incomplete. But the mistake is fateful, for it can delegitimate otherwise possible modes of coexistence of diverse peoples. And it always gives the high ground to the proponents of separatist nationalism when they offer their more narrow universes as the only way the state can function as a modern, democratic entity. It is a curious but unfortunate fact that the thought of Pierre Trudeau, the former Liberal prime minister of Canada, and that of Jacques Parizeau, the leader of the separatist Parti Québécois, tend to converge on the issue of the place of communities within the nation. One senses, either in their overt expressions, or in their whole attitude, their lack of sympathy for aboriginal calls for self-government, for instance. This shared uniformitarian assumption, played out in its two possible variants, is literally tearing Canada apart.

But fortunately, the outcome is not yet decided. The debate goes on. And we will go on benefiting from the contributions of Laforest, who has already done a great deal to shape it.

Bibliography of the works of Charles Taylor

BOOKS

The explanation of behaviour (London: Routledge and Kegan Paul, 1964)
Pattern of politics (Toronto: McClelland and Stewart, 1970)
  A section reprinted in Thomas A. Hockin, ed., *Apex of power* (Scarborough, Ontario: Prentice-Hall, 1971)
Hegel (Cambridge: Cambridge University Press, 1975)
  German translation: *Hegel* (Frankfurt: Suhrkamp, 1978)
  Swedish translation: *Hegel* (Stockholm: Symposion Bokförlag, 1986)
Erklärung und Interpretation in den Wissenschaften vom Menschen (Frankfurt: Suhrkamp, 1975)
Hegel and modern society (Cambridge: Cambridge University Press, 1979)
  Japanese translation (Tokyo: Iwanami Shoten, 1980)
  Spanish translation: *Hegel v la sociedad moderna* (Mexico: Fondo de cultura economica, 1983)
  Italian translation: *Hegel e la società moderna* (Bologna: Il Mulino, 1984)
  Chinese translation (Taipeh: Modern Foreign Press, 1988)
  Swedish translation: *Hegel och det moderna samhället* (Göteborg: Röda Bokförlaget, 1991)
Social theory as practice (Delhi: Oxford University Press, 1983)
Philosophical papers, I: Human agency and language (Cambridge: Cambridge University Press, 1985)
Philosophical papers, II: Philosophy and the human sciences (Cambridge: Cambridge University Press, 1985)
Negative Freiheit (Frankfurt: Suhrkamp, 1988)
Sources of the self: the making of the modern identity (Cambridge, Mass.: Harvard University Press, 1989)
The malaise of modernity (Toronto: Anansi, 1991)
  Republished as *The ethics of authenticity* (Cambridge, Mass.: Harvard University Press, 1992)
  French translation: *Grandeur et misère de la modernité* (Montréal: Fides, 1992)
Multiculturalism and 'the politics of recognition', Amy Gutmann et al. (Princeton: Princeton University Press, 1992)
Rapprocher les solitudes: écrits sur le fédéralisme et le nationalisme au Canada, ed. Guy Laforest (Québec: Les Presses de l'Université Laval, 1992)
  English translation: *Reconciling the solitudes*: essays on Canadian federalism and nationalism (Montréal: McGill-Queens University Press, 1993)

258

ARTICLES

(with Michael Kulman) 'The preobjective world', *Review of Metaphysics*, 12, 1 (September 1958)

Reprinted in *Essays in phenomenology*, ed. M. Nathanson (The Hague: Martinus Nijhoff, 1966)

'The ambiguities of marxist doctrine', *The Student World*, 2 (1958)

'Ontology', *Philosophy*, 34, 129, (April 1959)

'Phenomenology and linguistic analysis', *Proceedings of the Aristotelian Society*, 33 (supplementary volume, 1959)

(with André Raynauld, ed.) 'L'Etat et les partis politiques', *Le role de l'Etat* (Montréal: Les Editions du Jour, 1962)

'Nationalism and the political intelligentsia: a case study', *Queens' Quarterly*, 22, 1 (Spring 1965)

(with Bernard Williams and Alan Montefiore, ed.) 'Marxism and empiricism', *British analytical philosophy* (London: Routledge and Kegan Paul, 1966)

Reprinted as 'Marxismo e empirismo' in *Filosofie analitica inglese* (Rome: 1967)

'Mind–body identity, a side issue?' *Philosophical Review*, 26, 2 (April 1967)

Reprinted in *The mind/brain identity theory*, ed. C. V. Borst (London: Macmillan, 1970)

'Psychological behaviourism', *Encyclopedia of philosophy*, ed. Paul Edwards (New York: Macmillan, 1967)

'Relations between cause and action', *Proceedings of the seventh inter-American congress of philosophy* (Québec: Les Presses de l'Université Laval, 1967)

(with Peter Laslett and W. G. Runciman, ed.) 'Neutrality in political science', *Philosophy, politics and society*, third series (Oxford: Basil Blackwell, 1967)

Reprinted in *The philosophy of social explanation*, ed. Alan Ryan (Oxford: Oxford University Press, 1973)

Reprinted in *Social structure and political theory*, ed. William F. Connolly and Glen Gordon (Toronto: Heath, 1974)

Reprinted in *La filosofia de la explicación social*, ed. Alan Ryan (Mexico: Fondon de Cultura Economica, 1976)

'Two issues about materialism', *Philosophical Quarterly*, 19, 74 (January 1969)

'Explaining action', *Inquiry*, 13 (1970)

'Explanation of purposive behaviour', *The behaviour sciences*, ed. R. Borger and F. Cioffi (Cambridge: Cambridge University Press, 1970)

'How is mechanism conceivable?', *Interpretations of life and mind*, ed. Majorie Grene (London: Routledge and Kegan Paul, 1971)

French translation: 'Comment concevoir le mécanisme?', *Théorie de l'action*, ed. Marc Neuberg (Liège: Mardaga, 1991)

'The agony of economic man', *Essays on the left: essays in honour of T. C. Douglas* ed. L. Lapierre et al. (Toronto: McClelland and Stewart, 1971)

Reprinted in *Canadian political thought*, ed. H. D. Forbes (Toronto: Oxford University Press, 1985)

'Les cercles vicieux de l'aliénation post-moderne', *Le Québec qui se fait*, ed. Claude Ryan (Montréal: Hurtubise HMH, 1971)

'Interpretation and the sciences of man', *Review of Metaphysics* 25, 1 (September 1971)

Reprinted in *Explorations in phenomenology*, ed. David Carr and Edward S. Casey (The Hague: Martinus Nijhoff, 1973)

Reprinted in *Understanding and social inquiry*, ed. Fred Dallmayr and Thomas McCarthy (Notre Dame: University of Notre Dame Press, 1977)

Reprinted in *The philosophy of society*, ed. Roger Beehler and Alan Dregson (London: Methuen, 1978)

Reprinted in *Die Hermeneutik und die Wissenschaften*, ed. H.-G. Gadamer and Gottfried Boehm (Frankfurt: Suhrkamp, 1978)

Reprinted in *Interpretive social science: a reader*, ed. Paul Rabinow and William M. Sullivan (Los Angeles: University of California Press, 1979)

Reprinted in *Critical Sociology*, ed. Paul Connerton (London: Penguin Books, 1976)

'What is involved in a genetic psychology?', *Cognitive development and epistemology*, ed. T. Mischel (New York: Academic Press, 1971)

'Conditions for a mechanistic theory of behaviour', *Brain and human behaviour*, ed. A. G. Karczmar and J. C. Eccles (Berlin: Springer, 1972)

'The opening arguments of the phenomenology', *Hegel: a collection of critical essays*, ed. Alasdair MacIntyre (New York: Doubleday, 1972)

'Peaceful coexistence in psychology', *Social Research*, 40, 1 (Spring 1973)

Reprinted in *Social Research* (Spring/Summer 1984)

'Socialism and *Weltanschauung*', *The socialist idea*, ed. Leszek Kolakowski and Stuart Hampshire (London: Weidenfeld and Nicolson, 1974)

'Force et sens', *Sense et existence*, ed. G. Madison (Paris: Les Editions du Seuil, 1975)

'Neutrality in the university', *Neutrality and impartiality, the university and political commitment*, ed. Alan Montefiore (London: Cambridge University Press, 1975)

'The politics of the steady state', *Beyond industrial growth*, ed. Abraham Rotstein (Toronto: University of Toronto Press, 1976)

'Responsibility for self', *The identities of persons*, ed. Amélie Rorty (Los Angeles: University of California Press, 1976)

'What is human agency?', *The self, psychological and philosophical issues*, ed. Theodore Mischel (Oxford: Basil Blackwell, 1977)

'Hegel's *Sittlichkeit* and the crisis of representative institutions', *Philosophy of history and action*, ed. Yirmiahu Yovel (Reidel: Dordrecht, 1978)

Swedish translation: 'Hur lar vi av historien?', *KRIS*, 20/21 (Stockholm: 1981)

'Marxist philosophy', *Men of ideas*, ed. Bryan Magee (London: BBC Publications, 1978)

Turkish translation: *Milli egitin basimaki* (Istanbul: 1979)

'The validity of transcendental argument', *Proceedings of the Aristotelian Society*, 79 (1978–79)

'Action as expression', *Intention and intentionality: essays in honour of G. E. M. Anscombe*, ed. Cora Diamond and Jenny Teichman (Ithaca, N.Y.: Cornell University Press, 1979)

'Atomism', *Powers, possessions and freedom: essays in honour of C. B. Macpherson*, ed. Akis Kontos (Toronto: University of Toronto Press, 1979)

'Sense data revisited', *Perception and identity*, ed. G. F. Macdonald (Ithaca, N.Y.: Cornell University Press, 1979)

'What's wrong with negative liberty?', *The idea of freedom*, ed. Alan Ryan (Oxford: Oxford University Press, 1979)

    Reprinted in *Readings in social and political philosophy*, ed. Robert M. Stewart (New York: Oxford University Press, 1986)

    Reprinted in *Liberty*, ed. David Miller (Oxford University Press, 1991)

'Why do nations have to become states?' *Philosophers look at Canadian confederation*, ed. Stanley G. French (Montréal: Canadian Philosophical Association, 1979)

'Leader du NDP-Québec', *Robert Cliche*, ed. Alfred Rouleau (Montréal: Les Editions Quinze, 1980)

'The philosophy of the social sciences', *Political theory and political education*, ed. Melvin Richter (Princeton: Princeton University Press, 1980)

'Les sciences de l'homme', *Critique*, 399–400 (August-September 1980)

'Theories of meaning', *Man and World*, 13, 3–4 (1980)

'Understanding in human science', *Review of Metaphysics*, 34, 1 (September 1980)

(with Alan Montefiore) 'From an analytical perspective', introduction to Garbin Kortian, *Metacritique* (Cambridge: Cambridge University Press, 1980)

'Growth, legitimacy and modern identity', *Praxis International*, 1, 2 (July 1981)

'Understanding and explanation in the *Geisteswissenschaften*', *Wittgenstein: to follow a rule*, ed. S. Holtzmann and C. Leich (London: Routledge, 1981)

'Consciousness', *Explaining human behavior*, ed. Paul F. Secord (Beverly Hills: Sage, 1982)

'The diversity of goods', *Utilitarianism and beyond*, ed. A. Sen and B. Williams (Cambridge: Cambridge University Press, 1982)

    Reprinted in *Anti-theory in ethics and moral conservatism*, ed. Stanley G. Clarke and Evan Simpson (Albany, N.Y.: State University of New York Press, 1989)

    Portuguese translation: 'A diversidade dos bens', *Revista de communicaçao e linguagens* (1992)

'Rationality', *Rationality and relativism*, ed. M. Hollis and S. Lukes (Oxford: Blackwell, 1982)

    Italian translation: 'Razionalità', *Ragione e forme di vita: razionalitá e relativismo in antropologia* (Milan: Franco Angeli, 1990)

'Theories of meaning', *Proceedings of the British Academy*, Dawes Hicks lecture on philosophy', 16 (1982)

'Hegel's philosophy of mind', *Contemporary philosophy: a new survey*, ed. G. Floistad (The Hague: Martinus Nijhoff, 1983)

'Political theory and practice', *Social theory and political practice*, ed. C. Lloyd (Oxford: Clarendon Press, 1983)

'The significance of significance: the case of cognitive psychology', *The need for interpretation*, ed. S. Mitchell and M. Rosen (London: Athlone, 1983)

'Use and abuse of theory', *Ideology, philosophy and politics*, ed. Anthony Parel (Waterloo: Wilfrid Laurier University Press, 1983)

'Foucault on freedom and truth', *Political Theory*, 12, 2 (May 1984)

    Reprinted in *Foucault: a critical reader*, ed. David Hoy (Oxford: Blackwell, 1986)

    French translation: 'Foucault, la liberté, la verité', *Michel Foucault: lettres critiques* (Brussels: Deoeck-Wesmael, 1990)

    Spanish translation: 'Foucault sobre la libertad y la verdad', *Michel Foucault* (Buenos Aires: Ediciones Nueva Visiòn, 1990)

'Kant's theory of freedom', *Conceptions of liberty and political philosophy*, ed. A. Pelczynski and J. Gray (London: Athlone, 1984)

'Philosophy and its history', *Philosophy in history*, ed. Richard Rorty, J. B. Schneewind and Quentin Skinner (Cambridge: Cambridge University Press, 1984)

'Alternative futures: legitimacy, identity and alienation in late twentieth century Canada', *Constitutionalism, citizenship and society in Canada*, ed. Alan Cairns and Cynthia Williams (Toronto: University of Toronto Press, 1985)

'Humanismus und moderne identität', *Der Mensch in den modernen Wissenschaften*, ed. Krzysztof Michalski (Stuttgart: Klett-Cotta, 1985)

'The person', *The category of the person, anthropology, philosophy, history*, ed. Michael Carrithers, Steven Collins and Steven Lukes (New York: Cambridge University Press, 1985)

'The right to live: philosophical considerations', *Justice beyond Orwell*, ed. Rosalie S. Abella and Melvin J. Rothman (Montréal: Les Editions Yvon Blais, 1985)

'Les droits de l'homme: la culture juridique', *Les fondements philosophiques des droits de l'homme*, ed. Paul Ricoeur (Paris: UNESCO, 1986)

'Leibliches Handeln', *Leibhaftige vernunft*, ed. Alexandre Metraux and Bernhard Waldenfels (Munich: Fink 1986)

'Die motive einer verfahrensethik', *Moralität und Sittlichkeit: das Problem Hegels und die Diskursethik* (Frankfurt: Suhrkamp, 1986)

'The nature and scope of distributive justice', *Justice and equality here and now*, ed. Frank S. Lukash (Ithaca, N.Y.: Cornell University Press, 1986)

'Sprache und Gesellschaft', *Kommunikatives handeln: Beiträge zu Jurgen Habermas' Theorie des kommunikativen Handelns*, ed. Axel Honneth and Hans Joas (Frankfurt: Suhrkamp, 1986)

  English translation: 'Language and society', *Communicative action*, ed. Axel Honneth and Hans Joas (Cambridge: Polity Press, 1991)

'Zur Uberwindung der Erkenntnistheorie', *Die Krise der Phenomenologie und die Pragmatik des Wissenschaftsfortschritts*, ed. Michael Benedift and Rudolf Berger (Vienna: Osterreichischen Staatsdruckerei, 1986)

'Dialektika segodnya ili struktura samootritsaniya', *Philosophia gegelya: problemy dialektiki*, ed. T. I. Oiserman and N. V. Motroshilova (Moscow,: Nauka, 1987)

'Overcoming epistemology', *After philosophy: end of transformation?*, ed. Kenneth Baynes, James Bohman and Thomas McCarthy (Cambridge: Mass.: MIT Press, 1987)

  French translation: 'Le dépassement de l'épistémologie', *Critique de la raison phénomélogique*, ed. Jacques Poulain (Paris: Les Editions du Cerf, 1991)

'Algunas condiciones para una democracia viable', *Democracia y participación*, ed. R. Alvagay and Carlos Ruiz (Santiago: Ediciones Melquiades, 1988)

'The hermeneutics of conflict', *Meaning and context: Quentin Skinner and his critics*, ed. James Tully (Cambridge: Polity Press, 1988)

'Inwardness and the culture of modernity', *Zwischenbetrachtungen: im Prozess der Aufklärung*, ed. Axel Honneth, Thomas McCarthy, Clauss Offe and Albrecht Wellmer (Frankfurt: Suhrkamp, 1988)

'Le juste et le bien', *Revue de métaphysique et de morale*, 93, 1 (January–March 1988)

Spanish translation: 'Lo justo y el bien', *Revista de ciencia politica*, Universidad catolica de Chile, 12, 1–2 (1990)
'The moral topography of the self', *Hermeneutics and psychological theory*, ed. R. Alvagay and Carlos Ruiz (Rutgers, N.J.: Rutgers University Press, 1988)
'Cross-purposes: the liberal–communitarian debate', *Liberalism and the moral life*, ed. Nancy L. Rosenblum (Cambridge: Mass.: Harvard University Press, 1989)
French translation: 'Quiproquos et malentendus: le débat communautaires-libéraux', *Lieux et transformations de la philosophie*, ed. Jean Borreil and Jacques Poulain (Paris: Les Presses Universitaires de Vincennes, 1991)
'Embodied agency', *Merleau-Ponty: critical essays*, ed. Henry Pietersma (Washington, DC: University Press of America, 1989)
'Explanation and practical reason', *Wider working papers*, Helsinki: World Institute for Development Economics Research of the United Nations University (August 1989)
'Hegel's ambiguous legacy for modern liberalism', *Cardozo Law Review*, 10, 5–6, (March/April 1989)
Reprinted in *Hegel and legal theory*, ed. Michel Rosenfeld and David Gray Carlson (New York: Routledge, 1991)
'Marxism and socialist humanism', *Out of apathy: voices of the new left thirty years on*, ed. Robin Archer, Diemut Bubeck, Hanjo Glock, Les Jacobs, Seth Moglen, Adam Steinhouse and Daniel Weinstock, (London, Verso, 1989)
'The Rushdie controversy', *Public Culture*, 2, 1, (autumn 1989), pp. 118–22
'Comparison, history, truth', *Myth and philosophy*, ed. Frank E. Reynolds and David Tracy (Albany, N.Y.: State University of New York Press, 1990)
'Exploring "l'humaine condition"', *Fermentum massae mundi*, ed. N. Cieslinska and P. Ruszinski, *Jackowi Wozniakowskiemu w disdem sziesata rocznice urodzin* (Warsaw: Agora, 1990)
'Les institutions dans la vie nationale', *Les institutions québecoises: leur rôle, leur avenir*, ed. Vincent Lemieux (Québec: Les Presses de l'Université Laval, 1990).
'Invoking civil society', Working paper (Chicago: Centre for Psychosocial Studies, 1990)
'Irreducibly social goods', *Rationality, individualism and public policy*, ed. Geoffrey Brennan and Cliff Walsh (Canberra: Australian National University, 1990)
'Modes of civil society', *Public Culture*, 3, 1, (autumn 1990), pp. 95–118
'Rorty in the epistemological tradition', *Reading Rorty*, ed. Alan Malachowski (Oxford: Blackwell, 1990)
'Die beschwörung der civil society', *Europa und die civil society*, ed. Krzysztof Michalski (Stuttgart: Klett Cotta, 1991)
'Civil society in the western tradition', *The notion of tolerance and human rights*, ed. Ethel Groffier and Michel Paradis (Ottawa: Carleton University Press, 1991)
'Comments and replies', *Inquiry*, 34 (1991), pp. 237–54
'Comprendre la culture politique', *L'engagement intellectuel: mélanges en honneur de Léon Dion*, ed. Raymond Hudon and Réjean Pelletier (Québec: Les Presses de l'Université Laval, 1991)

'The dialogical self', David Hiley, James Bohman and Richard Shusterman ed., ·
    The interpretive turn: philosophy, science, culture (Ithaca, N.Y.: Cornell
    University Press, 1991)
'Les enjeux de la réforme constitutionnelle', *Les avis des spécialistes invités à
    répondre aux huit questions posées par la commission*, Submission to the
    Commission sur l'Avenir politique et constitutionne du Québec (Québec:
    Québec government publication, 1991)
'The importance of Herder', *Isaiah Berlin: a celebration*, Edna and Avishai
    Margalit (London: Hogarth Press, 1991)
'Lichtung oder lebensform. Parallelen zwischen Wittgenstein und Heidegger', *Der
    Löwe spricht ... und wir können ihn nicht verstehen*', ed. Brian McGuinness et
    al. (Frankfurt: Suhrkamp, 1991)
'Shared and divergent values', *Options for a new Canada*, ed. Ronald Watts and
    Douglas Brown (Toronto: University of Toronto Press, 1991)
'Les grandes lignes d'une solution constitutionelle', Présentation à la Commission
    d'étude sur toute offre d'un nouveau partenariat, Québec, 23 March 1992
'Can Canada survive the charter?', *Alberta Law Review*, 30, 2 (1992)
'Explanation and practical reason', *The scientific enterprise*, ed. Edna Ullman-
    Margalit (Boston: Kluwer, 1992)
    Expanded in *The quality of life*, ed. Martha Nussbaum and Amartya Sen
    (Oxford: Clarendon Press, 1993)
'Heidegger, language and ecology', *Heidegger: a critical reader*, ed. Hubert
    Dreyfus and Harrison Hall (Oxford: Blackwell, 1992)
'The politics of recognition', Working paper (Chicago: Centre for Psychosocial
    Studies, 1992)
    Amended version in *Multiculturalism and 'the politics of recognition'*, ed. Amy
    Gutmann (Princeton: Princeton University Press, 1992)
'Quel principe d'identité collective?' *L'Europe au soir du siècle*, ed. Jacques
    Lenoble and Nicole Dewandre (Paris: Les Éditions Esprit, 1992)
'To follow a rule', *Rules and conventions: literature, philosophy, social theory*, ed.
    Mette Hjort (Baltimore, Md.: Johns Hopkins University Press, 1992)
'Der Begriff der "bügerlichen Gesellschaft" im politischen Denken des Westens',
    Gemeinschaft und Gerechtigkeit, ed. Micha Brumlik and Hauke Brunkhorst
    (Frankfurt: Fischer Verlag, 1993)
'The deep challenge of dualism', *Québec: state and society*, ed. Alain Gagnon
    (Toronto: Nelson, 1993)
'Embodied agency and background in Heidegger', *The Cambridge companion to
    Heidegger*, ed. Charles Guignon (Cambridge: Cambridge University Press,
    1993)
'Hegel and the philosophy of action', *Selected essays on G. W. F. Hegel*, ed.
    Lawrence Stepelevich (New York: Humanities Press, 1993)
'Wie viel gemeinschaft braucht die Demokratie?', *Transit*, vol. 5 (winter 1992–93)

Index

" Trees"
Howard Nemerov

Collected Poem Univ. Chicago Press